The Outhouse War and Other Kibbutz Stories

The Outhouse War and Other Kibbutz Stories

Shimon Camiel

Writer's Showcase
San Jose New York Lincoln Shanghai

The Outhouse War and Other Kibbutz Stories

All Rights Reserved © 2001 by Shimon Camiel

No part of this book may be reproduced or transmitted in any form or by any means, graphic, electronic, or mechanical, including photocopying, recording, taping, or by any information storage retrieval system, without the permission in writing from the publisher.

Writer's Showcase
an imprint of iUniverse.com, Inc.

For information address:
iUniverse.com, Inc.
5220 S 16th, Ste. 200
Lincoln, NE 68512
www.iuniverse.com

ISBN: 0-595-16572-9

Printed in the United States of America

Contents

1958: Grandfather's First Appearance—Berkeley, California 1
January 1959: From Brooklyn to Piraeus 6
1959: Piraeus 14
1959: Piraeus to Haifa 19
1959: Love in Beit HaAlon 26
1959: Heading for the Galilee 37
1959: Sending for Ruthie 44
January 1960: Ruthie Arrives 49
1960: The Man in the Apple Tree 54
December 12, 1960: Bottom line? 59
1961: South of Rosh Pina 60
1961: From Here to Istanbul 66
1961: My Big Mouth 72
1962: The Battle of the Children's Farm 82
1962: Equality 94
May 3 and 4, 1963: Replenish, Replenish. 104
1963: The Girl in the Apple Tree 105
1963: Nights of Terrorists and Wolves 118
1963: More Volunteers From Abroad 128
1964: To Serve Our Country 137
1965: Going Outside 149
1965: The Things We Cling To 171
1966: Grapes and Bullets 181
1966: Why Do They Hate Us? 185
1966: The University of the Vineyard, Part 1 203
1967: The University of the Vineyard, Part 2 207

1967: Those Heroic Days	212
June 7, 1967: Of Bombs and Mules	218
June 9, 1967: I Thought the War Was Over	221
June 10, 1967: A Walk Up the Golan	225
June 10: 1967: Thou Shall Not Plunder	230
1967: The Aftermath	236
1968: The Outhouse War	247
1968-73: To School and Back	273
1973: Yom Kippur	288
1973: Blackout	293
1973: Ruthie	299
1973-1975: Of Personal, Local and National Depression	301
1976: Tracking Down Saba	313
1993: Slivovitz and Judaism	320
1996: Close Call	331
1996: The Three Rebels	335
1997: 50th Anniversary	343
1998: Turtle Doves	351

To my children and grandchildren.

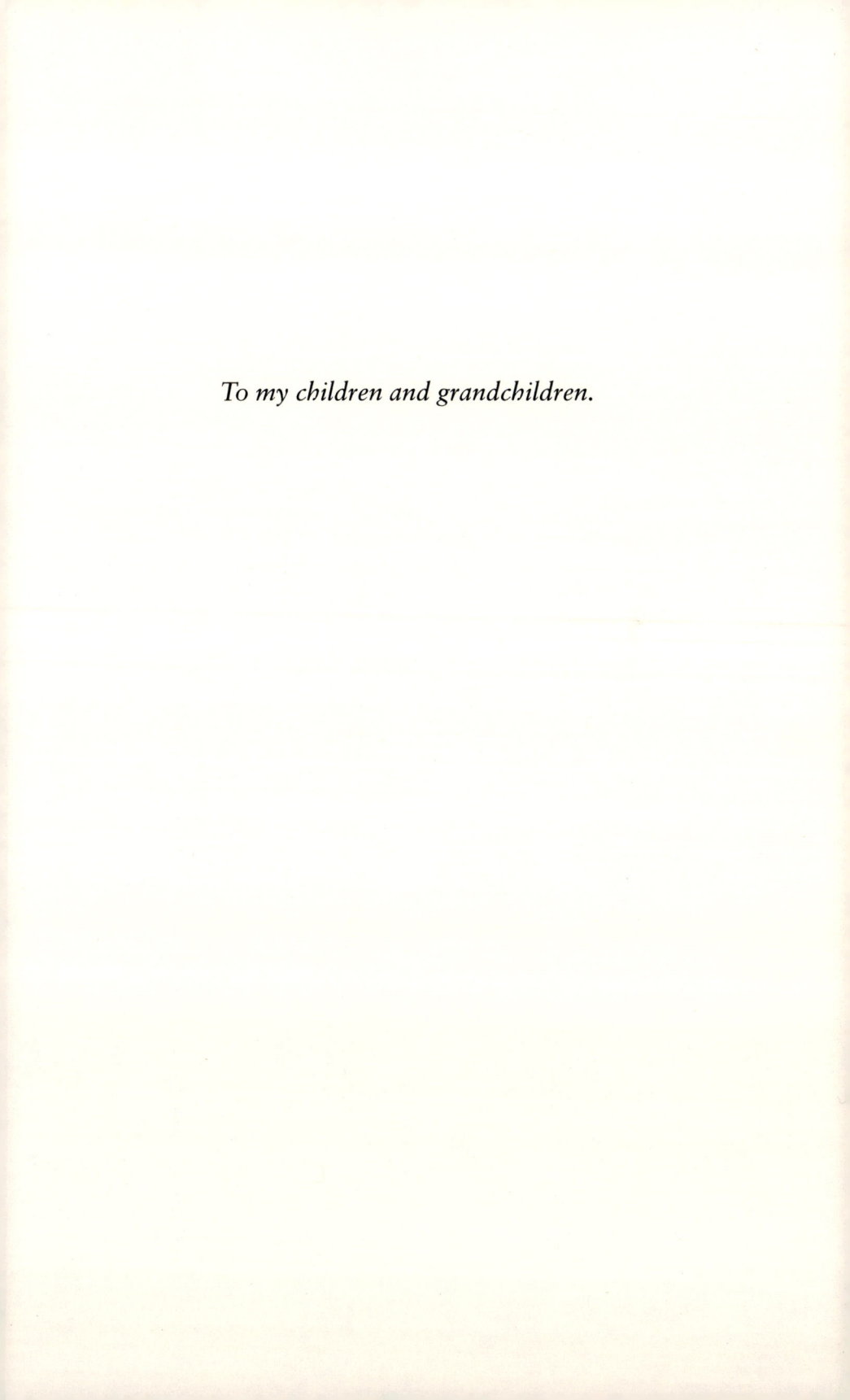

Proverbs 30:11

Two things have I asked of Thee;
Deny me them not before I die:

Remove far from me vanity and lies;
Give me neither poverty nor riches;

Feed me with my allotted bread;
Lest I be full, and deny, and say:
'Who is the Lord?'

Or lest I be poor, and steal,
And profane the name of my God.

I gratefully acknowledge the following heroes:

Joyce Camiel - Editor, CEO
Doug and Alice Diamond - Jacks of all trades
Stefan Schumann - Computer wizard extroardinaire
Robyn Conely Weaver - Also editor
The Amazing Writers Group - Mentors and critics
Jean and Laura Walcher - Ace publicity agents
Gert Thaler - Historian
Members of a certain Galilee Kibbutz
Rebecca Geiss - Cartoonist
Alan Douglas, Jane Meis, Joan Bigge, Joy Hanna - Guinea Pigs and typo control
David Rogers, Rivka Keilson - IUniverse gurus
Yehuda and Hannah Chmiel - Research assistants

1958: Grandfather's First Appearance—Berkeley, California

At dawn, the door of my bedroom opens and my paternal grandfather enters. I have always imagined him as an old orthodox Jewish man wearing a *yarmulke,* a wrinkled black suit, a stained waistcoat, and long fringed *tsitses* hanging down from a dull white *talit katan* undershirt. But on this first morning visit to me, he appears dressed in the uniform of a pre First World War Russian cavalry soldier. His reddish beard is clipped. On his right side, a sword rests in its scabbard, reaching down to the top of his military boots. The boots gleam even in the dimness of my Berkeley apartment, the only light coming from a hint of sunrise sifting through a dust covered window shade. I note our family resemblance: the triangular face, the straight, sharp nose, the long ears, and the mischievous brown eyes.

"I thought that I might try wearing this again," says my grandfather, framing his military jacket with his thin and white talmudic hands. "Haven't had it on since 1906. "Good as new," he exclaims as he straightens his black billed military cap. I notice that the hair under his hat is thick but graying. He looks to be about 60 years old.

I sit up in bed, and blink hard, trying to clear up the slight possibility that I am still dreaming. After all, Grandfather Yisroel died in the Holocaust twenty seven years ago, along with Grandmother Rivka, Uncle Daniel, Aunt Blüme, and most of the rest of the Chmiel family members who had the misfortune to still be in Ostrolenka at the outbreak of the Second World War. Am I in Berkeley or am I in Poland? But I've never been in Poland.

"I hear you're going to *Eretz Yisrael*," says Grandfather sitting himself down at the foot of my bed. He speaks English with a hint of a Polish accent.

"Yes, I am."

"I also hear that your parents don't like the idea."

"True."

"They think that you are throwing away all those years of education that they paid for, eh?" he continued, in a somewhat-non-judgmental tone, the kind where you know that judgement might still be on its way.

"Yes, especially since I'm leaving school a month before I'm supposed to get my degree."

"Nu, why are you doing this?" he asks as he stands up, stalks around the bedroom rubbing his hands together and enjoying the sound of his army boots on the wooden floor.

"Because, I thought it would make you happy."

"You thought you would make *me* happy?" he muses. "Why would it make me happy? Do you know how dangerous it is over there in the Holy Land? Do you know that your father, Zelig, left Ostrolenka and came to America to find a safe place for his family to live? Do you know that he tried to bring all of us over to America so that we wouldn't have to die at the hands of the Nazis?—may their memory be erased! Do you know that we would have come ourselves to America if we had the money and if we could have finished the paper work and the visas in time? Why would I want you to risk your life in Israel? Haven't they had enough wars over there yet?"

"Only two, so far."

"They'll probably have three or four more by the time you figure out what's good for you."

He puffs at my ignorance and then sits down on the bed.

"You know, Grandfather, even though I've never met you before, even though I've only fantasized who you were, I felt that we had a bond of some kind together. I felt that you would want me to do something for our people. Consider what happened to you and our family in Poland. We have to protect our new country, especially since *Eretz Yisroel* is so new, so vulnerable. And this is the first time we've had our own nation for the past two thousand years. Why shouldn't I go help?"

"Listen to me," he leans over me and softens his voice, "I think that this thing that you are planning is very foolish and dangerous. You should stay here and finish your schoolwork. You should become a doctor, or a lawyer, eh? Or maybe just open up a grocery store like your father—as long as you make an honest living. You can donate money to Israel, but why risk your life. Believe me, life is very precious.

He sighs with impatience realizing that he might as well be talking to the bedpost.

"But, I know that you won't listen. Some people have a stubborn and capricious nature. They don't think things through and they don't plan well. And they don't like to accept the world as it is. I've been following your behavior for almost twenty years now, through letters from your parents when I was alive and through other ways since I've been dead. You're always dreaming adventures and you're thinking about trying to change the way that things are. No, I'm not encouraging you to do this and I don't approve of your going against your parents' will, but…" he hesitates.

"But what?"

"Shhh! I've decided to go with you," he whispers. "You're going to need some protection. You have no background in facing danger, growing up here in America. Yes, I'm going with you. We have a tradition in our family; we take care of each other."

"How are you going to come with me?"

"That's my problem," he states, "You can just be sure that I'll be there when you need me. Maybe like a messenger, maybe like a shield. You're not as strong or wise as you think you are. Also, outside of taking care of you, I want to have a look around and see what kind of a State we Jews have created for ourselves."

The chimes on the Campanile bell tower sound their seven o'clock bongs.

"Got to go now, *boytchik*," he says and kisses my cheek. "Don't worry. I know you've already bought your ticket to Israel, but I won't tell your parents. I'll see you on the ship."

I get a whiff of pipe tobacco and boot polish and he's gone.

January 1959: From Brooklyn to Piraeus

My adventure begins on a rain-swept pier on the shore of the East River, Brooklyn, New York. The sky is a dismal gray, but I am full of sunlight and great expectations. I'm wearing a new, dark blue trench coat and a black beret and I'm on my way up a gangplank. My fancy education taught me that the origin of the word gangplank comes from the Old English verb, *"Gangan"* meaning 'going' and I can hardly wait to be *gangan*. You see, I'm not merely *gangan* onto the ship, but *gangan* out of my country of birth, *gangan* out of apple pie and baseball, out of the Western Hemisphere and out of my former identity. The good ship *A.K. Galilee*, sporting the blue and white naval banner of the State of Israel sounds its Hebrew horn, pulls up its gangplank, and steams past the Statue of Liberty. I feel a great burden lifting off my shoulders: done with America, done with Capitalism, done with McCarthyism and Ike, done with my past, done with conformity, even done with the Statue of Liberty. And why am I doing this?

Do I really want to please an exterminated grandfather?

Or do I want to avoid becoming a lawyer, a doctor or a CPA?

Do I want to be the rugged pioneer defending the border?

Or do I just want to escape for the sake of escaping?

The shores of America are fading...

On the first day out, I size up the sparse population of passengers on our New York-Gibraltar-Piraeus-Haifa crossing. Here is Manya: she's another immigrant to Israel, baby-faced and homely, insecure yet adventurous. She is nineteen and has read every book about the glorious new State of Israel. No one is seeing her off, either. Like me, she sails off the map of her past. Here are Nik, Thomas and Sid, three Greek sailors deported to their homeland after being caught as illegals in the USA. Here is Mike, an Israeli-American, returning home to inherit a gas station in Tel Aviv. Here are Mr. and Mrs. Margolis, American tourists. Mrs. Margolis has a phobia about flying in airplanes. There are others but, strangely enough, not many others.

Hopefully, Mr. and Mrs. Margolis do not have a phobia about rough seas because it is mid-January and on the third night of the voyage the ship is fighting its way across the Atlantic in stormy seas. The dining room of the ship is empty except for Nik, Thomas, Sid, Manya and me. All the other passengers languish seasick in their cabins and the chicken soup cure isn't working. Manya makes a valiant attempt to dine with us, but when the first course turns out to be a goat cheese plate, she bites her lip and then vomits into her dinner napkin. We move to a different table, on the other side of the dining hall; after all, we are the only diners and can take our pick. Manya, ashen-faced, makes an embarrassed exodus to her cabin where she will spend the next few days. The *A.K. Galilee* plunges into a trough in the waves and then lurches obliquely to the side but we pay it no mind. We are full of *Ouzo* (from the Greek sailors' private stock) and goat cheese and we are hungry for the next course. It might be squid and cotton candy for all we care since we are a team of three macho Greeks and one soon-to-be Israeli, heading toward Athens.

After feasting on mountains of food cooked for the absent passengers, we linger at our table, joke telling, card playing, and tall-tale spinning. We form a table-wide academy of obscenities, teaching each other lewd oaths in Spanish, Hebrew, Greek and English. We leave the dining room for our cabins, weak from ribald laughter accompanied by the crazy rock and roll of the *A.K. Galilee*.

During the next few days, I spend my time wrapped in a blanket on the empty, pitching, careening tourist deck. I read books in glorious solitude having discovered the ship's library, stocked by someone who loves Georges Simenon's detective stories. After Simenon, I digest *The Good Soldier Schwiek*, while I wait for the reappearance of the rest of the voyagers but they remain closeted with their upset stomachs.

On one particularly tempestuous day, who should appear on deck but my deceased grandfather, Yisroel, marvelously balancing himself on the rolling deck as he makes his way toward my chair. This time he is unseasonably dressed in a zippy white suit, alligator shoes and a Panama hat. Four ritual fringes, however, are hanging out of his pants indicating the presence of the *Talit Katan* under his dandy outfit. He spills himself down on the deck chair next to me and, true to the Chmiel family tradition, wastes no time getting to the point.

"What are you going to do when you get to *Eretz Israel?*"

"Go learn Hebrew," I reply. "I'm signed up to go to an *Ulpan* on a kibbutz."

"*Kibbutz, Ulpan,* that's already Hebrew" says Grandpa, "but what means this?"

"It's a place where I'll learn Hebrew half-day and work on the kibbutz the rest of the day."

"How much do you have to pay to go to the *Ulpan*?"

"Nothing," I answer, "you break even with the kibbutz. They teach you Hebrew and you work for free. Also you get free room and board and free trips around the country."

"Very clever," says Grandpa, "I tell you the truth, I was worried that you wouldn't have enough money to get started over there. You only had $2.50 in your bank account, last time I looked."

"You looked in my bank account?"

"Oy, I shouldn't have mentioned it."

"How?"

"Ghosts have some privileges," he replied, shrugging his shoulders and opening his palms to either side. "So what next after the *Ulpan*?" he ignores the astonished look that lingers on my face.

"What do you suggest?"

Grandpa Yisroel thinks about this for a few seconds, and says, "You have family in Israel, Chmiel cousins, my Brother Asher's children. They went to the Holy Land before the war broke out. You should go see them, get to know them. Maybe one of them has a nice daughter, a *shayne yiddisha meidlach*. Maybe we can make a *shiddukh*, a matchmaking."

He pauses to think this scenario out for a bit.

"Yes, you should get married to a nice girl from a good Ostrolenka family," he muses. "What kind of girls do you like? Rich? Poor? Blondes? Pug-nosed? Big hips? Small hips…"

To my amazement, I hear my own deceased grandfather sifting through his own catalog of feminine preferences as he disappears in front of my eyes like Alice's Cheshire cat.

"…Make sure she knows how to make a good borsht…"

He fades out completely, and I'm left alone, a salty wind blustering against my face.

A few more days of rough seas and a few more raucous nights pass; more bottles of *Ouzo*, *Retsina* and sweet kosher wine, and more heaps of food for the four of us and suddenly, almost biblically, the sea is calm. A few passengers, seasick and cloistered for most of the crossing, timidly creep out of their cabins and begin to stroll along the decks. Mr. and Mrs. Margolis say *"shalom."* The clouds part and the sun makes an appearance. One night, the lights of the Portuguese coast sparkle in the distance and the dining room is reinhabited. The next day we anchor in Gibraltar.

Mike, the guy who inherited a gas station in Tel Aviv, appears out of his seasick quarters and the two of us take a walking tour of downtown Gibraltar, a city the size of a postage stamp. We pop into a few souvenir shops and find that most of their proprietors are Sephardic Jews. When they hear where we are bound, they say, "*Shalom*, can you look up my cousin in Tel Aviv?" I return the greeting, promise to look up their cousins and buy another beret just for memories and Jewish solidarity. The merchant gives me ten percent off for ethnic unity. Then, we take a bus tour of the Rock of Gibraltar, all fourteen hundred feet of it, and look over at Africa across the straits.

On the way back down the Rock of Gibraltar, we have a glance at the fortress and then head back to the ship. I am full of the romance of my first encounter with Europe, the Old World and the Mediterranean, but Mike is too preoccupied with plans for the gas station in Tel Aviv. He wants to try a long distance phone call to Israel to talk to his lawyer.

A surprise awaits us as we arrive back at the ship. In our absence, several hundred Moroccan Jews from the Atlas Mountains have boarded our ship, for most of them it is their first journey beyond their remote villages in the mountains of Eastern Morocco. The men are wearing long white *Jelabiya* robes and the women wear black shawls and black dresses over brightly colored blouses. A few of the younger men and women wear Western style clothing as misinterpreted by inhabitants of the Atlas Mountains.

A.K. Galilee sails out of Gibraltar bound for Israel. Moroccans, Israelis, and we few American immigrants gather in the ship's synagogue for afternoon prayers. Its small space cannot hold many worshipers and many of the passengers must pray in the corridors.

Some even pray on the deck. Although the language of the prayers–Hebrew–is familiar to most, accents and melodies vary greatly. I listen to the vast cacophony of thanksgiving prayers and shed tears with most of the others, celebrating about the miracle of our return to homeland, even though we have not yet reached its shores.

"*Baruch Ata Adonai, Elohainu Melekh HaOlam, Shehekheyanu, v'Kiyamanu, v'Higianu lazman haz'e*," we chant the prayer of joyfulness and redemption as the ship chugs out of Gibraltar Bay. Blessed is *Adonai*, our God, ruler of the universe, for giving us life, for sustaining us, and for enabling us to reach this joyous day.

As the prayers continue I notice a tall, red-bearded man standing in the front of the sanctuary close to the ark containing the ship's Torah scrolls. His head is covered by a *tallit* and his body sways forward and backward while chanting the Hebrew prayers. I note that he keeps extraordinary balance considering the rough side to side dance of the *A.K. Galilee*. Because of the crowd (I am mashed against the wall nearest to the door of the synagogue) I can't approach the man though. But strangely, I feel drawn toward him. He turns his head away from the ark for a second and I see the face of my Grandfather Yisroel. He nods to me and then faces back around to the ark and continues his prayers. We finish the *Aleinu* prayer, chanting the ancient words that sometimes give me solace and sometimes annoy me:

"*She-lo assnu k'goyei HaAratzot, v'lo samanu c'mishpakhot HaAdama*...Praise God...He has not made us like the nations of the lands and has not placed us to be like the other families of the earth; for He has not assigned our portion like theirs nor our lot like all their multitudes."

After the service, the ship's synagogue empties out but I lose sight of my grandfather. I figure he was there to revel, as I did, in the fiery feeling of peoplehood with these exotic Jews from the Atlas Mountains.

At night, the Moroccans huddle together below decks, perhaps afraid of the darkness over the waters and of the unknowns they will face on their three-day voyage to the Holy Land. Crewmembers make the rounds and gently explain that lighting cooking fires on or under the ship's decks is forbidden. Several of the Arabic speaking crewmembers try to explain to the heads of families how to operate the flush toilets, but not before some of the new immigrants have stashed their cucumbers and tomatoes in the toilet bowls and peed into the sinks.

I spend the rest of the voyage trying to communicate with the new passengers in my poor Hebrew or in my even poorer French. But many of them have come from areas so remote from the densely inhabited areas of Morocco, that they speak only incomprehensible Berber. I spend a lot of time on deck staring from afar into the eyes of a beautiful Moroccan girl with long black braids. I fantasize becoming a Moroccan immigrant, just so I can marry this princess of the Atlas Mountains.

The Mediterranean decides to give us a tranquil voyage all the way to the harbor of Piraeus, Greece, where, after a short adventure, the *A.K. Galilee* and I will continue on to the land of my dreams with grandfather as a spiritual stowaway.

1959: Piraeus

I have a day and a half to see Greece. The romance of being on the ship with a few hundred tribal Jews from the Atlas Mountains is beginning to wear off, given the ripe smells of onions, body odors, Gauloise cigarettes, old prayer books, sacks of old clothes, strange spices, and unflushed toilets. The Princess of the Atlas is not allowed out of her parent's eyes and so I decide to descend the gangplank, take a bus up to Athens and plant my flag on the Acropolis.

Once on the wharf, I hear my name called and see Nik and Sid, two of my Greek sailor friends, standing by their sea bags.

"Hey, Shimon, come over here, come with us," they say. "Come have an *Ouzo* with us."

Why not? I accompany them a short distance down a street lined by white buildings with blue doors. We stop at a tavern and enter a dark bar room leading to a patio. We sit down and order a bottle of *Ouzo* 90°. A cat climbs on Nik's sea-bag and I pick it up to examine what a Greek cat might look like.

"Every good Greek *taverna* has its cat," says Nik profoundly.

"And every Greek cat has its fleas," adds Sid.

I discard the cat, pour a little water into the *Ouzo* and watch it curl milky white into the colorless, gasoline-like beverage before I bolt it down. Ahhh.

"Where are you going today?" asks Sid.

"I thought I would go to see the Parthenon." I answer. "How do you get to Athens from here?"

"The bus station is close by," says Sid, "but why are you in a hurry? Come with us and we'll show you some interesting things in Piraeus."

"What?" I asked

"Oh a surprise, it's something just down the block," Nik explains. "A surprise for you."

After a few more shots of *Ouzo*, my friends pay the bill—I don't have any *Drachmas*, yet—and we head, a little unsteady, down the block to another blue doorway into a two-story house. In my innocence, I think it might be Nik's home. I'm thinking that it would be great to observe Nik's reunion with his family...local color, you know.

If it *is* Nik's home, he certainly has a lot of sisters. We enter a sitting room with couches lining all four walls. A woman, whom I recognize as Madame Hortense from *Zorba the Greek*, sits in an armchair at one end of the room. After the three of us recline on a couch, Madame Hortense smiles and commands one of the "sisters" to pour us some Greek coffee. Sid and Nik carry on a short discussion with Her Majesty and although my Greek is non-existent—except for a few obscenities learned crossing the

Atlantic—I finally figure out that this is going to be a homecoming of a different type, especially after I see a quick exchange of *Drachmas* between Sid and Nik on one hand, and Madame H. on the other. A few minutes of polite sipping of coffee and my two shipmates leave the room accompanied by two "sisters." As Sid passes by me, he winks and says, "We pay for you, Shimon, have fun."

A red headed-woman, somewhat older than I am sits next to me and smiles. She has a gold tooth and a very white thigh sticking out of her red skirt.

"I am Simona," says she of the red hair, gold tooth, white thigh, red dress and green fingernails. I speak English."

"I am Shimon," I say, "are you Greek?"

"No, I Romania, from Bucharest...Sheeemon," she tries out my name. "Like Simona - we the same name. I make you good love. Go upstairs now?"

Thinking quickly and not willing to insult Simona or any of the staff, I say: "I am very hungry. I want to eat now, love maybe later. You and I go to good restaurant? Change money, too?"

She looks at me quizzically, thinks for a few seconds and says, "OK, I very hungry too. I show you to restaurant and money change."

We are sitting in the *taverna*, the one with the cat and the blue door. Shimon and Simona having lunch. Simona is tearing apart a roast chicken and I am eating Greek salad with good tomatoes, feta, red onions, anchovies and lots of peppers. We drink beer.

Simona and I are getting friendly. We are temporary soul mates with the same basic first name.

"Where you go?" she asks between bites.

"Israel"

"Ah, Holy Land."

"Not holy for me," I protest. "I'm a Socialist."

"*Sotzializm*, not good. I know." She says with fervor. "I Romania. *Sotzializm* very bad. Stalin. Anna Pauker. Make me run away."

"Not that kind of Socialism," I correct her.

"I am for Democracy. Social Democrat. I am going to join a kibbutz."

"What is kibbutz?" Simona asks and gnaws voraciously on a drumstick as I think about my answer.

"A Kibbutz is a communal farm in Israel. Everyone on the kibbutz is equal. Doctors and farmers get the same pay. Women and men get the same pay. Jews and Christians get the same pay. Children grow up together in children's houses. Everyone works where they want to." (I'm a little uncomfortable spouting all this propaganda to her, even though I truly believe it. Does she think that I'm a nut?

"You crazy," she says. "Leave America and go to *Kolkhoz?* You American no?"

"I'm also a Jew." I say, "this is the first time in 2000 years that my people have their own home. I want to be part of it. You know about pioneers?"

"Pioneers," she sneers, "Very bad. Communists try to trick Romanian children with Pioneers. I know. I was pioneer. White shirt, red bandana on neck, blue skirt. My leader force me to have sex with him. Very bad, pioneers. Let's go back to house. Your friends pay me to make you happy. Now, I'm sad. You will be sorry that you go to Sotzialism. Bad. Bad. Too bad."

I take Simona back to the brothel as ordered and leave her at the blue door. I head back toward the wharf and look for the bus station. During the forty-five minute ride to Athens, I lean my head against the window and fall into a half-sleep where I am continuing to explain my ideology and dreams to Simona so that she will understand. As Athens and the hill of the Acropolis swing into view, the thought strikes me that Simona might be having similar musings about me.

"Crazy American," she might mutter.

1959: Piraeus to Haifa

The last leg of my Odyssey begins as the *A.K. Galilee* plows through the choppy Aegean Sea past the Cyclades and Crete. Europe is now behind us and the Middle East is approaching. Somewhere between these two worlds, the reality of what I am about to do sets in. I slip out of tourist mode and begin to think of myself seriously as an immigrant to a new land. I lean against the rail looking east toward a still invisible coast.

"Any regrets, Shimon?" My grandfather asks. I hadn't noticed him standing next to me also facing toward the New World to the east. He holds fast to his Panama hat so that the sea breeze won't blow it into Lebanese waters, but his *tsitses*—his ritual fringes—flutter in the breeze unhindered.

"No regrets, Grandfather. I'm ready for a new life, come what may. I'm feeling like Cortez. I've burned my ships behind me, dropped out of college, and said goodbye to all my girlfriends. I've dumped all my belongings except one suitcase and, as soon as I get on shore, I'll get rid of my American passport as well. So I'll be a crazy Israeli instead of a crazy American."

"Oh, I don't think you're crazy," says Grandfather, "just immature. Sometimes what seems to be the safest and sanest way turns out to be the craziest way. Look at your Grandmother and me. We tried to keep all of our children in Ostrolenka. We thought that they would lose their religion if they went to America. We thought that things would get better under the Polish flag. We thought that Hitler would go away. We thought that if there was going to be another world war that we would somehow survive, just like we did in the First World War. Look what happened...A Holocaust. Your mistake is leaving your parents, giving up the chance to make a good living, bringing yourself over to a war zone, and, worst of all, planning to give up your American citizenship. All of this just to become a hero. Anyway, what's the use of telling you all of this, we're only a short distance from the Holy Land now and it's too late to turn back."

He sighs, stares out at the sea a bit, takes a deep breath, and then slowly a little smile appears on his sensual lips.

"Now tell me a little about the good time you had in Piraeus with the red-head?" asks my grandfather, stroking his beard with a sudden sparkle in his eyes."

I get up early the next morning and hurry out on deck to get my first sight of the Israeli coast, but a line of fog blocks my view of the horizon. I know what I'm looking for from all the books I've read and pictures I've obsessed on: a view of Mount Carmel, the golden dome of the Baha'i Temple half way up its slope, and the white buildings of Haifa. I switch on my newly bought battery-powered portable radio hoping to hear the Israeli Broadcasting Station. Maybe they will be playing *Hatikvah*, my new national anthem. Wouldn't that be a glorious first direct contact with my homeland?

I get the Israeli radio station, loud and clear, but they are not playing Hatikvah. I hear a Hebrew voice with a strange, Germanic accent barking out the Hebrew numbers: *"ehad, shtaim, shalosh, arba,"* (1-2-3-4), and repeating *ehad, shtaim, shalosh, arba,* and repeating them again. Then, I hear *"Yadaim L'malla"* (hand's up), then again *"ehad, shtaim, shalosh, arba...."* My spoken Hebrew is still rough but I know enough to understand that I have picked up the morning exercise group, doing their stuff on the beach in Tel Aviv. So much for high drama, but I am elated with the idea that Jews are exercising at 6:00 a.m. The fog slowly dissipates and I am looking at my new homeland, Mt. Carmel, the Bahai Temple and Haifa, as advertised.

The *A.K. Galilee* docks in Haifa port and I am *gangan* on my way with my lone suitcase, down the gangplank, across the concrete wharf and into an enormous customs house. Not far behind me, I think I see Yisroel, my grandfather, bending over to plant a kiss on holy soil, in this case the concrete wharf. My passport is stamped and a customs officer peers into my suitcase. He's dressed in khaki, and has a wall-to-wall mustache. To my joy, he has a Star of David on his officer's badge. I'm here in the Jewish State! He sifts through my meager pile of ragged Levi's, old shirts, underwear, and socks. He picks up the portable radio, takes it out of its case and examines it for lethality.

"That's all you brought from America?"

"That's it, that's all I need," I explain.

"How much money did you bring with you?"

I show him my wallet and produce a $20 bill.

"That's it." I declare.

"How do you expect to settle in Israel with only $20 in your pocket?"

"I'm going to a kibbutz." I explain.

"Which one?" He asks.

"Beit HaAlon," I say, mentioning the kibbutz that I had been assigned to by the Jewish Agency representative in Los Angeles. "What's the best way of getting there?"

"I'm a customs officer, not a tour guide," he says gruffly, giving his mustache an impatient tug. "When you get out of this building, go to the main street, turn right and walk to the Zebulon Cafe. There you can ask how to get to Beit HaAlon. When you get to the kibbutz, say hello to my brother, Chaim Shachori. Tell him Yossi sends his greetings. He'll take care of you. Now go. My tourist office is closed. Next!"

Outside of the customs shed, a short guy with a battered Brooklyn Dodgers baseball cap calls me over.

"Hey you, American, you got any dollars you want to change?"

I sense a rip off and decline his offer. "Where's the Zebulon Cafe?" I say in Hebrew. He shifts gears and says to me, in Hebrew: "Where you going?"

"Kibbutz Beit HaAlon"

"OK, crazy American, going to a kibbutz, eh? Come on, I'll take you over to the Zebulon. I have to go that way anyway. You'll get lost and end up in Lebanon. Kibbutz eh, no wonder you don't have any money to change. You won't get any more where you're going either," he chuckles.

He grabs my free arm and marches me to Port Street, the main commercial thoroughfare in downtown Haifa. We turn right and half a block later I am prodded into a smoke-filled cafe. The cafe is full of small tables with one or two guys sitting at each one. There is the loud noise of wheeling and dealing. The tables are piled high with pieces of scrap paper, crumpled documents, Israeli currency, and cigarette butts.

"Over there, the guy in the white shirt with the bald head, his name is Eric. He'll get you to where you want to go. Also, when you get to the kibbutz, say hello to Amnon Cohen from Yaacov Goldstein, his brother-in-law. *B'Seder?* (OK)."

"*Toda raba, l'hitraot* (thanks, see you again)," I say, pleased with myself for sticking to my Hebrew vocabulary through the entire conversation.

I walk over to Eric's table. He looks at my suitcase and motions me to sit down. A cigarette dangles from the corner of his mouth as he leafs through his pile of papers and money.

"You're an American?" he asks in German accented English without interrupting his search through the mountain of paper.

His cigarette wiggles as he talks. I notice that he has a number tattooed on his left arm.

"How do you know?" I ask.

"You look like one. You want to go to Kibbutz Beit HaAlon to learn Hebrew?"

"How do you know that?"

"You think you're the first one to be sent to me? I'm the treasurer of the Kibbutz Beit HaAlon. This table is my office. In fact, this cafe is the office of every treasurer of every Kibbutz in the Galilee. But I'm not going back to the kibbutz until tomorrow so I can't transport you. You see that red truck across the street? Take your suitcase, get into the truck and wait. The truck belongs to us. You'll be in the Beit HaAlon in less than an hour. The driver's name is Zelig."

"What do I do when I get to the kibbutz?"

Eric sighs, throws his cigarette butt on the floor and squashes it. "When you get there, get out of the truck, go into the kibbutz office and ask for Chaim Shachori. He'll take care of you."

"Is he the brother of the customs officer?"

Eric laughs, "Right, I see you're on the way to become a kibbutznik. You already know everyone and everything and you just landed. Go, sit in the truck." Eric gets up and heads for the men's room leaving the papers and bills on the table.

I take my suitcase, leave the Zebulon, wait in the crosswalk and, after observing that none of the cars stop at the crosswalk, and dodge my way across the street. I climb into the unlocked, empty truck cabin. After a few minutes Zelig, the truck driver, climbs into his side of the cabin. Like Eric, he also has a cigarette dangling out of the side of his mouth. He wears a faded blue porkpie idiot's cap, a sleeveless sweat stained undershirt, dusty blue work shorts, and even dustier sandals. He starts the truck and without saying a word shifts into gear. The truck groans and rattles down Port Street, heading east toward the kibbutz and the Jordanian border.

1959: Love in Beit HaAlon

After only a few days in the kibbutz, I will have fallen in love— not with Democratic Socialism, collective farms, nor with the State of Israel, but with a redheaded, freckled-nose Irish girl from Cork. She will appear, as if by magic, on the third day of my arrival at the *Ulpan* (Hebrew language school).

I have plunged furiously into the rhythm of work life on the kibbutz. Beit HaAlon is a community of some one thousand people situated on a low ridge overlooking the *Yizrael* valley in central Israel. This valley is paradise. Gentle, multicolored, rolling fields of cropland stretch across the valley, ending at the bare mountain ridge of Gilboa.

It's the same spot where King Saul and his troops perished at the hands of the Midianites, just a few millennia ago. The kibbutz sits on a hill on the north side of the valley separated from neighboring settlements by wheat fields and olive groves. On the eastern horizon, the Mountains of Gilead, property of the Hashemite kingdom of Jordan, mark the valley of the Jordan River as it flows from the Galilee down to the Dead Sea. The kibbutzim to the East, and the immigrant town of Beit Shaan are at the foot of Mount Gilboa. They are frequently exposed to bombardments and small arms fire from the Jordanian army across the frontier. We hear the noise- booms and bumps- from our safe perch five miles back from the border.

Beit HaAlon's members live in red tile-roofed cottages grouped around a large, central dining hall. Each cottage has a tiny garden and a bit of grass planted around it. A luxuriant lawn with islands of rose bushes and shade trees surrounds the dining hall. The dining hall itself is the largest and most important building in the kibbutz. There, the members eat their meals, and conduct their New England style town meetings with a Middle Eastern brashness. They read their newspapers, argue their politics, sip their afternoon tea, play chess, and plan their future.

The children's houses nestle between the dining hall and the members' cottages. How dear these children are to the kibbutz! Nothing is spared to make the children's houses safe, friendly and pleasant for the youngest generation of kibbutzniks.

"After all," say the members of the kibbutz, "they are our future."

Each age group has its own house where the children sleep, learn and work. Each of the children's houses has it's own crew of adult helpers and educators to ensure the best possible care. I look forward to having my children born in a kibbutz. But who will their mother be?

The backside of the kibbutz is a muddy hodgepodge of small workshops, silos, tractor sheds and manure piles that contrast with the organized and manicured quality of the living area. This is where the religion of work is the only ethos and the only sins are lethargy and the evil desire for personal, rather than collective, gain. Here are the flourmill, the sandal maker, the work coordinator's shack, the garage, the chicken houses, the sheep pens and the stable. Here, also, is the kibbutz pigpen, carefully hidden from the medieval eyes of any kosher inspectors that may wander in from the much-hated Ministry of Religion. Here is what the kibbutz is all about: Jewish pioneers, building a new life by the sweat of their brows.

I wake up at 5:30 in the morning and get into my work clothes: the traditional blue pants, blue work shirt, idiot's cap, gray work socks and heavy work shoes. I brush my teeth in an outdoor sink, just beyond the bare cabin that is my new lodging. Later, I make my way to work in the flourmill.

There I put in a ten hour day shouldering ponderous sacks of flour, barley, corn and fishmeal, mixing the grains for feed, and stacking the burlap sacks in the granary. Tractor motors are revving up in the kibbutz garage and from every direction, blue clad *Chaverim* (kibbutz members), puffing on their morning cigarettes, are on their way to work sites. Some are going to the sheep and cow pens, some to the olive canning factory, some to the vegetable fields, some to the children's houses, some to the dining hall to set up for breakfast. Others, like Zelig the driver, proceed to their trucks ready to haul goods back and forth to Haifa, Tel Aviv or Jerusalem.

I arrive at the flourmill a few minutes early and Chaim Shachori, the miller—and brother of the Haifa customs officer—has coffee ready. Chaim is an older kibbutz member. His hair is white with grain, dust and age. Originally from, Poland, he joined the kibbutz in the mid-1930s when it was only a camp of tents on a ridge above a swamp. While we sip the strong, coarse brew, called *café botz* (mud coffee), Chaim hands me the list of grains to be milled, and instructions for sacking and storage. Today we prepare sheep fattening feed and I need to measure out Milled

Roughage, Maize Meal, Feed Lime, Urea, Sulfur and Salt to get just the right mixture for our horned ruminant comrades.

Coffee *botz* hurtling through our veins, we are up and at our work until 8 a.m. Breakfast time. We shake the feed dust off our clothes as best we can and head for the central dining hall. Several hundred *Chaverim* are already at the tables, wolfing down the typical winter breakfast of hot cereal, Israeli salad, rough bread, herring, goat cheese, and tea. The morning papers are floating around the dining hall and loud political deliberations are roaring at the tables. This is not an English tea party. These are the new Jewish peasants who believe in Socialism, worship manual labor, despise bourgeois manners, defend the borders, and vigorously join in the political struggles of a new nation. I feel honored to be among them, even with a sore back.

Five more hours of heavy work in the flourmill and I am covered with a thick layer of flour and sweat. We take a half-hour for a heavy lunch, eating voraciously. Late in the afternoon, I return to my cabin in back of the *Ulpan,* take a towel and clean clothes and head for the communal shower. The men's side of the shower facility reminds me of my high school gym back in San Diego: ancient shower heads, steam, and the pungent smell of sweaty underwear and socks hanging on hooks.

I can hear the damp click of wooden clogs on wet cement floors. Except that here, the men are arguing over the future of the country, not the results of a football game. They scrub their bodies with square bars of rough yellow soap and lufa. Their Hebrew is still too fast for me but I pick out words and names: Ben Gurion! Sinai! Begin! Yigal Alon! Abdul Nasser! Crazy Americans! Eisenhower! Bulganin! Khrushchev! Hussein! Castro!

Sotzializm! Capitalizm! A few of the young guys peek at the women's side through a small hole in the wall and I hear a whistle and the words *takhat yaffa,* meaning 'nice ass.'

After my hot shower, I put on my clean shorts and a short sleeved white shirt and head back to the *Ulpan*. A cool, late afternoon breeze feels refreshing and the waning sun paints the Gilead hills. My muscles are gratifyingly sore after the day's physical labor. Approaching the school, I see Zelig's truck and several new *Ulpan* students passing suitcases down from its platform. Among them, I see a flash of red hair, a white skirt and the back of a woman's comely legs. My love has arrived…with an Irish accent.

My eyes meet the green eyes of this lovely girl whose long red hair falls like silk to her waist. She has an angelic, tiny nose covered with freckles. She wears a peasant blouse and a simple white skirt. She has firm and full breasts and a sweet little Irish bottom. Her green eyes laugh at me, but not a word passes between us. I smile and climb on the truck to help with unloading the suitcases. I hand one down to the Irish girl and get another glance at her beauty.

In the evening, I visit Chaim, the miller, and sip pomegranate wine made by his wife Sarah. I am hearing Chaim's stories about the difficult early days of the kibbutz ("…when *we* came here, we all lived in tent…") but I'm thinking Ireland and freckled noses. I return to the *Ulpan* area and sit on the wooden steps leading up to the classroom cabin listening to jackals howling their greeting to the night and frogs singing their green wake-up songs. Then God creates a miracle, and Fionna, the Irish girl, appears and sits down next to me on the wooden steps.

Fionna starts up the conversation.

"Beautiful night" she says in her Irish accent, and I am done for.

"Yes, beautiful night" is what I say. I love you and will always love you is what I think.

She tells me about her life in Cork. Her father is Jewish but he has hidden his identity. She has argued with him about her Jewish American boyfriend. The boyfriend is studying medicine at the Royal College of Surgeons in Ireland and her father is a big muckimuck on the faculty. The father has threatened to expel the boy from the school if he doesn't leave his daughter alone. In anger, she leaves home and comes to Israel to discover her roots. I tell her about my own search for roots, my unwillingness to fall into the mold that society has prepared for me, et cetera, et cetera, but it's all blather, irrelevant to what is really going on—my becoming lost in her eyes, her silky red hair and her Irish lilt.

We go into the dark classroom, ostensibly to turn on the ancient radio and hear the news from BBC, but within seconds we are in each other's arms, holding each other, our loneliness melting away. My senses blur, hours seem to pass before I hear the BBC, and the jackals and the frogs start up again. Nothing exists for me outside of this lovely woman...no *Ulpan*...no kibbutz,...no Israel,...no world but her soft hair falling across my face.

The next morning, on a cold but clear February day, the *Ulpan* courses commence. I am in the advanced class and Fionna, being Hebrew-less, is in the beginners' class. The students in my class are new immigrants from Bulgaria, Rumania, Argentina, Brazil, Ireland and the USA. The first lesson taught by Esther, the headmistress of the *Ulpan,* concentrates on a map of Israel hanging in front of the blackboard. Esther expounds, in basic Hebrew, upon the natural borders of our new homeland. Pointer in hand, she identifies and carefully pronounces the regional names: the *Negev,* the coastal plains, the Jerusalem highlands, the Yizrael valley—where our kibbutz is located—the Galilee, the Beit Shan valley guarding us to the east, and the Jordan River valley. Next, incredibly, Esther traces the pointer along the Litany River, deep in Lebanon.

I raise my hand and ask in my stilted prayer book Hebrew:

"Is not the Litany River in Lebanon?"

"It is now," Esther fires. "But the Litany River has to be considered our natural frontier for the future. Now that we have a country, we must be prepared to defend it. Now, repeat after me: The Litany River is our...."

I gulp but I'm not going to get into an argument with the teacher on the first day of class. Besides, my mind is very much elsewhere. I am wondering if Fionna has freckles on her knees as well. My pulse races!

In the early evening, Fionna and I stroll out to the fields, walking the paths between the vegetable gardens and the citrus groves, hand in hand. We watch the sun dip over the Western Galilee and then we turn to the east and watch the last windows glowing in the Jordanian villages across the Jordan. Fionna and I hug and embrace, looking into each other's eyes for long stretches of heart-pounding time. Such tenderness, such passion!

Two pulsating weeks pass in our romance. The *Ulpan* students are given a breather from their grammar books, dictations, constipated conversations, and border smashing map sessions. We have two days off and Fionna and I accept an invitation to visit the home of Ibrahim, an Arab friend who works as a hired electrician in the kibbutz olive cannery. We take a bus to Nazareth and sleep, in separate rooms, in the sprawling house of the Abu Nawab clan. In the morning, the young children of the house pull us all through the town, showing us the holy places, the churches, the grottos and Mary's Well. At night, Ibrahim slaughters a sheep in the family courtyard in our honor and we eat *humus*, pickled vegetables, *kabob*, *shashlik* and *pita* to our hearts' content. The next afternoon, we set out for the Sea of Galilee. We hitch rides on army jeeps, produce trucks and a tourist bus.

In Tiberius we splurge on a fish dinner at a lakeshore restaurant, feeding ourselves, and an army of Jewish and Arab cats that demand their share of the catch. I am growing a beard and, dressed in my rough kibbutz clothes. I fancy myself as one of Jesus' disciples and offer to walk on the water for Fionna.

She is wearing her peasant blouse with an Israeli army jacket, and a plain blue skirt. With her sparkling green eyes, lovely hips and spicy Irish manner, who can she be but Mary Magdalene herself?

We return to the kibbutz, learn more Hebrew, and a few weeks later set out together once more, this time to Jerusalem. Fionna has Irish friends in the capital and I have orthodox cousins there whom I have never met. Twilight finds us walking, hand in hand, looking over to the church towers and minarets that jut above the old city wall. As the sun sets in Jerusalem, the walls turn a burnt red, the Christian bells peal and the muezzins call out the Moslem evening prayers. It is all a wonderful dream except for the saddening effect of the barbed wire, sand bags and alert sentries marking the dividing line between Israel and Jordan through the middle of the city.

Three ecstatic months go by at Bet HaAlon for us and I maintain an insatiable appetite for my Irish-Jewish love. The hard work in the granary has changed both my body and my perception of myself. I am lean and brawny and beginning to look like a true proletarian. My skin is bronzed from toiling outside in a new job. I am now the kibbutz gravedigger and I keep very busy because the founding generation of Bet HaAlon is beginning to pass on to the big commune in the sky. I found out that the soft-looking earth of this valley has a hard layer of gravel under it. It takes a whole day of pick and shoveling to hack out one grave.

I have taken another step in becoming an Israeli and discarding my American identity. Now officially my last name is no longer Camiel. I am now Shimon Chamiel, the grandson of Yisroel Chmiel and son of Zelig Chmiel. In three generations, our family name has shifted from Yiddish to English to Hebrew. And now we are back in our Promised Land. I imagine the applause and joy of a long string of ancestors. Free at last.

Fionna is working indoors, keeping her white Irish body out of the sun. But in spite of her precautions her skin is burning and blistering. Her nose is peeling and she is working in the kibbutz sewing room. I notice that she is putting on weight; her arms are puffy but still sweet. OH, those freckled elbows!

One early summer's day, Esther, the Hebrew teacher, draws me aside after class.

"When are you two getting married?" she asks in her blunt, but motherly style.

"I don't know," I answer, surprised by Esther's question.

"I hope it's soon. I can make the arrangements with the Rabbi in Afula for you," she offers.

"We really haven't talked about marriage. Right now we're just friends." (Gulp)

"Well, your friend is pregnant." Esther observes, as if she was talking to someone who is a little dense.

Late that afternoon, Fionna and I take our stroll out of the kibbutz living areas to the fields opposite Mount Gilboa. Fionna and I sit on the edge of a newly plowed field and watch a line of storks stalking the furrows in search of little fat mice and bugs.

"Are you really pregnant?" I ask

"Yes, I am. I came here pregnant," she answers.

"Who is the father?" I stammer sadly, knowing it wasn't me.

"Oh, my boyfriend, Richard, in Ireland." She goes on as if we were discussing the storks instead of my life. "You see, my father threatened to kick Richard out of medical school if we tried to get engaged or married. Father might have really ruined Dick's career, so we decided to force the issue by me getting pregnant. I didn't have the nerve to stay and face my father; he can be a fearsome ogre when he's angry. I decided that I should come here to Israel until Dick could break the news to my dad, after graduation of course. Then, he is to come here to pick me up and off we'll go to New York. I'm sorry Shimon, I didn't have the nerve to tell you."

Her green eyes fill with tears and so do mine.

The storks, perhaps feeling our sadness, begin, one by one, to leave the field, slowly spiraling up the warm currents, moving down the valley to wherever storks sleep.

1959: Heading for the Galilee

The *Ulpan* in Beit HaAlon ends, Fionna is gone, and my Hebrew is much improved. It's time to move on. Every bush and every tree, every stork and every goat, every cloud and every sunset remind me of Fionna. There are few people my own age among the younger kibbutzniks, and they are all off in the army. I am lonely and restless. I say goodbye to Esther, pack my suitcase, put on my idiot's hat, and head for the Galilee. I have decided to scout out the far northeast corner of my new homeland and work on a kibbutz in the Upper Galilee, the seven-mile wide thumb of the Jordan River valley that sticks up between Syria and Lebanon.

On a bone-dry August day, I hitch rides up the Jordan valley, past the Sea of Galilee, and through the steaming heat of Tiberius. At the Tiberius bus station, I climb aboard a smoke belching, gear grinding, *Egged* bus and head north up the steep basalt plug leading to the Hulah Valley. The bus is jammed full, standing room only, with a cargo of kibbutzniks, Moroccan immigrants, Arab farmers, Russian old-timers, Swedish pilgrims, Australian tourists, black Cochin Jews from India, gold toothed Romanian shop keepers, and live chickens. Only in Israel will you find a busload like this: a melting pot of people piled on top of each other with no air conditioning and no deodorant.

A Moroccan and his chicken get off at Rosh Pina and I lurch into his seat in the back of the bus. Who do I see sitting next to me but Grandfather, dressed in blue work clothes and an old Israeli army jacket.

"I'm sorry about your broken romance on the kibbutz," he says. "But after all she was only half Jewish, it wouldn't have worked out anyway. You look good, healthy as a Cossack, stronger. Are you still on your way to being a hero?"

"You look good, too, Grandpa. Are you enjoying Israel?"

"Well, I see some good and some bad in what's going on here." He cogitates and pulls on one of his ears.

"Tell me about the bad."

"First, hardly anyone prays to God, especially up here in the Galilee and especially in the kibbutzim. We had Socialists and Communists in Ostrolenka, so it's not that I'm seeing them for the first time. But up here, everyone seems to be a Socialist. I even saw a picture of Stalin in the dining hall on one kibbutz. Another bad thing is, of course, the danger. There are little children and mothers living too close to the border. I'm used to armies. They used to pass through our village all the time, Russians, Germans, Poles…but they didn't bring their children up to the front line. What will happen if there will be a big war? I wouldn't want my grandchildren living in a place like that. Another bad thing are the crazy drivers on these roads. Give them enough time and they'll kill more people than all of the bombs and bullets put together."

My gut reaction, as a new immigrant and a super patriot, is to dispute Grandfather, point by point. After all, look had what happened to his family in Poland. How can we protect our own country unless we are willing to run risks? We can't let the enemy intimidate us. If we pull back our settlements along the border, the Arabs will encroach upon our land, little by little or maybe all at once. Then, what will become of us? We have to stand fast. And as far as praying to God for help is concerned, if that strategy had worked I might have a live grandfather sitting next to me rather than the ghost of one. But I didn't try to argue with him, especially with his fears about his great grandchildren who have, incidentally, not even been born yet. He still has much to learn about our fledgling country.

"So you think you know more than your Grandfather?" he says, with a touch of patriarchal humor. "We'll see. I've got plenty of time to keep an eye on you."

He puts his hand over mine and gives it a squeeze. The bus pulls to a stop near an abandoned Arab village. Grandfather gets up and moves toward the open door.

"Incidentally," he says as he departs, "I've learned some more Modern Hebrew. You can call me *Saba* from now on. Grandfather is too formal for the two of us. *L'hitraot* (see you later)."

Next, I unfold my map of Israel, and pick a Kibbutz located conveniently in the center of the valley...it doesn't make much difference to me which one I go to, so why not Cfar Moshe?

After about ten minutes, I jerk on the bell rope. Stepping over the chickens in the aisle, I get off the bus and find myself at a junction where the road to Cfar Moshe heads East across the Hulah. I am alone by the side of a one and a half lane road. A rusty road sign points to Cfar Moshe and Frontier Settlements. A hot wind is blowing down from the Golan. The asphalt is sticky, melting in the brutal heat of the day. A cow watches me from behind a barbed wire fence, perhaps thinking, here comes more cannon fodder. Eucalyptus trees line the road, planted so that the Syrian artillery observers will have difficulty tracking Israeli troop movements. A few minutes later, a giant Mack truck, painted orange, pulls off the main road and whooshes to a stop. A sign on the door panel states in Hebrew "*Upper Galilee Truck Cooperative.*" The driver motions me up and I climb into the cabin.

"Going to Cfar Moshe?" I ask. The driver nods his head and off we go. He is a dark skinned Cochin Jew with a dreadful overbite, originally from the south coast of India. His name turns out to be Eliyahu (Elijah), and although his destination is a border kibbutz further down the road than I need to go, he will let me off at the gate to Cfar Moshe. A great start, I muse, personally delivered by Elijah, the precursor of the Messiah. The truck whisks down the narrow road at a furious speed. God help us if a vehicle comes from the other direction. In a few minutes we cross a Bailey bridge and scream to a stop next to a gate and a sentry box.

"This is it," proclaims Elijah in his strange Indian accent. "Say hello to my friend Eliezer for me. He works in the pig farm."

"Thanks for the ride," I call, suitcase in hand, as Elijah and his truck gnash gears, envelop me in dust and exhaust, and roar off to the east.

The sentry pays no attention to me as I pass through the gate and walk into the kibbutz past a row of carob trees facing a parallel windbreak of cypress trees. A windbreak guards the long rows of an apple orchard and the trees are heavy with their dusty fruit. Alfalfa fields, green as a golf course, spread off to the east. Down the internal road, a little farther, I see the first line of one-story apartment buildings painted white with red tile roofs, four families to a building. Past the first apartments, I see a wooden cabin marked *Mazkirut* (Secretariat).

I put my suitcase down on the porch and go in to speak to the kibbutz *Mazkir* (Secretary General). He is sitting behind a scratched, wooden desk cluttered with an Everest of papers. The office reeks of tobacco, heat and the faint odor of bat dung. The *Mazkir* is dressed in blue work shorts and a sweaty gray undershirt. A cheap, kibbutz-issue cigarette dangles from the side of his mouth and I note his bare feet and hairy legs under the desk.

"What can I do for you?" he says politely in English with the trace of a Central European accent.

"I would like to stay on your kibbutz and work." I respond in my best Hebrew, somehow conscious that every word I say might influence my future life.

"You are from California?" the *Mazkir* continues in English. Obviously he is a master of accents.

"I am," I answer in Hebrew.

"Did you do any manual labor in California?" The Secretary General asks with a twinkle in his eye, knowing that I hadn't, but this time, at least, he addresses me in Hebrew.

"No, I was a student in California, but I've worked six months in the flourmill at Kibbutz Bet HaAlon."

"Well, we don't have a flourmill here. How would you feel about picking apples?"

"Why not?" I say.

Switching to politics, the *Mazkir* asks, "Do you think that Jewish youth from the United States will begin to immigrate to Israel now?"

"No, I'm afraid not." I answer, shifting into political gear with him. "Unfortunately, you can't look at *me* as being the first wave of an immigration: I'm just an odd ball American that hates Capitalism and wants to help build the Jewish State. My family and friends think I'm crazy."

"So did mine," comments the *Mazkir* sadly, "but they're all dead in Czechoslovakia now, thanks to Hitler, and I'm alive, here in Israel."

A bit of silence passes between us.

"Well, take your bags over there." The Secretary General points to another small cabin visible through the dusty and flyspecked window screen. "Go over there to Malka. She's in charge of new immigrants. Tell her to give you a room in the volunteers' quarters. You start picking apples at 6:00 tomorrow morning."

I'm in!

"Shalom," I say, picking up my suitcase and heading toward the door. "Incidentally, my name is Shimon."

"Incidentally, my name is Amnon," says Amnon. "Find your way over to my house for tea this afternoon. We'll have some Johnny Walker Black Label that I've saved for a wandering Californian."

"I'll find you and thanks," I say, "*L'hitraot*, see you later."

I step outside the door and begin my seventeen years as a kibbutznik in Cfar Moshe.

1959: Sending for Ruthie

"How do you like our Kibbutz so far?" says Amnon, as he pours me another cruel shot of Slivovitz.

"No complaints, Amnon."

"Not even one? Do you like your work in the orchards? I know that in America you aren't used to waking up at five in the morning. What about the food we serve in our dining hall? Too bland compared with your Mexican food in San Diego? Are the dishes clean enough for you? Do you lack anything?"

"What is it that you want to ask me, Amnon? I've been in Cfar Moshe for four months now. If I didn't like it here I would have left already."

"I understand," says Amnon, "just teasing a little. People do like you here. You have more patience with people, maybe because you're an outsider, or maybe because you come from such a relaxed country. We're not used to Americans who haven't had a hard life like many of us. Look, even my dog Dasha has taken a liking to you."

Indeed, Amnon's airdale is happily lounging under my chair, snuggling her doggy chin between my felt slippers. Although Amnon, Dasha and I are pleasantly warming ourselves with the help of a kerosene heater and the Slivovitz, it is a miserably cold and wet day outside in the Galilee.

"This Slivovitz is a hell of a lot better than that bad shnapps that Chanoch sells in the communal storehouse. Where did you get it?"

"I have my sources, Shimon. But I don't mind telling you that I got a few bottles of the stuff when I was in diplomatic service in Hungary during the 1956 revolution."

"Was that a good year for Slivovitz?"

"No," Amnon laughs, "but it WAS a good year for getting Jews out of Hungary."

Amnon had been on hush-hush service behind the iron curtain in 1956. Since this is only 1959, I figure that Amnon still has a major stash of the Balkan intoxicant. But of course, no one would know anything about that, except the entire Kibbutz.

"But getting back to my original question, Shimon, do you think that you will be applying for membership in our little community? You know that you're eligible to do so after six months of being a resident here."

"Maybe."

"Maybe?"

"Well there's a little problem that I have about staying on in Cfar Moshe; the same problem that I had in Beit HaAlon, the first kibbutz I was living on."

"Let me guess," says Amnon. "You're frustrated because there is nobody here your age. Our own kids are too young for you and our *vatikim*, our old timers, we're all too old to be of any interest to you. Some of us are even into our 40s."

"You got it Amnon. It seems like the only eligible female here is Konga the Mule."

"Not your type, eh. But what about all those girlfriends you had in the USA. Don't any of them want to live in our little Utopia?"

"Amnon, you don't know anything about our American Jewish girls. Most of them are spoiled rotten. None of them would ever think of coming to Israel, much less a frontier settlement like this."

"Not even one of them?"

He pours another shot glass full of the greenish poison. A full-blown rain now soaks our Galilee soil.

"Hope this weather will be over before the potato harvest is due to start," says Amnon.

"Sure is getting warm in here." I say, trying to push Dasha off my slippers.

"Incidentally," says Amnon, "you've certainly made my neighbor Franta the postman happy, allowing him to steam off the nice stamps you get from your American friends?"

"Actually, Franta was steaming them off anyway so I just gave him permission to do it."

"He told me that the postmarks are all from Beverly Hills, California. Any connection to one of those ex-girlfriends of yours?"

"That's what I like about this kibbutz. Who wants privacy anyway?"

"Well?"

From shoe-level Dasha looks up at me, as if she too wants to know who the hell I'm getting mail from?

"OK, I have got this one ex-girlfriend in mind. Ruthie is her name. But I'm still wondering whether she would be willing to come here or not. Her Dad sent her to Israel a few years ago and she liked it. She liked me a lot at one time, although she has been dating some other guys. Her Dad is a big guy in Hollywood. Makes movies. Beverly Hills family."

"How does she look?"

"Pleasant. Tall. Dark hair with a little stripe of grey. Wonderful eyes. Very down to earth type. Hates the whole Beverly Hills scene. Well, maybe she would be willing to try to live with me on the kibbutz."

"Sounds just right for you, Shimon. How are her legs?"

"Why do you ask?"

"In the long run, good legs are very important."

"Better lay off the Slivovitz, Amnon."

January 1960: Ruthie Arrives

HaOlam Shel Machar Newspaper

Upper Galilee, January 15, 1960: BEAUTIFUL AND SPOILED BEVERLY HILLS GIRL ARRIVES IN THE KIBBUTZ...

...states the leading Israeli scandal magazine; its yellow journalistic odor emanates from the fleshpots of Tel Aviv.

Ruth Brand, daughter of Herman Brand the famous Hollywood producer, has tossed away her rich Beverly Hills life-style for a new life on a border kibbutz (name withheld) in the north of the country. A blue eyed, leggy blonde and former model, Miss Brand joins her kibbutz lover (name withheld) after a torrid romance, which began in the affluent circles of Hollywood and was consummated in a dangerous border kibbutz along the Golan Heights. Dressed in simple but obviously expensive American jeans, wearing kibbutz-issue sandals and a kibbutz work shirt, she answers our reporter's questions with great personal charm, subtle sexiness and aristocratic elegance as she feeds the pigs in the kibbutz's covert pigpen.

Our Reporter: How did your parents react to your immigration to Israel?

Ruth (now nicknamed Ruthie): My parents *encouraged* me to come here. They are both life-long Zionists. My father is even planning to make a new Hollywood movie here in Israel starring Merlina Mercouri and Eva Marie Saint.

Our Reporter: Why did you choose to live in a kibbutz instead of Tel Aviv. Don't you like our nightlife and our beaches?

Ruthie: Well, as you know, my boyfriend, S. (name withheld), is a kibbutznik; he's also from the USA. He is so passionate about his work up here on the frontier. Neither of us would want to live in the city. Neither of us have interest in nightlife beyond what we like to do in our little wooden shack next to the River Jordan. (She grins sexily.)

Our Reporter: Tell us about your boyfriend here in the kibbutz. What attracted you to chase after him all the way to Israel?

Ruthie: Well, he's very good looking, very tender, big muscles, romantic, heroic, intelligent, and thoughtful, wants children. What's not to like?

Our Reporter: What about the bombs and other dangers along the border. Wouldn't you be safer in the city or back in Beverly Hills?

Ruthie: No way! I feel much safer here. Beverly Hills is full of all kinds of freaky, selfish people. Here, everyone helps everyone else and everyone trusts everyone else. Besides, we all have to do our part for the State of Israel. Some people like to donate money to Israel; some people want to build luxury villas down in Tel Aviv. I like being up here in the front line. Living on the kibbutz is my way of contributing to our new Jewish homeland.

Our Reporter: What are your plans for the future?

Ruthie: Stay right here and have lots of babies! And as soon as possible!

****

"Jesus Christ, Ruthie, how did that reporter find you all the way up here?"

We are standing on the sidewalk in front of the Baby House where Ruthie works raising the latest batch of future kibbutz members.

"He didn't."

"He didn't?"

"No he didn't. I never even talked to the guy."

"You've got to be kidding."

"I'm not kidding at all...I never met the guy. The first time I heard about the interview was when *Zahava* brought the damn magazine over from the kitchen just a few minutes ago. My Hebrew isn't good enough yet to read the thing, but *Zahava* translated it for me."

"I can't believe it, Ruthie! They faked a whole interview with you. They even made you into a blonde!"

"Now all the people in the packing house will think that I dye my hair black."

"Black with a few wisps of grey, if I'm not mistaken. I love your hair as it is. You better not become a blue-eyed blonde. What about the professional model thing? Something in your past that you didn't tell me about? You have nice legs but they're not model class!"

"You don't think so?"

"Actually they are. Several of the apple orchard guys were talking about them in the dining hall and I'm getting jealous."

"I thought everyone was supposed to share here," she says as brazen as could be.

"We're not at that stage of Socialism yet," I say.

"Getting back to the article, what do you have to say about that little added touch," says Ruthie, "where the article has me working in the pig-pen instead of here in the baby house?"

"And how about my passionate work out in the fields, when I really *am* working in the pig-pen?" I say.

"How about your father making a new Hollywood movie here in Israel?"

"How about the thoughtful, romantic, big muscled kibbutz hero?"

"And how about the lots of babies thing?"

"Well Shimon," she smiles her teasing smile," that may be the little touch of truth in the whole non-interview. How 'bout meeting me after work at our little cabin next to the Jordan River?"

"But our cabin isn't near the Jordan River, it's clear across the kibbutz from that stinky river."

"Never mind, it's close enough," says my Ruthie."

1960: The Man in the Apple Tree

It is 5:30 on a December morning and Kibbutz Cfar Moshe is draped in darkness. Not everyone here has an alarm clock. Those of us that don't can ask the night guard to give us a wake-up call. The guard, a young Turkish immigrant named Baruch is anxious to finish his job and go to sleep after prowling the kibbutz periphery all night. His call is not a docile one. *Boker tov* (good morning) he shouts as he bangs upon my door. I curse Baruch, and his Ladino speaking ancestors. What will he be dreaming of as he drifts off to sleep in his warm room while I stumble out of bed and go out to work in the freezing apple orchard?

Seen from the air, the kibbutz looks like three concentric squares. First, there is the inside square: the dwelling area with red roofed, one-story cottages for the older members, prefabricated shacks for the newer members and a few public buildings nestled within a forest of pine and eucalyptus trees. The second square, surrounding the first, is that of the industrial area with the packinghouse, the cold storage building, the carpenter's shop, the armory, the shoe factory, the tractor sheds, the garages, the alfalfa mill, the turkey coops, the children's farm and the beehives. Beyond that lies the third concentric square surrounding the other two. This is the vast, outermost square of the agricultural areas - the orchards, the alfalfa fields, the cotton fields, the fish farms, the vineyard, and the wheat fields. If you are working anywhere within the agricultural area, you are treated to two gifts: The first gift is a spectacular view of the two mighty ridges on the east and west sides of the valley. The ridge of Naftali, inside the Land of Israel, looms benignly on the west; and the Golan Heights, in Syria, staring menacingly down upon us on the East. To the north there is an even more dramatic view of snow-covered Mt. Hermon, Syrian army fortresses and a ruined crusader castle visible on its limestone slopes.

The second gift of working in the agricultural square is the gift of hard labor in the fields, so long denied to most of the Jewish people. Now agricultural work itself is the symbol of the new Jewish pioneers who, at least on the Zionist calendars, march proudly to work with their scythes, shovels and pitchforks over their shoulders, singing songs of Zion. At least in the movies.

Beyond the legend, the pioneers are more likely to be like me this morning, staggering along, half-asleep, on the way to a long day of work, thinking about how warm it had been in bed until Baruch, the Turk, crowed his wake-up call.

Officially at work, a few dozen of us stand outside the tractor shed, sipping strong coffee. It has been mercifully prepared by Ziggi, a red haired man, with the kibbutz's best mustache. He wakes up a quarter hour earlier than we do to bring us the gift of caffeine.

Tractor motors warm up in their shed giving a hint of heat along with a whiff of carbon monoxide. The orchard branch manager, Amos, reads our assignments from a clipboard between puffs on his pipe.

"Gad goes to '*Aleph*' orchard with Meir (the kibbutz clown) to prune the Jonathan apple trees, Ziggi and Shimon go to '*Daled*' orchard to finish pruning the Golden Delicious trees, Clarita and Adva go to '*Tet*' orchard to check for tiger moth larvae in the bark of the trees."

A slice of sun peeks over the Golan Heights without interrupting the cold, but bringing the illusion of warmth in its presence. The strong taste of coffee helps, too. I start up the orchard committee jeep while Ziggi loads our equipment in back - pruning shears and knives, ladders and saws, tar and brushes, cigarettes and coffee cups. He pops into the front seat, lights a cigarette and we are on our way. Heavy dust rises from the dirt road as the jeep speeds along the side of the cotton fields toward '*Daled*' orchard.

Arriving at the orchard tool shack we take down a harsh gulp of medicinal cognac from a bottle stashed in the first aid box. We both grunt as the near toxic schnapps hits bottom. The defrosting process has begun in earnest.

Soon Ziggi and I are standing on the metal rungs of ladders on opposite sides of a bare-branched, still dormant apple tree. Our pruning shears click away and branches crash down to the floor of the orchard. The hard work heats our bodies, but it's still too cold to remove our work gloves. The sun crawls a little higher and we begin to talk to each other between the limbs of the tree.

Yesterday, I had been answering Ziggi's questions about my life in California: girlfriends I left behind, surfing adventures and mischievous pranks with the other fraternity guys at college. It is Ziggy's turn today and I ask him to tell me the story of his youthful days.

"You know, Shimon," he says from the other side of the tree, "I never had a adolescence like you did. I left Danzig when I was only 11-years-old. My parents took me down to the railroad station. It was 1939, and they put me on a train full of children that turned out to be the last train out for Jewish kids before the war began. I still had my knickers on and looked just like any German kid. I said goodbye to my mother and father through the window of the train and we were gone. I never saw my parents again."

We feel some warmth now as the sun rises three fingers above the Golan Heights. We both unbutton our work coats and toss them down to the bottom of our ladders.

Ziggi continues in his matter-of-fact voice, "So, the train brought us to a port city in Romania and I was put on a ship and sent off to Palestine. The boat was crowded and there was nothing for me to do. We had to hide down below every time another ship would come near us because we were coming illegally to Palestine. The British navy was blocking refugee ships in order to pacify the Arabs, who didn't want any more Jews in Palestine. We almost made it to the coast of our new homeland but a British destroyer caught us and forced us to follow her into Haifa port. We were interned for a few days, looking at Palestine through a barbed wire fence, and then British soldiers loaded us onto a freighter that took us through the Suez Canal to the island of Mauritius in the Indian Ocean. On the island, we were kept in a prison camp with British guards all around the periphery. I don't know what they thought a few hundred unarmed Jews could do to them. There wasn't much food and there was nothing to do for a kid. I spent eight boring years on Mauritius."

As Ziggi tells me more details about the drab life, isolation, bad food and bad health in the camps on Mauritius, the sun asserts its authority and we both peel off our work sweaters and gloves and drop them down to the base of the tree.

"Then," continues Ziggi, "in 1948, the English let us go on to Palestine. When we got there, a few days after Independence had been declared, they sent a few other kids and me from Mauritius to this kibbutz, *Cfar Moshe*. It wasn't very long before we were put into the army, given a rifle and sent out to the battlefield. I was in *Mishmar HaYarden*, a village right next to the Syrian border and, with all of my bad luck, the village was overrun by the Syrian army. I was wounded in the battle and a Syrian soldier picked me up and carried me to safety, but I ended up rotting in a Syrian army prison for three years. That's where I learned to eat onions and olives and to swat flies. We were exchanged back to Israel in 1951, and I started my life again here on the kibbutz. I realized, then, that I had lost my childhood and youth somewhere between Danzig and Damascus."

I don't exactly know what to say to Ziggy. "I guess I wasn't the only one who had some adventures," I toss out, weakly.

We prune together in silence for a minute, standing on top of our ladders. I can see Syria from where I stand. The great ridge of Naftali, to the west, burns ochre as the sun touches its face. Ziggi pulls his pipe out of his pocket, and stuffs some kibbutz-issue pipe tobacco into it. He hoists a lighter out of his jacket pocket and angles the flame into the bowl. The smoke smells good in the cool morning air of the apple orchard.

"Shimon," he sighs, "I'd trade lives with you any time."

He puffs on his pipe a few more times and then goes on pruning the tree, opening the center branches to the rays of the sun.

December 12, 1960: Bottom line?

Socialist ideology?
Pioneering?
Equalitarianism?
Love of the land?
Guarding the borders?
Making a living?
All of the above, but it is especially about having children.

With no children, the people of the kibbutz will age and die and the dream will pass away into history.

The children of the holocaust are gone, murdered in the forests with their parents.

A new generation of children must arise.

Be fruitful and multiply and replenish the earth, says the author of Genesis.

The new Israeli government gives cash bonuses to large families.

Replenish!

Our daughter Galila is born December 12, 1960

1961: South of Rosh Pina

South of the hamlet of Rosh Pina, the north/south road leads down a serpentine descent through a vast plug of basalt rock to the Sea of Galilee.

The Jordan River feeds this biblical body of water, beginning its path at the fountains emerging from Mt. Hermon's snows. It flows through the twin-ridged Hulah valley and then plunges through white water narrows to the below sea-level basin of the harp-shaped lake. The sea has had many names in its long history of settlement, among them: Genesserat, Yam Kinneret, Lake of Tiberius, Bahr Tabariya, and Sea of Galilee.

This sea, really a lake, shows different faces depending on the weather. During the heat of summer, it is a pale, unmoving gray mirror, barely alive, windless, small comfort to the dreary sweat-armpitted population of its shores. Other times, especially in the spring, it is a bright blue, lively, playful body of water with its own waves and froth, almost imitating a real sea. In the winter, it can decide to be rough and dangerous and even the bold fisherman of Tiberius will take the day off and read the paper in bed.

The strange natives of Tiberius, called *Tverianim*, are an odd mix of fisher-folk, falafel-stand vendors, hot springs operators and provincial government officials. These people, in their false glory, call their city the capital of the north. We Upper Galileans, north of Rosh Pina, consider the mystical city of Safed to be our urban hub. Only the *Tverianim* with their ubiquitous flies and hoards of wharf cats could imagine that their town is some kind of capital. We avoid the place, especially in the summer.

But sometimes one does have to go Tiberius. Reasons vary. The regional branch of *Kupat Holim* (the Israeli labor federation's health plan), the draft board, the regional department of motor vehicles, some courthouses, and the nearest optometrist are all down in this usually torrid and unpleasant place.

In all fairness, some people like Tiberius. It does have a flourishing tourist business, spawned by the desperate attempts of residents of Tel Aviv to escape the humidity of the coastal plain. They arrive in Tiberius by the hundreds on Friday afternoons and stay until the Sabbath ends on Saturday evening. The men throw themselves into the cool waters of the lake like enormous white, hairy-backed lemmings. The women sit on the rocky shore in black bathing suits, soaking their puffy urban feet in the shallows. They eat their picnic lunches of cheese sandwiches, herring and apples and then bake in the sun, suffering momentous sunburns. This may not sound like fun, but at least they have found a respite from the steamy, noxious air of Tel Aviv.

On this particular summer day in 1961, I have two appointments in the heat-oppressed, so-called capital of the north. The first one is with the draft board to take a psychometric exam that will decide whether or not I am eligible to join the Israeli Defense Forces. The second appointment is for my 6th driving lesson (out of 20) forced upon me under the Israeli motor vehicle licensing law (even though I had been driving in California for fifteen years).

The bus ride from Kiryat Shmonah has taken about an hour and it is seven a.m. The sun is three fingers above the South Golan Heights on the other side of the lake; its yellow rays are already dancing over the wavelets of the sea. I descend from the *Egged* bus a few blocks before its final terminal.

The draft board office opens at eight a.m. so I buy the morning newspaper and sit on a bench in a little park next to the grave of *Maimonides*.

This great philosopher and physician of the eleventh century had reached Tiberius after a series of wanderings and expulsions from Spain and Egypt. Just how he got to Tiberius (or if) is a matter of debate and conjecture, but one thing is true, his grave has not become a Mecca for tourism. I put a little pebble on this wise Rabbi/Physician's sepulchre, if only to show solidarity against the ultra-orthodox yeshiva boys who have been known to trash the grave from time to time—for obscure theological reasons.

I think I hear a small voice from under the gravestone say,

"Thanks, Shimon, at least someone in Tiberius appreciates me."

After visiting Maimonides and reading about the latest disasters in the Israeli government, I hike up the hill to the draft board. Inside, I find myself in a dismal, Social Democratic renaissance cube dedicated to inducting more soldiers into our courageous Israeli army. I am sitting opposite a sweet looking Moroccan girl with sergeant's stripes on her khaki sleeves. She has a rich supply of jet-black hair under her army cap, eyes like moonbeams, and teeth like the snow on Mt. Hermon during the winter. She looks vaguely familiar.

"English or Hebrew?" She asks and smiles a dazzling smile as she offers me the test booklets.

"Hebrew," I assert, trying to prove to her that I'm not just a crazy, illiterate American.

She waves me into an empty room overlooking the lake to the east, and someone's striped laundry flapping in the breeze to the south. I check off answers to the stupid questions on the exam. The exam seems to be written by a bachelor's degree psychologist and mostly addresses my childhood relationship with my parents. Only the health questions might have some validity as to whether or not I could fire a rifle or dig a foxhole.

"No, I've never had syphilis," I check.

The Sergeant collects my completed form. With her brown arms, black eyes, raven hair, shapely tush and khaki uniform, she takes the document back to her lair to wait for expert analysis by the draft board psychologist, who lives in Haifa but is expected sometime later today. I guess I can leave now, and I do. Time for my driving lesson.

The driving instructor picks me up next to *Maimonides'* tomb and we have fun touring the west shore of the lake at about 20 miles per hour over the speed limit. When we get back to Tiberius, the instructor compliments me on my progress and takes the kibbutz's money. At least I have done something for the Israeli economy by keeping the driving instructor in business, especially since he is Amos' cousin. Now I'm only fourteen lessons short of earning my license.

After the lesson and an early lunch at the King of Falafel's lunch stand—by this hour he could also be called the Lord of the Flies—I report back to the heartbreakingly beautiful sergeant at the draft board, just in case the military shrink has finished my psychoanalysis. To my great surprise, he *has*. He arrived early from his cuckoo nest in Haifa and my confession just happened to be on the top his stack.

The sergeant gives me that smile again.

"Don't I know you from somewhere?" I ask, hopefully.

"You don't recognize me?"

"Great *Elohim*!" I slap my head. "You're the Princess of the Atlas on the boat from Gibraltar."

She nods her head and laughs. "You're the American with the black beret that kept staring at me on the *A.K. Galilee*. Don't think I didn't notice."

Talk about quick adjustments to Israeli life! Me, a kibbutznik and the Princess of the Atlas with three stripes on her sleeve. We talk a bit more and then part. Such is life in a small country like ours. As we shake hands to say, "see you again," she hands me a pink mobilization slip requesting that I begin my service in the Israeli Defense Forces in a couple of weeks. For me, it is a big milestone, and I rejoice. A new immigrant like me is only a pseudo-Israeli until he has served in the army. My beloved Moroccan sergeant asks me to countersign my mobilization order.

"You're in the army now, you're not behind the plow." I have a sudden glimpse of myself heroically sprawled behind a machine gun holding the border against the Syrian tanks, just like Robert Jordan did holding off Franco's fascists in the conclusion of *For Whom the Bell Tolls,* or just like John Wayne did mowing down the Japanese hoards in *Back to Bataan.*

As I initial the pink slip, I hear a little voice, possibly emanating from my pal Maimonides in his humble tomb down the street.

"Shimon, don't be so frivolous. You may be signing your death warrant."

1961: From Here to Istanbul

Early in October, the kibbutz newsletter reports that last year's potato harvest was Cfar Moshe's largest ever and that this year's crop is likely to be even more bountiful. The editor of the newsletter, Eliezer, who is also the boss of the pig farm, claims that if you lay all of last year's potatoes end to end, they would stretch all the way from our Hulah valley to Istanbul, Turkey. Maybe this year, they will reach Vienna or Prague.

Normally, the people on the kibbutz that work in the Field Crops/Potatoes branch, numbers ten or fifteen members, supplemented by school children and some volunteers from abroad. The harvest itself, however, involves almost everyone. The chief of the Field Crops branch is a small wiry man nicknamed Sharik. Like many other kibbutz members, the nickname is all he is ever called by and a newer member might never know Sharik's horrible birth name (Heinrich). He is a quiet man in his mid-forties and lives only for his work, driven by the intense desire to build his community and his country through perfecting the art of growing potatoes, alfalfa, and cotton. When you see him, what you see is a glimpse of dust, tractor grease, work clothes, and a dangling cigarette, hurrying toward the fields.

As the harvest season grows closer, Sharik always develops a tic in his shoulder, a sure sign that the growing pressure of bringing in a safe, abundant harvest is beginning to show on his otherwise quiet composure. Harvesting potatoes is a complex job involving the coordination of large numbers of people, time, and machinery. A good harvest entails overcoming the risks of inclement weather, defense emergencies, transportation problems and other unknown and unexpected troubles. Nothing can be taken for granted until the spuds are safely deposited in the potato storehouse or sent on their way to the markets in Tel Aviv, Haifa and Jerusalem.

One early morning in late October, I find myself sitting on the ground in the middle of a potato field that stretches from the alfalfa mill all the way down to the apple orchard, about a third of a mile to the south. The open ground is dark, and moist. Tractors and harrows have removed the potato plant foliage; clusters of potatoes are peeping up on the surface of the field like bones popping up out of a grave. The sky is clear and the temperature is crisp. There must be at least two hundred kibbutzniks: women, men and children, waiting for the harvest to begin. They sit on piles of empty burlap sacks alongside the long rows of partially plowed up potatoes,

You need three tools to work with in order to bag potatoes. One tool is the burlap sack itself. The second tool is a rust-colored, square metal frame with two hooks on its top and two more hooks on its bottom, used to hold the burlap sack's hungry mouth open. The third and most important tool is your own hands and arms, used to toss the potatoes into the mouth of the bag until it is filled. You hook the sack onto the frame, straddle the empty bag, bend over until you can reach the potatoes on the ground and then toss them backward into the bag.

The sun climbs up a notch above the Golan Heights and strong coffee is served from large aluminum canisters into plastic cups as we sit on our piles of burlap sacks. I feel the warmth of the hot coffee as I talk to my friend Yitzhak, who sits next to me.

Yitzhak begins telling me his life history. He was born in Argentina. His family immigrated there from Poland in the nineteen twenties. They crossed the Atlantic to one of the few countries that seemed interested in accepting Jewish refugees. His family settled in the capital city, Buenos Aires. The father worked as a *cuentanik*, a door-to-door salesmen traveling around rural areas of the country, selling his wares out of a suitcase. The rural villagers could not afford to buy a new shirt outright, or a pair of pants, or a comb and brush set and Yitzhak's father would revisit each customer several times a year to collect the payments. Often, months would pass between the time that the father set out on his rounds to remote settlements on the pampas and his return to the small apartment where his wife and four children lived. I ask Yitzhak how he decided to leave Argentina for a new life in Israel, but our conversation is interrupted by the noise of tractor motors.

A string of red Ferguson tractors, each with a plow-like device attached behind it, can be seen and heard in the distance poking out from behind the tractor sheds in the work area of the kibbutz. After four or five minutes the first tractor reaches the edge of one row of the potato field, lowers its plow blade and begins advancing down the line of half submerged potatoes. The tractor creeps along at a slow place and behind it you can see clumps of fat potatoes emerging from the Galilee earth. As the tractors pass each worker down the line, the worker straddles the line of upturned potatoes with the burlap sack and bags the spuds, pulling the sacks along the ground as they hunch forward.

The sun rises higher over the rich fields of the Hulah valley.

Yitzhak and I watch while the tractor and its plow creep through the row segment that we are responsible for. We wave at the tractor driver, in this case, Sharik, the boss himself, and Meir, his plowman. Meir is perched precariously behind Sharik on the harvesting apparatus. The two of them must keep the tractor going in a straight line and the plow blade at the right depth. The plowman has a handle that controls the depth of the blade so that the deepest potatoes can be brought to the surface but without digging up too much dirt. Too much dirt pulled up with the potatoes will make work tough on the harvesters and will slow the tractor down. Not plowing deep enough will leave them buried in the field, diminishing the harvest. This is the art of potato harvesting.

As the tractor and its crew pass us, Yitzhak and I take our place straddling the upturned potatoes and tossing them at a furious rate into the burlap sack. As the area in front of me clears of spuds, I wobble forward to the next clump, dragging the sack along with me. As soon as my sack is full, I unhook it from the metal frame, set it aside, stand the heavy sack on its bottom, grab an empty sack from the pile, hook it onto the frame, bend over, straddle the sack and begin to bag more potatoes. By the time I have cleared my segment of the row, I hear the tractor creeping up behind me one row over to my right. More potatoes surface demanding to be bagged. On with it!

Bend and bend and bend again. The potatoes seem heavier in each new row. The sacks complain. They want to stay where they are. Pull and pull again and the sacks creep forward. The sun climbs higher and the cool air of morning departs. Look forward along the line of workers and what do you see? Potatoes and butts and legs. Male butts and legs, female butts and legs, skinny butts and skinny legs, fat butts and skinny legs, fat butts and fat legs.

Break time. The tractors are silent and we rest for fifteen minutes. I see long lines of kibbutz workers sitting among the full sacks of potatoes, wiping the sweat off their faces and sipping the lemonade ladled into plastic cups by the younger school kids, out in their blue work shorts and their undershirts.

Next to me, Yitzhak continues his story:

"How did I get to Israel? The first interest I had in Israel came from meeting Jewish farmers in Argentina. When I was a little kid, six years old, my father took me with him on a business trip to Moisesville, a Jewish agricultural community in one of the northern States of Argentina. There, for the first time, I saw a place where everyone was Jewish. They were almost all farmers, some working with modern machinery and some still using plows and oxen. My father noticed how excited I got seeing this sight and he said to me, "Isaac (the name I had before I took my Hebrew name), someday you can be a farmer too, but only in your own land, the Land of Israel."

From then on my path was clear. When we returned from our trip my parents enrolled me in a Zionist Youth group. Twelve years later, I was in Israel on the way to this kibbutz..."

I want to hear more about Zionist Youth groups in Argentina, but the tractors have started up their motors again and the potatoes are waiting to be sacked.

It is noon, two hours after the last break; we are covered with dust. Our collective backs are killing us. I curse the burlap bags, the dust, the potatoes, the life of a farmer, the diesel fumes from the tractor, the sun, and God himself. I look up and see Yitzhak's fat Argentinean ass with a potato sack trailing behind it, filling it up as his hands pitch the spuds backward. His upside-down eyes meet mine and he gives me an upside down grin.

"What do you say about Zionism now?" he yells over the noise of the tractors.

The potato harvest lasts for two weeks. If only we could bag our sweat and sell it.

1961: My Big Mouth

I

Amos, the head of the orchard committee comes over for afternoon tea and makes me a proposition.

"Shimon," says he, "I hear that you are going to France for your sister-in-law's wedding. I wonder if you could bring back something for me?"

I know that Amos likes good vodka and I figure that he has come to ask me to pick him up a few bottles of Stolichnaya, till now unavailable in Israel.

"Eighty or a hundred proof?" I ask.

Amos is a *vatik* - an old timer in the kibbutz - a tall man in his early forties, already bald under his blue idiot's cap. He rarely removes the cap outside his apartment, on the relatively plush eastern side of the kibbutz...the side with the hot water.

"Not vodka," Amos corrects me. "Cranberries."

"Canned or fresh?" I add, somewhat surprised by the strange request. After all, Amos is a Czech, not known for his observance of American Thanksgiving rituals.

"Neither, I want you to bring back cranberry plants," says Amos in a hushed voice. I notice that he is sweating under the brim of his idiot's cap, despite the coolness of the late afternoon.

"Why? Where from? How? When?" I hiss back, as if Syrian intelligence officers are listening in from the hills of the Golan Heights to the east.

"I want you to go to Italy," he explains, "to pick up cranberry plants at a tree nursery near Bologna and bring them back into Israel. Then we'll grow them and corner the Israel market. There's a big demand for cranberries among the Arab population and they spend a lot of money importing them. Why shouldn't we have their business?"

"Another monopoly for Cfar Moshe," I comment. "Out of season apples, kiwis and now cranberries...but why me? Why don't *you* go to Italy? My sister-in-law's wedding is in France."

"Shimon," answers Amos in a conspiratorial tone, "remember when you told me the adventures that you had smuggling liquor across the border from Tijuana, Mexico, to your home in San Diego? And remember when you told me that your father's family was in the smuggling business in Poland before the war? *You* are just the right one of us to do smuggling for Cfar Moshe. It's in your blood. Even better, you still have that honest, naive American look about you and, most important of all, you still have your American passport."

"But I was just a wild sixteen-year-old kid when I did the Tijuana thing and my smuggling ancestors disappeared in the Holocaust. And why are we talking about smuggling the cranberries? Is it illegal to import them?"

Because," says Amos, taking a deep breath as if he would like to avoid disclosing the next detail of information about his plan, "if we don't smuggle the plants in through customs, we won't be able to create our own little monopoly on the berries. Every customs agent has an uncle on some other kibbutz. The news will get out and then everyone will be getting into the cranberry market. You can make yourself look like a typical American tourist. The customs officers won't even look in your bags."

I think critically for about half a second and then plunge recklessly into my adventure mode.

"Why not, I'll do it," my big mouth says.

The plan we work out is as follows: Ruthie and I will fly to France, for the family wedding. She will return straight to Israel and I will fly to Italy and pick up the cranberry plants at a certain tree nursery. Then I will cut the plants into one-bud segments and buy a large vase. The vase will be packed with excelsior chips, supposedly to prevent it from damage during its transit to the Galilee. I will mix the cranberry bud segments in with the excelsior. The Israeli customs officials will think that I'm a just a crazy American bringing a vase to my beloved family in the Holy Land and voila, the beginning of a Cfar Moshe monopoly on cranberries. Amos will wait for me with a kibbutz car outside the airport terminal. And I'll be the hero!

II

The wedding in Paris is over, Ruthie returns to Israel and I take an afternoon flight to Milano. This is my first time in Italy. I take the train to Bologna. Five train hours later at exactly eight p.m. (thanks to Mussolini) I descend from a railroad coach at the

Bologna depot. A cold wind snaps through the city as I search out a restaurant to alleviate my hunger. Across the dark street from the station I spot a neon sign -*Rosteria*. My carnivorous instinct tells me that something may be roasting over there. Post haste, I cross over and peek through the *Rostaria's* window. A recently deceased boar's head stares out at me, with its blood exuding slowly out of his mouth. Despite 3000 years of moral kosher training, the craving to eat the rest of the boar conquers all.

After the pagan dinner, I happily take a cab to the *Italia* hotel and plunge into sleep with dreams of conspiracies, heroes' medals, and Amos' strategies rolling through my brain.

In the morning, I call the tree nursery to tell them I've arrived. I shower and shave and a driver mysteriously appears to take me out to where I will purchase the cranberries. After a long drive through mountains, woods and valleys, the taxi arrives at the ornate gates of the tree nursery. We cruise by rows of experimental pear trees all trained to grow like grapevines at shoulder level.

How clever of these Italians, I muse, and fantasize possible future smuggling operations for *Cfar Moshe*.

The nursery office is a large three-story building surrounded by poplar trees. I am greeted at the door by Sophia Loren. She takes me to the nursery owner's office. His secretary, a Gina Lollobrigida twin, welcomes me and I do my best not to look at her breasts popping out of a low-cut, but otherwise business-like, dress. I'm asked to have a seat and, within a few minutes, a cup of espresso appears on a tray surrounded by a blonde woman who belongs in a *seraglio*. It suddenly strikes me that I haven't seen any males since I arrived in the office building.

How lecherous, I think, with some jealousy.

After the espresso, the boss man of the nursery, Mr. DiPasta greets me. He is dressed in an expensive suit and tie, very unlike the blue work pants, blue work shirt and blue idiot's cap worn by Amos. The two of us sit down to a light breakfast in his office served by no less than Ingrid Bergman in her prime. After breakfast we begin our deliberations, Mediterranean style.

"How are things in Israel?" he asks, as we finish our bacon and *polenta.*

Very good," I reply, "We are staying alive despite our crazy drivers. How are things in Italy?"

"As usual, chaotic," he offers. "But we have enough to eat. Do you have a family in Israel?"

"Yes, I do," I answer proudly. "I have a wife and a daughter. And your family?" I ask politely.

"Ah, my family is very good. Four daughters and a son."

End of Round one.

Round two topics include my admiration for Mr. DiPasta's orchards and nurseries, the beauty of its setting, the magnificent office building and its furniture, and the beauty of Italy - especially Bologna.

He discusses his visit to Israel last year - the wonders of the Holy Land, the bravery of its inhabitants, and the high quality of its developing agricultural industry.

End of round two.

At the beginning of round three, he pats his ample pouch and smiles at Grace Kelly as she brings in the bill for the cranberry plants. She is followed by a smiling, busty redhead (Rita Hayworth?) who brings the cranberry plants all wrapped and ready. I hand him a check from the inconspicuous, ultra-religious Israeli bank that the kibbutz uses for "sensitive" purchases. The deal process lasts only a few minutes and I am in the taxi on returning to Bologna.

Back in the city I head down to a *tchotchke* store and buy a nice vase for my Israeli "cousin." The store clerk carefully packs the vase in excelsior. I return to the hotel to unwrap the cranberry plants. My heart drops. They are scrawny twigs and the dormant buds are microscopic and fragile. Even an inexperienced cranberry farmer like me can see that cutting up these twigs into small segments might kill the damn plants. I look at the miserable things for a minute to see if they might, magically, grow fatter before my eyes. Perhaps a Hail Mary would help. But no miracles occur.

If God won't help this smuggling expedition, I'm left with the Devil and with the logical agronomic thing to do. I empty my own things from out of the suitcase, and stuff the plants in whole, without cutting them up. I put on my tourist clothes and leave the rest of my wardrobe in the closet, an offering for the poor of Bologna. I stick my Israeli passport into a zippered compartment in the suitcase and haul out my green passport with the American eagle on it.

"On with the adventure and the Devil take the hindmost," I tell myself, full of bloated self-bravado and James Bond images. I head for the checkout desk.

III

Rain pours down on the tarmac at *Leonardo da Vinci* International Airport and I am climbing the slick boarding ramp into an El Al, Israel bound jetliner. As usual, armed Italian soldiers ring the access to the plane, ready for any terrorist attacks. I'm grateful for the security but apprehensive about the cranberry shoots in my carry-on suitcase. I hear the voices of these fragile twigs saying, Shimon, hurry up. Get us to your kibbutz before we dry up and die. What will be their fate? Will it be safe delivery into the rich soil of the Galilee, or incarceration in Israeli customs along with their human courier?

A heavy oriental man in a black overcoat hurries up the ramp ahead of me. He slips on the wet stairs and falls flat. His valise tumbles down to the bottom of the ramp. Instinctively, I put my carry-on down and help the guy up. Someone else brings his bag back up to him, and I carefully retrieve my suitcase with its secret cargo.

Mr. Sato, my rescuee, turns out to be Japanese. We are sitting in adjoining seats with my contraband laden suitcase in the rack above our heads. He thanks me in perfect English for my help. We both listen to the plane's loudspeaker singing *Hava Nagila*. The flight attendant tells us, in Hebrew and English, about what to do if we have to land in the Mediterranean Sea. Mr. Sato is a short man, in his forties. He asks the flight attendant for a towel and nervously wipes the rainwater off his valise. Like most Israelis, I can't help but wonder if there is anything ticking inside of it.

Once in the air, Mr. Sato wants to talk about Israel. He explains, in a quiet and polite voice that this is his first visit to Israel. He is an official in a Japanese Labor Federation, invited to Israel by the *Histadrut,* our giant Israeli labor federation, the pearl of our Social Democratic system. He questions me about the kibbutz movement, the development of agriculture, the status of the Arab minority, and the political situation. When he asks me about the Labor Federation, I fill him full of praises about our health benefits, our worker owned factories, the Federation's power in the government, etc. Why should I go into critical detail with him about the *Histadrut's* seamier side, especially its army of creaking, dust-covered bureaucrats? Instead I tell a popular joke.

"A story is told about a lion escaping from the Tel Aviv Zoo, sneaking into the Labor Federation's headquarters on Arlozoroff St. The lion finds an empty office and converts it into his lair. Every morning, the lion flashes a paw out the door and snags a bureaucrat for breakfast. A year passes and nobody notices the lion's presence nor the missing labor officials. Finally, the lion eats the worker who serves tea to all of the offices and the animal is immediately detected and returned to the zoo."

Mr. Sato laughs at the joke and says that it's not much different from his organization, the Japanese National Union of Workers. We are friends now and he turns out to be no less than the headman of the Union himself.

Three hours later, we land on the holy tarmac of Israel at Lod airport. The security gentlemen board the plane with a big show of weaponry and eye the passengers for terrorists. No problem, we're all kosher and we deplane into the airport bus. More security guys with more bulges in their pockets then board the bus with us. After a short trip through the airport, the bus discharges us at the door of the terminal where even more security troops scan every move we make. Welcome to Israel.

Now the cranberry plants are whispering from their dark hideaway. "Gevalt, something is up. The customs inspectors are going to open everyone's suitcases. They are on special alert. Do something Shimon. You're supposed to be a hot shot smuggler."

I notice that there are two lines passing by the customs officials, one for arriving dignitaries and one for all the rest of the passengers. In the regular line, the officials are inspecting everything down to the belly button lint. I also notice that there is only one person in the dignitary line, who else but Mr. Sato, my Japanese fellow passenger. Smugglers' instinct guides me to walk over to him with my precious suitcase and discuss more mutual interests and tell a few more jokes. Watching the other passengers having their baggage torn apart by the inspectors, I try to hold my sweat inside of my skin.

"Be calm, Shimon," whisper the cranberries.

A minute later, still jabbering with Mr. Sato, I begin to smell approaching bureaucrats: None-other than the Secretary General of the *Histadrut* shows up with a big entourage, minus the lion, to pick up the distinguished Japanese guest. Introductions and handshakes take place and Sato introduces me as his friend, savior and mentor, Mr. Shimon. I smile and shake their hands. What the hell, I *did* consider voting for the Labor Party in the last elections. A miracle happens. A side door opens and all of us dignitaries pass through it into the main terminal sans passport checks or customs inspections. I am in the middle of listening to a joke told by Mr. Sato about Japanese bureaucrats. His arm is around me as we stride out of the main terminal door. I introduce him to Amos who is nervously awaiting the cranberries and me. Amos shakes Sato's hand and I place my baggage in the back of the Cfar Moshe's orchard committee jeep waiting by the curb, with it's motor running. We roar off and I wave to Mr. Sato, but *he* is busy with the heads of the labor organization. And isn't that Golda Meir standing next to him in her black dress and cigarette?

1962: The Battle of the Children's Farm

I

Yeshai is the boss of the Children's Farm. He is one of our few Argentinean *Vatikim*–old timers–having come to the kibbutz in the early 1950s, when South Americans were rare birds in the country. He had grown up in a Jewish Agricultural Colony on the Pampas, was a hard worker and an experienced farmer. He blended in nicely with the original Middle European settlers.

In the late 1950s, a flock of exuberant young Argentinean Zionist Youth Movement immigrants arrived in the kibbutz, chattering away in singsong Spanish and raising the noise level in the dining hall by a thousand percent. The *vatikim* welcomed the new immigrants as a boost to the workforce but grumbled about their raucous behavior, and lack of manners. 'Lack of culture' the *vatikim* called it. After all, the Argentineans weren't Europeans like them. But at least Yeshai had been born in Poland and was thus half civilized.

Here, it must be said that even though all the members of *Cfar Moshe* are technically equal, there is still a pecking order. New people like myself are at the bottom of the order (although being the only Americans around gives my Ruthie and me a few points over the rest of the newcomers). The young Argentineans are next up the pecking order with their ideological uniformity and their clannishness, most of them having spent many years together in their youth group back in Buenos Aires. Next up the pecking order, are people who had dribbled into the kibbutz during the mid-1950s. They were a mixture of individuals and families from a variety of places: India, South Africa, Denmark, and the USA. The true aristocrats of *Cfar Moshe* are the Czechs and the Germans. They are the cultured ones who eat at their own tables in the dining hall.

Of course, the children born in Cfar Moshe are immune from such classification. No matter where their parents were born, their children grow up in strict equality. They are considered the children of all the kibbutz members and the hope for its future.

The Children's Farm is an important institution in the kibbutz, not only for its economic contributions, but also for its educational role. Here the children, from kindergarten age through early adolescence, are taught the Torah of collective labor through the milking of goats, the tending of newborn chicks, the growing of vegetables and fruit trees, the care of horses, mules and donkeys, and the cleaning of stalls, pig-pens, and poultry cages. You will see them on their way to their farm at any hour of the day not claimed by formal school activities. They return from the farm to their age-graded children's houses with the rank smell of goats and chicken shit on their clothing.

Yeshai is the Tolstoy of the Children's Farm. In his patient manner, he assigns the children to their jobs and monitors their progress toward becoming the future farmers of Israel. He sits with them in the clubhouse that the children have built under his direction and talks about the responsibility of being the first generation of Jewish farmers in their own land. He swaps jokes and stories and brews them tea. He explains the importance of working together rather than competing with each other. He teaches the older children how to gently teach the younger ones. He enjoins them to beautify their farm by planting flowerbeds, by keeping the pens, fences and corrals freshly painted and maintained, and by keeping the farm clean and neat. He talks to them, as they sip their tea, about the heroes of Jewish Agriculture, A.D. Gordon, Aharon Aronson, and, of course, the *Halutzim* (Pioneers) who drained the swamps, cleared the stones, paved the roads and plowed the fields of this Socialist Holy Land.

There is a secret growing in the Children's Farm that even Yeshai himself doesn't know about. Last year, when my smuggling expedition to Italy had come to its successful conclusion, Amos, the head of the orchard committee, had clandestinely planted the cranberry stock in pails in a far off corner of the Children's Farm. The Italian cranberry plants enjoyed being with us in our paradise and early in the spring they were already making a robust showing, sending down formidable roots through the bottoms of their aluminum containers.

From time to time, Amos visits the far corner of the Children's Farm and gazes at the cranberry plants' progress, the wheels spinning in his head about what miracles will occur because of our triumphal evasion of the law and our impending monopoly on the cranberry market. He ponders about where he will plant these rapidly maturing cranberry plants.

"They like bogs," he thinks to himself out loud. "They need bees for cross pollination. Hmm, the beehives that we keep over on the south edge of 'D' orchard might be a good place. The ground water is high there. The cranberries like cool air and sunlight, maybe in the shade of the cypress tree windbreak, but not too far in the shade."

Then he switches to fantasizing product lines and marketing strategies: juices, honey, relishes, marmalades, candles soap, perfumes, cosmetics, garnishes, table decorations all ending up in handsome profits, all with the *Cfar Moshe* label, of course not right away. In the meantime the Arabs are the market. I have to find out what they do with those berries."

He takes his pipe out and treats himself to some good tobacco brought from America to the kibbutz by his cousins during their last visit. He looks out over the golf-course-like fields of alfalfa and the cypress tree wind breaks of *'Daled'* orchard.

The alfalfa is Sharik's kingdom," says Amos to himself, "but the orchard and the cranberries are mine."

Farming is a tough business and Amos is a tough guy who has seen it all. But nothing prepares him for the disaster that is about to happen.

Baruch, the Turk, is starting a new career in the beehive business and I drop in on him to see how things are going. I enjoy the sweet and sour smell of the little shack where the main office of the beehive department is located. There, the Turk cranks the honey-extracting apparatus and then dollops the golden stuff into jars proudly marked with a miniature picture of Mt. Hermon and the words: "*Eretz HaDvash* (Land of Honey) Product of Kibbutz Cfar Moshe." This business is one of the small enterprises on the kibbutz, not like the big cash crops, the orchards, the turkeys and the alfalfa, just a little branch of work that maybe will pay for itself and maybe won't. Other worksites of this humble variety are the toy factory, the pottery barn, the bookbindery, and the vineyard. The economic gurus of the kibbutz don't think much of these enterprises, but what is one to do when the religion is work and work is not available? Open a pottery barn and hope for the best.

I help Baruch fill a dozen bottles or so of *dvash* and, along with most other Israelis, we listen to the radio news on the hour.

"Beep, beep, this is the voice of Israel from Jerusalem." (What bad news now?)

Suddenly we hear two loud voices screaming at each other, not over the radio, but over at the far end of the Children's Farm. Is someone's foot caught in a tractor motor? Did someone sit on a scorpion? We rush outside and look over the fence of the Children's Farm. There stand Amos and Yeshai.

"Idiot!" yells Amos.

"Maniac!" screams Yeshai.

"Saboteur!" shouts Amos, his face as red as a baboon's ass.

"*Mamzer, Bastardo,*" growls Yeshai, reverting to his native languages, Yiddish and Spanish. I see him eye a pitchfork propped up against the fence.

"Idiot!" yells Amos, returning to the top of the denunciation cycle and raising his fist.

The Turk and I intervene before Yeshai goes for the pitchfork. We climb through the fence wires into the Children's Farm and stand between these two premeditators.

"*Chaverim, Chaverim,*" chides Baruch, his outreached palms planted on each of their breasts, "comrades, don't hurt each other. What has happened to the two of you? Are you crazy, are you *meshugaim?*"

Amos blows out a mouthful of air and lowers his fist. He points down the fence to the corner of the Children's Farm where the two of us had stashed the cranberry plants six months ago.

"He tore them up. He murdered them," growls Amos, his face redder than ever before.

"Not true," protests, Yeshai, "we just moved them."

"You tore the roots out!" Amos yells, his fist moving up again.

"Amos, put your fist down," I bravely say from between the two combatants, but I'm also getting ready to duck, knowing Amos' famous temper.

"The roots, the roots." He groans, "The roots went through the bottom of the pails. Then you moved them and you tore them out..." Amos shouts and then turns around and begins to stride around the little Children's Farm.

He kicks a tire of Yeshai's Ferguson and gives Konga the mule a deadly look. He snarls at the chickens in their coop and chases a wandering goat out of his way. Then he disappears out the gate into the orchard tractor barn, muttering and swearing, his hate still lingering in the air.

"What happened?" We ask Yeshai.

"Well, it was like this," says Yeshai, beginning to regain his cool. "The children and I wanted to start a garden down in this end of the farm. I saw all these pails of rootstock and decided to move them. Some of them were mine, some came from I don't know where. No one said anything to me about them. I sent some of the kids out to move them. The kids moved them all to the other side of the farm. They heard the roots tear but I guess they didn't pay any attention to them. I looked at them later and saw that these enormous roots that had gone right through the bottom of the pails. Great *Elohim*, I've never seen such roots. I didn't know what they were. They looked like Cedars of Lebanon. Today, Amos comes by looking for the plants. I show him what had happened and, you know him when he explodes! The rest you heard and saw. Do either of you know anything about what those plants were?"

"Cranberries," I say, feeling sick to my stomach. My whole Italian adventure is now in shambles along with those poor plants.

"Cranberries?"

"Cranberries," I repeat sadly. I am beginning to feel like socking Yeshai myself.

II

Later, in the evening, I set out for a walk through *Daled* orchard just to brood on the cranberry plantation that could have been. I meet my sainted Grandfather, Saba Yisroel. He's back in his kibbutz costume, blue work pants, light blue work shirt, a blue idiot's cap, and scruffy work boots.

"Nu..." he questions, "what will be your next act of heroism, now that your smuggled plants are dead?"

"It wasn't heroism, Saba," I lied, "the kibbutz needed me to do it because with my American *punim* (face), I could get through the damn customs agents."

"And look what happened," says Saba mischievously, "the whole thing was a fiasco, the Wages of Sin. Trying to cheat your own government. Isn't that nice?"

"I seem to remember that you were in the smuggling business, too, at one time."

"True, true," Saba confesses, "but that was in Poland under the Czar's reign. We really didn't see that government as being ours. A Jew had to do all sorts of things to remain alive in those days. But the Israeli government is supposed to be on your side, including the agricultural inspection officers that you so cleverly avoided."

I have the impression that Saba is toying with me and, after all, is proud of my sinful achievements.

"Smuggling is just smuggling," I retort.

"I disagree," he says, "sometimes it is legitimate. Let me tell you a story to illustrate the point."

We both sit down on the a furrow of Hulah valley earth and Saba's story begins:

"Once, there was a Jew who needed to escape from the Czar's secret police. He had been active in the Bolshevik underground and someone had betrayed him. We'll call him Yankel. Yankel's father gave him a generous sum of money, blessed him and off went the young man, to seek safety in America. He was only a few steps ahead of the Secret Police. He had to cross Poland and then get over the German border. Once over the border he would head for the port of Königsberg and from there he would take a boat to Hamburg and then to America. The closest place to the German border was a small city called Ostrolenka. It was a town where 90% of the people were Jews. Yankel decided that he had better get advice from the local people about how best to go over the border. He walked through the streets and tried to find someone who was knowledgeable and trustworthy. A tall man with a reddish beard walked up to him and asked where he was going? Yankel, for some strange reason, felt that he could trust this man and he blurted out the naked truth.

'I'm trying to get over the border into Germany to escape the Russian Secret Police. I have a large sum of money with me. What is the best way to get across?'

The man with the reddish beard, let's call him Shmuel, put his finger to his lips and beckoned to Yankel to follow him. They went into Shmuel's house on the main square of the town and sat at the table inside. Shmuel's wife poured some tea and Yankel received the following instructions from Shmuel:

'Listen, *boychik*, there's no problem crossing the border from here to Germany. We can give a little bribe here and there and the border guards will let you cross; they don't like the Czar's government either. The problem comes if you have any money with you. Believe me, if they see your money, they'll take it all, without any hesitation. Do you want to get to Königsberg and buy a ticket on the boat? Do you want to go to America with nothing in your pocket? Then don't try to get across the border with a wad of rubles.'

'So how can I get my money to Königsberg?'

'Give it to me,' says Shmuel. 'But don't ask any questions. You'll just have to trust me to get to you after you have crossed over the border.'

'Yankel thought about this for a few minutes. 'I think I can trust this Shmuel, but what if he fails? What if he gets caught himself? And what if he really isn't trustworthy? And what will happen to me if I get to Germany without a *pfennig* in my pocket? Well, I guess that the worst thing that can happen is that a Jew will get my money instead of the customs officer or a policeman. At least I'll be out of the Czar's hands.

"Yankel fished out the rubles (and there were a lot of them) from his pocket. Although he was a Communist, he said a silent prayer that everything might somehow turn out for the best. The next day, Shmuel hitched his horse to a small wagon and drove Yankel to the border, only about 10 miles away. Shmuel approached the guards and whispered in their ears. A bag changed hands then Shmuel approached the German guards in the same manner. Both sets of guards waved the young man over and the Czar missed a chance to hang another Communist, especially a Jewish one.

"Yankel waited for as long as he dared on the German side, and with a sinking feeling set out for Königsberg with some small change he had in his pocket. Goodbye rubles. When he got to Königsberg, he bought a ticket for Hamburg using the last few rubles secretly stuffed into his *tuches*, and hoped for the best. Maybe he could work for a while in Hamburg and then make his way to America. Maybe and maybe not.

"A few days passed in Königsberg and it was time to get on the ship. Yankel was very sad that he had trusted the red-beard in Ostrolenka. He had looked so honest and sincere, the *goniff*.

'Cursed be Shmuel's name,' he thought in his accumulated rage.

"As he went on board, the ship's horn sounded and the dockworkers began to remove the gangplank. Shmuel leaned on the rail, closest to the gangplank and mourned this latest betrayal.

"Suddenly his eye caught a movement down the wharf. A man in a long coat and a red beard was running down the dock at full speed. The man clambered up the gangplank and reached the top just as it was about to disconnect from the ship. He yelled at Yankel and thrust a large envelope toward him. Yankel took the envelope, felt its weight and his spirits lifted. He looked at the man on the gangplank. It was Shmuel, the Jew from Ostrolenka.

Yankel opened the envelope with shaking hands and saw the wad of Russian banknotes.

"Shmuel waved at him and yelled: 'Good fortune in America.'

"Then he headed back down the gangplank, marched down the wharf and disappeared.

"Nu, Shimon, how did you like this smuggling story?" asks my grandfather.

"Great," I reply. "Who was this Shmuel anyway?"

"It wasn't Shmuel at all," Saba answers, "it was me, your Saba, Yisroel Chmiel, the smuggler. Do you still think that smuggling is always just smuggling?"

1962: Equality

I

"How equal does equality have to be?" asks Eliezer-the-pig-farmer at the Town Meeting of Kibbutz Cfar Moshe. "Why shouldn't each member get an equal sum of money at the end of the year so that he can do whatever he wants with it? I'm tired of having to go to the storehouse to beg a bar of soap from Chanoch-the-Storekeeper every time I run out."

"I agree," says Chanoch-the-store keeper, "Why do I have to argue with Eliezer-the pig farmer every time he comes into the storehouse to drive me crazy? Let him buy his own soap. I'm not interested in why he needs it, although I think I have an idea."

The crowd of kibbutz members, sitting around the dining hall tables, buzzes and laughs at that one. Eliezer turns scarlet and averts his eyes toward the window of the dining hall.

Shamai, the ideology man, raises his hand and Dvorah, now the Secretary General nods her head in his direction. "How equal does equality have to be?" he echoes and everyone braces for another of his interminable orations. He stands and commences his onslaught with his thick Argentinean accent:

"We are trying to build a model of equality for the rest of the world to see. The world does not know what equality is and will not discover its virtues unless **we** show them the way. If not us, then who? That's why we should not compromise on building perfect equality. No, no, not even for the sake of Eliezer's need to have more soap allotted to him than someone else."

He sat down with a look of purity on his face. There was a murmur of amazement among the members only because Shamai's speech had been so short. They hardly had time to yawn.

Gad, a second-generation kibbutz member, just out of the army stands without being recognized and begins his remarks in his soft but icy voice. "I think that it's time that we all become responsible for our own personal decisions. The days when we didn't have enough possessions to even talk about are gone. We don't need to cut hard-boiled eggs in half any more. We have all the eggs we can eat. Now we can pay attention to our private needs, those that may be different from each other's. So what's wrong with just giving everyone a budget to make their own choices?"

Marta, the head nurse, raises her hand and, taking a deep breath, says, "I too think that people's needs are different. But Gadi doesn't go far enough. Some families need *more* things than others do. My husband and I have four children now, one in the army, one living in Tel Aviv and two in other kibbutzim. Sometimes they need a little financial help and we're tired of having to go to a committee each time that we need to send them some money. We should do more than change the way goods and services are dealt out. Why should *we* get the same as a bachelor that doesn't have any children?"

There is a collective gasp as Marta sits down and lights a cigarette waiting for hell to break loose. Unlike the other speakers before her, she is proposing a much more radical approach. In a community based on equality she is proposing institutionalized inequality.

Hell does break loose. People stand up and yell their message across the dining hall. Knitting needles fall. Kibbutz members sitting around individual tables quarrel with each other. Lots of people are lighting up their cheap kibbutz-issue cigarettes and smoke drifts under the ceiling of the dining hall. Dvorah calls for order, to no avail. Heresy is in the air.

And if that isn't enough, Clarita, the beautiful, stands up, tall and straight, glaring at the rest of the assembled kibbutz members as if she is about to announce the end of the world. We know that look. She is famous for telling it like it is. The rest of us leave off of our clamor and sit down to hear Clarita.

"As long as we're talking about serious changes, then let's talk about the most serious change of all," she begins. "I believe that its time to give up the system of having the children sleep in children's houses. They should be sleeping with their parents like normal families everywhere else."

A stunned silence falls over the dining hall of Cfar Moshe. Such words have never been publicly stated. We can all hear the clicking of the electric clock that hangs above the dishwashing unit. A lone hand slowly rises for permission to speak. Dvorah nods her head and the much-respected Amnon, a founder of the kibbutz, stands up to answer Clarita.

Amnon is considered the paradigm of what a kibbutz person is supposed to be. He is a brilliant intellectual and a humble man at the same time. He has worked in manual labor and he has also served the Israeli people as a diplomat on dangerous assignments. He is a handsome, tall man with clear blue eyes.

"I would like to answer Clarita's comments," says Amnon in a quiet and respectful voice, "I think that we are now stepping onto perilous ground. Let us ask ourselves why the children sleep in the children's houses in the first place. I say that there are many reasons. Some of these reasons came about because of certain situations. For instance, we needed to have the children sleep together so that they could be close to a bomb shelter if we were attacked. We needed to find ways of giving the children a decent place to sleep when we ourselves were living in tents or in one-room wooden shacks, sometimes more than one family in a room. We needed to have some way of taking care of the children when we all went out to work in the fields at sunrise and worked all day, sometimes into the night. I do agree that many of these problems have been solved. Thank God, almost all the family dwellings in Cfar Moshe have more than one room. And now we have a big enough work force so that some people, especially the mothers, could go to work later and *could* take the little children from home to the nurseries in the morning.

"I use the word *could* because there are very important reasons for not changing the system as it is. The main one is that we are not just a village trying to make a living for ourselves. We are also a community of people committed to an idea. We don't want people to be divided into the rich and the poor. We don't want to bow and scrape to each other. We don't want to live in a community where you can buy honor.

"We hoped that our children, from the beginning of their lives, would grow to be cooperative people, learning to respect work by working together for a common goal. We decided that our children were the hope for the future of our dream and that they were all part of the mutual responsibilities of the kibbutz members. Yes, the parents are the most important influence on our children, but we felt that the economic and educational responsibility for these children belonged to the community, to every *chaver* (member) and not just to the parents.

"Clarita, I understand that it can be a wonderful feeling to raise your children within your home. After all, except for the youngest *chaverim*, we *all* grew up in our parents' houses. Mine in Prague and yours in Montevideo. But now our parents are gone and the kibbutz is our home. We have to decide together how the children will be raised. And then, unfortunately, the issue of safety is still with us. We still need to be able to evacuate the children quickly down to the bomb shelters."

Pandemonium again. "*Shtuyot*," (stupidity), yells Marta. "What does being a good kibbutz member have to do with where a child sleeps? We can always build more bomb shelters in more places."

It's hard to hear anything above the noise of the crowd. Someone shouts: "If you don't like the kibbutz, go live in Tel Aviv."

Dvorah pounds her hands on the table and tries to quiet the *chaverim* down but to no avail. Only sheer exhaustion brings the shouting match to an end. Little by little, small groups of people leave the dining hall and walk through the Galilee night to their apartments, still arguing along the way. I look at the dining hall clock. It is one in the morning and I have to be at work at 4:30 a.m.

II

The next day, after a deep afternoon nap, my wife and I pick up our two-year-old daughter, Galila, at her children's house and go over to Chava and Yigal's apartment over on the East side of the kibbutz for our weekly coffee circle. Chava and Yigal have been our adopted parents for the past several years. Not showing up at their house on Friday afternoon would be unthinkable except for very extenuating circumstances, for instance, being called up to the army or being too sick to come out of the house. Our adopted parents are both Czechs and they have that delightful middle European cultural mix of tolerance, down to earth friendliness, and a healthy disdain for false pride. At the door, we politely knock and hear Chava's ringing voice say, "*yavow*" (please enter whoever you are). I lower Galila down from my shoulders and in we go. We are greeted not only by Chava and Yigal, but also by Peretz and Franta, two older bachelors who are also adopted "children" of this household, both of them part of the Czech constituency (some say the Czech *Mafia*) in Cfar Moshe.

"Ruthie, Galila, Shimon," they all call out. "Sit down. Chava has made a spice cake for us today. Have some coffee."

Galila climbs up on Franta's lap while Ruthie and I take our chairs around the coffee table. Franta cuddles and pinches Galila and then hands her over to Chava.

"Nescafé or *botz?*" asks Yigal. The question is only ceremonial because Yigal already knows that I drink *botz* and Ruthie drinks instant. He fills our coffee cups from the two kettles on the table.

Chava hands Galila over to Peretz and gets up to bring the spice cake out of the kitchenette. She places it on the table and cuts each one of us a slice. Refusing to eat any cake that Chava bakes would be unforgivable.

"Sugar or saccharine?" inquires Chava before she sits down at her traditional place on the chair closest to the kitchenette. There is no mention of a 'black coffee' alternative since no one in his or her right Israeli mind would drink unsweetened coffee. Except maybe a crazy American.

The greeting and the coffee ceremonies are now past and we turn to the real purpose of kibbutz people sitting around the table on a Friday afternoon; kibbutz politics followed by national politics.

"What's your opinion about the kibbutz meeting last night, Shimon?" Yigal asks. (Of course he already knows my opinion since we have a similar ideology about everything, but it's nice to be corroborated.)

"Disgusting," Chava breaks in.

"Abominable," says Yigal.

"Horrible," says Franta

"Perhaps there were some good ideas at the meeting," states Peretz—he's really with the rest of us, but someone needs to play the role of dissenter just to get the game going.

"What good ideas might those have been?" I ask, with a naïve tone to my voice, as if I am an observer in this hot kibbutz issue.

"Ah. Shimon, you're playing the neutral American card again," Yigal scolds me.

Turning toward the other philosophers in the room, he continues: "Don't you think that this will be the beginning of the end for the kibbutz? What will happen when some *chaverim* (members) get more than others do? At first it will be little things, like an extra can of Nescafé or a few more candy bars for the kids. Then it will escalate and one will have a car and another will have a better car. What will be left of the kibbutz ideology, *from each according to his ability, to each according to his needs?* Why should I work hard pounding nails in the shoe factory and smoking *Daphne's* when someone else is sitting in an office with his feet on the desk, smoking cigars?"

Franta pokes Yigal and says, "If it's a cigar you want, I have one left over from my sister-in-law's wedding down in Tel Aviv. It's only three-years-old."

Dasha, Chava's Airdale, nudges the outside door open and comes in for her afternoon snack. Chava cuts a small piece of the spice cake and pokes it into the dog's mouth. Galila, tired of being passed from lap to lap and, like most of the kibbutz-born kids, instinctively bored with ideology, climbs off Peretz. She accompanies her good friend Dasha outside to sit on the porch and play whatever Airedales and little kibbutz girls play.

The debate continues.

Peretz: "But why should it matter if I want a pear and you want an apple? Don't you trust us all to be reasonable in our choices? For instance, I don't smoke and the rest of you, except Ruthie, are smokers. What would you care if I want chocolate instead of cigarettes?"

Yigal: "Because you're a kibbutznik, not a capitalist."

Peretz: "If we don't begin to be a little less fanatic, our children will leave the kibbutz and we'll end up running an old age house for ourselves. Full equality but no one to do the work."

Me: "Don't you think that most of the kibbutz kids will want to keep the ideology like it is? If we get greedy, won't the children be greedy too?"

Peretz: "There's a difference between greed and the different needs of different people."

Yigal: "Once you let **that** door open, then you've let the bull out of his pen."

Chava: "Is letting the bull out of the pen worse than pushing our second generation out of the kibbutz just because they want to make a few changes?"

"Maybe," says Yigal.

"Maybe not," says Peretz.

Chava puts her hands down heavily on the edge of the table, a sign that she has had enough of philosophers and ideologues for the day. I realize that we have barely touched upon the subject of children's houses.

"Yigal and Shimon, what do your ideologies say about clearing the table?" she asks, not too politely.

May 3 and 4, 1963: Replenish, Replenish.

Our son Golan is born May 3, 1963 (ten minutes before midnight)

Our son Hermon is born May 4, 1963 (ten minutes after midnight)

Ruthie, Shimon and Cfar Moshe have a double bonus.

1963: The Girl in the Apple Tree

I

For years, German volunteers were not accepted in Cfar Moshe. The wounds of the Holocaust were still too fresh for some of the members of the kibbutz. Then, sometime during the mid 1960s, a German Social-Democratic peace group, composed of young people who had all been born after the Second World War, asked if they could come and work on the kibbutz as volunteers. There were a few difficult and emotional debates at the General Assembly meetings over the issue and, in the end all but one family accepted the idea of allowing selected German volunteers to contribute their labor to our kibbutz. Hanoch and Elsa were the sole dissenters. Both had grown up in the Rhineland and had lost their entire families in Hitler's death camps.

One crisp, late autumn day, my wife Ruthie and I are invited for tea over at Hanoch and Elsa's. We are sitting inside of their apartment on the veteran's side of the kibbutz around the warmth of paraffin stove. I notice that most of their bookshelf is stacked with German books and magazines. The paintings hanging on their wall are all of northern European landscapes, snow and forests, children on sleds, alpine villages with peaked roofs. I wouldn't think of bringing up the sensitive subject of the German volunteers, but Hanoch, to my surprise, brings the issue up himself after Elsa serves the coffee and homemade apple strudel.

"Well, Shimon, what do you think about the vote in the General Assembly meeting last night?"

"Which one?" I ask innocently, "the one about the new tractor for the orchard committee?"

"No, the one about German youth groups coming to our kibbutz," he says and sits back in his chair to light a toxic Daphne cigarette and listen to my answer.

"What do *you* think about it?" I parry.

"*Ach*, I'm tired of the whole argument. Everyone thinks that I'm too extreme about the ban on Germans coming to Cfar Moshe. I've fought this for years, but it's no use."

Ruthie says, "I guess that some of the members feel that it's OK this time, because the volunteers are all post war kids from a peace group. They didn't kill any Jews."

"I know that," says Hanoch, "it may surprise you that I don't hold any bad feelings about German young people. None at all. It's a new generation. Life goes on."

"Then why won't you accept them as volunteers?" Ruthie questions further.

"Very simple," Elsa interjects. "It has nothing to do with the young people themselves. We don't doubt their good intentions or their politics. It's the way that they speak German that is the problem. Hanoch and I can't stand to hear their voices."

I say, "You and Hanoch speak German to the other *Yekkes* (German Jews) in the kibbutz. I know because I sit at the *Yekke* table in the dining hall at lunch and I miss half the jokes because the punch line is in German."

"Yes," said Hanoch, "but we speak *our* German."

"Is it different from their German?" I ask.

"Same words, but different accent. *You* couldn't tell one from the other but *we* can." Elsa points out.

"So what are you going to do when the German youth group gets here?" asks Ruthie.

"Don't worry, Ruthie," explains Elsa, "we'll just take our yearly vacation in the city and then we'll visit our relatives over in Kibbutz Givat Haim. We don't want to create an incident. We really just can't stand to hear them talk. Maybe after more years have passed things will be different."

A few weeks later the youth group arrives and Elsa and Hanoch quietly go on their long vacation. It is late in the fall and the orchard team is pruning apple trees in the orchard over by the kibbutz cemetery. I report to the orchard committee tractor shed at the gloriously late hour of seven in the morning.—It is winter and it is still too dark to begin at our usual five in the morning starting time. We sip hot mud coffee before heading out to their labors. Here is Ziggy with his handlebar mustache and his lost childhood. Here is Clarita, an immigrant from Uruguay with the best legs in the kibbutz (we all like to watch her scamper up a picking ladder.) Here is Gad, one of the older kibbutz-born boys. And here is Meir, the kibbutz clown who spends his reserve duty time sharp shooting at Syrian sharpshooters who are shooting our sharpshooters. Here is Amos, the orchard branch manager, he of the red face and blue idiot's cap, still seething over the scandalous outcome of the cranberry bush affair. And here, on this historic morning, are six young Social-Democratic German maidens ready for their long awaited chance to prune apple trees on a kibbutz in the Galilee.

Each one of us kibbutz members is assigned to teach a German girl how to prune our Jewish apple trees. I draw a lovely, ripe blonde with an intense look on her Nordic face. I point to myself and say, "Shimon." She points to herself and says, "Annette." From this exchange, I assume that she doesn't speak much English. I load a couple of ladders into the back of a jeep and we head out to *Aleph* orchard. She is silent during the short ride, but her clear blue eyes are busy studying everything along the way. We arrive in the orchard and, gentlemanly, I start to unload the clanking aluminum ladders, one by one. To my surprise, in the time it takes me to place the first ladder against the nearest tree, Annette has unloaded the second one and has properly placed it against the other side of the tree. I immediately suspect prior training. I hand Annette pruning shears and she wets her finger and inspects the blade. This fräulein has worked in orchards before.

I start up the ladder and motion to her to do the same on her side of the tree. She does it gracefully. We are near the top step of our respective ladders looking over at each other through the top branches of the tree. She speaks, and her first words are, in perfect English:

"How can you forgive us for what we did to the Jewish people?"

I take a deep breath at this unexpected outburst from the blonde volunteer on other side of the tree.

"You speak English," I observe.

"I went to agricultural school in England."

"Did you learn to prune apple trees in England?"

"No, I learned that at home in our family orchard business near Hamburg. In England I learned farm mechanics. Is it so difficult for you to answer my question?"

"I can't answer it." I reply.

"Why not?"

"I'm not prepared. I haven't thought much about the issue."

"I have," she says. "My father was a German soldier."

"I've been a soldier, too."

"Did you ever kill someone?" she persists.

"Not yet, but since I'm in the army, I may have to some day."

"It's hard for me to understand this," she says, sadly. "I am a pacifist and I just don't understand how men kill each other so easily."

"I don't either."

"Maybe we should go ahead and prune these trees."

"We should talk about all this later." she comments and expertly snips a diseased branch off the tree.

"Yes," I reply, "let's talk about it later."

II

I decide to discuss this incident with my friends and mentors Amnon and Olga. Late in the afternoon I bike over to the older section of the kibbutz living quarters. At this time of the day you can see kibbutz families in front of every house: adults and kids, sitting outside around small tables, having a cup of coffee or a glass of juice, peacefully watching the little world of the kibbutz go by. Most of the members have just woken up from their late afternoon nap and are in their best mood after a long day of agricultural or industrial labor. Here they sit, dressed leisurely in their short pants, undershirts and sandals (or barefoot). They watch the passers by, greeting them with a *shalom* and, inevitably—and obsessively—discussing the local and national politics of the day. Lawns, kept green by the gardening staff, surround each row of red roofed houses. The younger children arrive home from their children's houses, sit down with the parents for a piece of cake or a cookie and then take off to play with their comrades. The sun moves west toward Lebanon and softly reddens the Golan Heights. Its tired rays peek obliquely through the cypress trees.

The day softens and there is a hint of the autumn night chill that will soon make us forget the warmth of the afternoon.

I prop my bike up in front of Amnon and Olga's house and knock on the door. They like to have their afternoon snack inside the house.

I hear Olga say, "*yavow*" and I open the door and step into the narrow hallway avoiding Dina the other Airedale (Dasha's sister) who is at her bowl munching last night's leftovers from the dining hall. Amnon, Olga, Gad their adopted son, Eliezer the pig farmer and his wife Dvorah, boss of the clothing warehouse, are sitting in the tiny living room. They are busy, after their coffee, drinking schnapps and eating *strudel*.

"Oh, Shimon, sit down," says Amnon joyfully, "We have something wonderful for you, just the fellow...Eliezer here doesn't drink *Slivovitz*, and I've been waiting for someone to join me."

He holds up an oval bottle with a pale green tint and slides a shot glass over as I take a seat at the table. He fills my glass with the lethal fluid and the two of us throw the awful stuff down our throats.

"Have some of Olga's strudel, too," he adds and pushes an empty plate over. Olga, within a millisecond plops a serious wedge of apple strudel onto the plate. *Better eat it* is the message. Dina comes over expecting her share of my strudel.

"What brings you to our side of the kibbutz?" questions Amnon, knowing that I usually show up at his place to discuss serious issues.

I tell the group the story about Annette's unsettling question up in the apple tree and end with, "what's your opinion?"

All of the assembled at Amnon and Olga's, except Gad, Dina the dog, and me, are of Central European origin and have lost most of their friends and relatives in the Holocaust. Eliezer and his wife are from Germany. Their families perished as well as Amnon's and Olga's. After the war, Amnon had participated in smuggling Jewish displaced persons out of Europe to Palestine. It seemed that most of the people in the room had the right credentials for getting advice about how to respond to Annette's question.

"This German girl asked you how you could forgive her for what was done to the Jews?" asks Eliezer.

"That's it."

"Amazing," agree the others and then there is a long silence.

Mental wheels go around and coffee cups clink as they are returned to the saucer. I fantasize that my murdered grandparents, cousins, uncles and aunts have moved into the room to hear the discussion. Dina the dog detects the somber note in the room and lies under the coffee table with a perplexed look on her face, as if she too is disturbed by the German girl's question.

"I would tell her this," says Eliezer, breaking the ice. "Most of us are too busy to spend time on questions of forgiveness. We have enough work building our country's strength so that this mass murder will never happen again. It only happened in Europe because we were unable to defend ourselves or, at least, unable to get out in time."

"I agree," Gad interjects, "if we had had our own army then, we could have prevented the Holocaust."

The others sigh at Gad's *Sabra* (Israeli born) naivete. He had been my drill sergeant in basic training. What could he know about Holocausts?

Dvorah responds, "Gad, out of everybody here, I am the only one that remained in Europe during that war. I saw my whole family go up in smoke and I still have a tattoo on my arm to remind me of it. I honor you for being a soldier and our protector, although, of course, we all have fought for this country in one war or another. Let's not have the illusion that we could have saved our families in Europe if we had had the guns and ammunition. We were too disorganized and too few of us were trained to be soldiers. And things happened too fast. But I agree with the others here that the way to remember the Holocaust is make sure that our people have a home here in Israel where they can be safe and where they can hold their heads high. We're not looking for apologies; it's too late for that."

Amnon speaks next. "We in the kibbutz movement have our own way of coping with the Holocaust. We're future oriented. But I think that we may be paying a price that we don't understand by ignoring the past. We force ourselves to live in an illusion. Look, don't we diverge from many the non-kibbutz Israelis in the way that we commemorate the day of the Holocaust? We call it the day of the Holocaust and Heroism, but we really prefer to focus on the heroism part. In our ceremony we invite ghetto fighters from the kibbutz down the road to come and talk to us about how many Nazis they killed, and how they escaped to fight with the partisans in the forests. But the truth is that most of our families and friends just went like sheep into the death camps. We don't like to deal with that reality."

Things are getting a little heavy and Dina moves out from under the table and asks to be let out on the porch. Perhaps she wants some relief from the sadness in the room. I get up to open the door for her and slip her a forbidden morsel of *strudel* before she exits. Then I return to the silence of the living room.

We all sigh. It seems like there is nothing more to be said. Amnon looks around, perhaps also feeling the presence of the murdered in the room.

"We probably haven't helped Shimon solve his dilemma," says Amnon. "Perhaps you could tell this German girl that it is too early for all of us to know what to think about her question. Invite her over to visit us. We'll adopt her during her stay. Maybe Olga and I can tell her some boring old stories about how the kibbutz was founded. And maybe some of our *Slivovitz* might do her some good."

III

When I get back home, a little tipsy from the firewater, it is just short of five in the afternoon. My wife Ruthie has gone out with the kids for a walk along the Jordan and my deceased Saba Yisroel is sitting in the rocking chair reading the Hebrew newspaper. He is dressed, to my consternation, in a white burial shroud.

"I'd like to talk to you about Germans," he says sternly.

Saba Yisroel never beats around the bush

"Yes…"

"I've heard about your conversation with the German girl. I don't want you to get angry, and I don't want to teach you a lesson. I know you well enough to understand that you don't listen if someone provokes or nudges you. But I also want you to think hard about what I am about to tell you and maybe you'll draw your own conclusions.

"In the summer of 1942 our family was living in the village of Stolin near the eastern edge of what used to be Poland. Those of our immediate family who were in Stolin were your grandmother Rivka and I, your Uncle Daniel and his wife and kids, and your Aunt Blüme and her husband and children. How did we end up in Stolin, of all places?

"When Poland was divided between the Germans and the Soviets in September 1939 after the defeat of the Polish army, our dear hometown of Ostrolenka ended up being on the German side of the border. Within a few weeks the Germans had expelled all the Jews from this town where we had lived our whole lives. They confiscated all our belongings and pushed us over to the Soviet side of the border. The Soviets put us on a train and we were sent to live in the remote village of Stolin and, for a while, we thought we were safe although the conditions were very difficult in our new location. We were hungry and cold in the winter, and plagued by mosquitoes from the nearby marshes in the summer. But at least we were alive.

"In June of 1941 the Germans invaded the Soviet Union and within a few weeks the Soviets were gone. Anarchy broke out. Bandit groups took over the area where we were living and caused us even more suffering. They robbed us and terrorized us. Not only were they bandits, but they hated Jews as well. But we were still alive.

"Later on, the German troops arrived. We lived under military law. Our food supplies were cut and we were forced into slavery from dawn until sunset, working on the roads, cutting trees in the forest, all without enough to eat and without a day of rest. Old people worked alongside the young and women labored alongside the men. But we were still alive.

"In June of 1942, we began to hear about massacres of the Jewish population in the larger cities in the area. To our horror, we found out from people who had escaped their murderers, that the German soldiers were marching the entire Jewish population of certain towns into a forest. There would be a clearing in the middle of the forest. In the clearing, the soldiers forced Polish and Ukrainian conscripts to dig a giant pit. There was a line of machine guns facing the pit. The Jews were made to stand in a line stretching back into the trees. The German soldiers would line up 50 or 60 people, men, women and children, at the edge of the pit. An order was given and the machine guns would shoot them. The line of dead and dying people would fall into the pit, dead or wounded, and then the next group was called. This would happen over and over until the pit was full or when there were no more Jews to kill.

"We heard these stories from those who had escaped and we tried not to believe them. Or we thought of reasons why we would be spared. Perhaps they were only killing the Jews living in large towns or cities? Perhaps the Jews of Stolin were to be preserved by a miracle? Perhaps…perhaps…

"On the first of July, regular German army troops, not the SS, came into the little ghetto of Stolin. They were people like you and me who had been drafted into armies; they were not professional murderers. They were good little German boys from farms and villages who had grown up in good families. But, obeying their orders like they had been taught, they threw us out of our little houses into the streets of Stolin. It was late in the afternoon. The sky was a beautiful blue. The weather was good. The Germans beat us into a line and we began our march to the forest, to the machine guns and to the pit…I'll spare you the details except that it was midnight by the time that our family faced the machine guns. We shouted good-byes to each other. I thought of you, my oldest grandson whom I had never seen, safe in California, and then the guns began to fire. This was the fate of our family. Could you forgive such a thing?"

Saba Yisroel stands up and walks out the door silently. I watch him walk toward the apple orchard opposite our apartment on the edge of the kibbutz; he and his white shroud disappear among the trees.

1963: Nights of Terrorists and Wolves

I

Every Jewish grandmother wants to give her grandchildren an apple. Jews greet their New Year (*Rosh Hashana*) with a ceremonial eating of apples dipped in honey. Why or where this love of the apple began, we don't know, perhaps in the Garden of Eden. (Although the biblical experts claim that there weren't any apples in the Middle East during those initial years). Anyway, it's all in the mind.

Cfar Moshe, during the 1960s, makes most of its income from several hundred acres of apple and pear trees. We have the most sophisticated cold storage unit in the country–giving us a monopoly on this precious fruit for several months out of the year. So much for Socialism.

In order to produce the apple crop, the orchard crew workers are involved in a never ending cycle of work: pruning, spraying, thinning, fertilizing, weeding, picking, culling, boxing, loading the fruit onto trucks, storing fruit in our refrigeration units, and marketing. Even kibbutz members whose jobs are not directly connected to the orchards are indirectly involved in the fruit tree cycle. The garage people keep the farm equipment in good shape.

The truck drivers transport the fruit to the markets in Tel Aviv, Haifa and Jerusalem. The accountants keep track of the profits and losses of our fruit business. The dining room staff brings the hefty farm workers' meals out to us in trucks and jeeps. The cooks set up rows of dining tables under the trees in the orchard.

Most of our orchard workers have been working for several hours before the clang of a metal pipe hanging from a cypress tree signals breakfast time. An onslaught of hungry orchard workers piles out of the trees and hurries over to the breakfast tables. The tractor drivers zoom to the eating area, shut down their vehicles and join the tree people. They all wolf down a meal of hot cereal, fried eggs, coarse bread, butter, jam, salads, sour cream, herring, anchovy paste, and other rustic delicacies. They eat, smoke bad cigarettes, tell dirty jokes, laugh, ogle the blond Scandinavian volunteer waitresses and argue politics until the metal pipe is clanged again. Then it's back into the apple and pear trees to do their duty for the economic welfare of the kibbutz.

By contrast, my own work, the spraying of pesticides in the orchards, is a lonely task. Because of the winds and the heat during the day, I need to begin my work around 9:00 in the evening and work until sunrise. To avoid contact with the toxic chemicals that I will be spraying onto the trees, I wear special clothing: a canvas *pancho* over my work shirt and pants, rubber gloves over my hands, rubber boots, a rain hat that covers my head and shoulders and a little black, rubber face mask that filters out the toxic chemicals and dust.

At the tractor garage, just outside of the kibbutz living area, I hook a bright red spraying rig up to the tractor, fill the tank of the machine with a mixture of chemicals and water, fire up the pump, drive over to my assigned orchard and enter each row of trees. I turn on the spray valves and a toxic mist blows out of the spray nozzles. I need to constantly watch behind me to see if all leaves of the trees are covered with excess spray. I regulate the tractor's speed so that I'll finish my nightly quota of trees according to schedule. When the tank of pesticides is empty, I return to the refilling station, usually at the edge of the orchard and dump more pesticides and water into the tank and off I go again. I have to do all these things and also remain awake while I'm doing them, otherwise I might find myself in a ditch with the tractor on top of me.

During the nights just before the fall picking season, there is always the chance that thieves will sneak into our orchards at night and steal the fruit of our labor. Some of the orchards are a few kilometers away from the living area of the kibbutz and it would not be much of a problem for some *goniffs* to bring a truck out to one of our lonely orchards and load it up with free apples. This picking season we are too short of labor to waste our time sitting around all night out in the orchards. We have decided to pay professional guards to do the job, rather than impose it on our own people. We hire a bunch of young Druze men, from the Lower Galilee, to guard our orchards at night.

The Druze are a Middle Eastern people who are neither Moslems nor Christians. They have their own religion with its closely guarded secret rituals. They live in mountain villages in Israel, Syria, and Lebanon. Those who live in Israel have been fiercely loyal to the Jewish State. They serve in the Israeli army. The men grow ferocious mustaches, and the women are invisible.

A week before picking season, I am out on my tractor on a particularly dark night, tugging along the spray machine and its poisonous content, heading out toward Aleph orchard. There are two major fears that I have about this unpleasant work. One is the possibility that I might spill some of the pesticide concentrate on myself while I am mixing the chemicals and water in the spray tank. Some of the pesticides we use, like *parathion*, for instance, are so toxic that a few drops of the concentrate on your flesh would be enough to kill you. Who is supposed to rescue me in the middle of the night in the darkness of an orchard has never been determined. (I have a little vial of stuff in my shirt pocket that I am supposed to inject into my skin if I spill *parathion* on myself, and this is supposed to help me stay alive until someone comes to my rescue.)

The other fear is that an enemy infiltrator from over the border will shoot me dead. Don't laugh. This fear is based on the reality of the 1960s in the Hulah valley. There were times, in the previous spraying seasons, when I had to go to work with a sub-machine gun hooked on the fender of the tractor, just in case. On some nights, both of these nightmares are on my mind. To make things worse, in order to see the effectiveness of the spray on the trees, my tractor is well lit by headlights and back lights. I am, basically, a sitting duck.

On this night, I don't have my Uzi with me and I am tractoring slowly, half-asleep, down a row of apple trees in one of the more remote orchards.

Suddenly, the headlights of my tractor pick up an Arab with a *kefiah* scarf draped over his face. He holds a rifle and screams at me over the noise of the tractor and the thunder of the spraying machine. Pow! My adrenaline kicks in. I ram the gearshift of the tractor into high gear and pop the clutch. Run him over before he can take aim. The tractor leaps forward and I see the surprised expression on the face of the Arab as my red Ferguson and the spray rig come hurtling toward him. He has no time to do anything with his rifle. I see the whites of his terrified eyes. He manages to duck between two apple trees, like a matador avoiding a blood-crazed bull. He takes to his heels into the dark.

As soon as the intruder disappears into the night, I slam on the brakes, bounce off the tractor and high tail it in the other direction to get lost in the darkness. Maybe I can make it back to the kibbutz to rouse the night guards. Heart pounding. I dash by the old corrugated iron shack that serves as the orchard kitchen during the daylight hours. A kerosene lamp is burning inside. I remember that there is a field telephone hanging inside. I plunge through the corrugated iron door and find four Druze night guards sitting around the table drinking coffee.

When they get over their startle, they greet me and, automatically, one begins to pour me some coffee into an empty cup. I recognize him as the man with the rifle that I had almost run over. He asks me, in Hebrew, why I had jumped off the tractor. My adrenaline drops significantly. I ask the one with the rifle why he had shouted at me out there between the trees.

"I heard you driving through the orchard with the spraying machine and came to invite you to drink coffee with us," He says politely and then adds with some sarcasm, "where did *you* learn to drive a tractor?"

For the rest of the apple harvest time, I have good Druze coffee waiting for me when I take a break from my lonely ride through the orchard.

II

During the winter dormant season, the apple trees have to be sprayed against the malicious mites that make their homes in the bark of our trees. This is a particularly nasty job. Your hands turn orange-yellow for several weeks from contact with the oil that has to be mixed with a miticide and water solution. You have to endure long, cold winter nights of the Upper Galilee sitting on the frigid tractor seat. The worst is when, in the middle of the night, your tractor gets stuck in the oozy mud of the sodden roads out to the orchards or, worse yet, somewhere in between the rows of trees–what a mess! It happens a lot during the rainy season. If you get stuck, you have to hike back to the kibbutz living area and wake up someone to come with a caterpillar tractor and a chain and pull you out. The people that must be woken up to help are not always enthusiastic about the rescue attempt in the middle of the night.

"*Cus Emak,*" they say, insulting your mother's anatomy, when you knock on their door at two in the morning.

The winter of 1963 turns out to be the coldest winter in many years. Mount Hermon, closing the north end of the valley, is covered with snow all the way down its slopes and, for the first time in many years, there is even a dusting of snow visible on the ridges of Naftali and on the Golan Heights. The paths around the residential area of the kibbutz are coated with slippery mud. Everyone, adults and children, wears rubber boots outside. At night, in their homes, people light their paraffin heaters, being careful to leave a window open to keep from being asphyxiated. Cats sleep on the beds worming their way in between the human sleepers. It is so cold that even the wolves, up on the frigid and windy Golan Heights in Syria, can't take it any longer and slink down, through the minefields and fortifications, to our valley, becoming, temporarily, Israeli wolves.

To my usual spraying wardrobe, I add to my work outfit a set of long johns, a heavy sweater, two pair of wool socks, a wool cap and wool gloves that fit inside the rubber work gloves. Does it help? Not really.

One frosty night, I hook the Ferguson up to the spray rig and fasten a cart full of mite poison and barrels of yellow oil onto the back of the rig. I'm again on my way to Aleph orchard. The first leg of the journey is a kilometer's drive up the paved west to east road across the valley. Then, I make a left turn and enter the dirt road that leads to the orchard. The lights of the tractor illuminate a morass of flooded potholes—plenty of mud tonight to add to my troubles! I maneuver the tractor onto the paved refilling ramp, dismount and toss a dose of miticide and a bucket of yellow oil into the churning tank of the spray rig. Then, I drive slowly through the first row of trees, spray valves open. The yellowish spray liquid coats the bare limbs and trunks of the trees. The mites die miserably and silently as the motors of the tractor and rig roar through the orchard.

A few minutes later, at the far end of the row, the headlights of the tractor pick up a couple of long-legged, gray canines. For an instant, as the lights shine upon them, their eyes are fiery mirrors. They stand maybe 100 feet away from me and then, in a dignified manner stroll on about their mischief. I know right away that these are not any of the good old dogs of the kibbutz, Humi, or Puki, or Lassie, out for their midnight pranks. These are wolves indeed. But I'm not afraid of the big bad wolves - they don't usually eat kibbutz pesticide sprayers (and after all, they are also communitarians). The lights of the tractor pointing off in a 360-degree circle will keep them away. I don't care if they are Syrian wolves either; I'm not about to check their passports. So for the next few hours, I have the thrill of watching these animals drifting through the orchard, once in a while having a look at me from far away. The tractor and spray rig motors drown out any growls, yips, or calls they might have been making.

But now *Elohim*, our local God, tests my complacency. Somewhere around row 26 of the Jonathan apple section, the tractor wheels plunge into a sea of mud and began to spin in the slime. Mud flies through the air and lands all over the tractor and me. I shift into neutral and curse my luck in Arabic.

"*Cus Emak.*"

Now I will have to make my way on foot to the kibbutz to wake up Avraham or Amos and have one of them pull my rig out of the mud. Neither of them is going to be happy about this.

What *I'm* not happy about is the idea of going on foot through the darkness of Aleph orchard with the Syrian pooches as company. A flashlight and an Uzi would probably make me feel better, but unfortunately I am not armed with either. I remember the field telephone hanging in the orchard shed only a few dozen rows of apples away. Then, I remember that the phone only rings in the kibbutz packinghouse, which is closed for the winter.

"Cus Emak," again.

What to do? The only alternatives are to sit on the tractor until daybreak, about seven hours away, or to hoof it back to the kibbutz, hoping that the wolves are not hungry. I weigh these alternatives and after a few seconds of meditation, I arm myself with the only weapon available, pipe wrench out of my tool kit. Now, I begin my lonely slosh through the wet orchard, back to the paved road, leading to the kibbutz. I hit on a morale-building idea of singing my way through the rows of trees. Surely the wolves would head in the other direction in response to my non-operatic voice making strange noises. To my own surprise, the first marching song that comes to mind is *"Marching Through Georgia."*

"Hurrah, hurrah..." I sing in my bravest baritone..."we'll bring the Jubilee, Hurrah, Hurrah, from Atlanta to the Sea..."

My rubber-booted legs take up the rhythm and I parade down row 10, Golden Delicious, with the heavy pipe wrench on my shoulder. I shift to more marching songs including, *The Song of the Palmach*–an Israeli, underground fighter's song.

Rishonim Tamid Anachnu...(We are always the first ones there...)

After this I do the *Battle Hymn of the Republic*. I like the last stanza best.

"In the beauty of the lilies Christ was born across the sea..."

Then I sing some Spanish Civil War songs learned from a Pete Seeger album back in Berkeley.

Venga jaleo jaleo
Sueño de ametralladora
Y Franco se va paseo
Y Franco se va paseo...

The wolves are nowhere to be seen. I fantasize that they are now on their way back to Syria escaping from my unmusical clatter.

"Better to suffer through the cold and ice on the Golan than to listen to that," the wolves say to each other.

As for me, I make it back, all aglow with my strident singing and heat creating marching. The first person I meet on the way is Max, the boss of the laundry crew, who is on guard duty all this cold night. He is waiting by the guard booth at the gated entrance to the kibbutz living area.

"I heard your concert coming for the last ten minutes and you're not Caruso," he says wryly. He had already figured out that the soloist was the crazy American coming back from the orchard with some kind of problem to be fixed. Probably stuck in the mud again.

"I'll go wake up Amos," he offers still giggling at my grand march and chorus. "*He* woke *me* up last week when the steam boiler broke down in the laundry house. He wasn't very delicate about it and I owe him one."

1963: More Volunteers From Abroad

I

Even though I am a relative newcomer to the kibbutz, it is my fate to be put in charge of orienting the stray English-speaking foreign volunteers that infrequently appear at the gate. After all, my Ruthie and I are the only Americans among the five hundred or so Central Europeans and Argentineans and others that make up the general kibbutz population.

"Shimon," the work chairman says to me, "you understand these Anglo-Saxons...do me a favor..."

The favor means finding the volunteers a place to stay in one of the wooden prefabs over by Turkey Row, finding them work, and acquainting them with the services and obligations due to them as volunteers. I also explain the rules governing the use of the dining hall, the laundry, the medical clinic, the public showers and the sanitation system. My orientation tour also includes identifying the site of the nearest bomb shelter and instructions on where not to wander at night, given the trigger-fingers of some of our night guards.

The kibbutz people, like most other people, are big on stereotypes, especially as they relate to the volunteers from abroad. On the negative side, French volunteers are thought to be un-hygienic. English volunteers are prone to alcoholism. South Americans are noisy and lazy. On the positive side, Scandinavian volunteers are perceived to be hard working and serious about life. Americans are something else altogether.

Leah K., who is both telephone operator and the editor-in-chief of the kibbutz newsletter for the year, drops by one day and asks me to write about some of the more "interesting" volunteers from abroad that have visited Cfar Moshe in the past few months. True to my nature, I wait until a few days before my assignment is due which means that Leah has to come by and plead with me several times during the week. But you know how kibbutz life is, since we are all equal, everything has to be done voluntarily. On Thursday, one day before the deadline, I have guard duty up on top of the alfalfa silo where I might be able to spot infiltrators in the unlikely case they attack Cfar Moshe. So I have four long hours to think about my writing assignment.

I come up with a few anecdotes about volunteers that I have known.

II

An American named Fred showed up in Cfar Moshe. He decided, after a week of working with the Alfalfa crew, that he needed to stimulate his sense of adventure. He was a big block of a guy, from Cleveland, Ohio, who had read 'Exodus' by Leon Uris, and was looking to find an exotic Israeli soldier woman who would lead him off to battle against whomever. He ended up crossing the border into Lebanon, being arrested by the Lebanese army and thrown into a military clink. All this created an international incident of epic proportions. Finally, with the aid of the United Nations Security Forces, he was released and sent back to America. Within a month, he dropped in to visit Cfar Moshe again. His visit lasted about ten minutes, the time it took Amnon, the kibbutz Secretary-General, to alert the police in Kiryat Shmonah that this undesirable maniac was back in our area. The police sent him south toward Tel Aviv with a recommendation that he be returned to America. Later, I heard that he had been caught crossing the border into the Hashemite Kingdom of Jordan, creating another diplomatic crisis and resulting in a much longer incarceration.

III

Another time, an English *meshuga* (madman), William, brought a barometer with him to the kibbutz and insisted on appearing at work only on days when the barometer was auspicious. He would wake up around six in the morning, squint at his apparatus, and, most often, bury himself back into his blankets. This proved to be unsatisfactory to his boss, Eliezer, the pig farmer, whose pigs needed tender loving care regardless of the barometric pressure. Eliezer sent William over to work in our gigantic cold storage unit where the apple crop was kept and where the climate was the same every day, about 3° Centigrade.

IV

Gary Cooper (no relationship) came to Cfar Moshe from Texas, disguised as a normal man. From the beginning of his stay, he made a real hit in the kibbutz. He said that he had fought in the Korean War. He worked like a horse, picked up a serious Hebrew vocabulary within a few weeks, and knew a lot about the history of Israel and the geography of the Galilee. He had a great Texas accent and a big following among some of the unmarried women of the kibbutz. He stayed with us for almost three months and became a frequent visitor in my apartment, playing chess with me, flirting with my wife, discussing the day's news, and asking serious questions about the every aspect of kibbutz life. Then, one day he informed me that he was going on a short trip to Greece, and asked me if he could I store his suitcase in the shed I had built along the side of our family apartment.

"Sure, why not, Gary. Hurry back, we'll miss you, bring back a bottle of *Ouzo*."

Months passed and Gary didn't return. I needed to put some more of my junk in my shed and I decided to move Gary's suitcase over to the big General Storehouse over next to the volunteers' area on Turkey row. Sarah, who was in charge of the Storehouse, insisted on opening the suitcase, over my protests that it belonged to Gary Cooper. I didn't want to poke into his private stuff. But she was a pioneer type who had been through it all and never took no for an answer.

"Either I open it or you can take it back to your apartment." said Sarah, making her point without disturbing the cigarette dangling out of her mouth.

She brought out her wire cutters and with one mighty *kvetch* cut the lock off the suitcase. She opened it up carefully and we both peered inside. What do we see but two pairs of underwear and a hand grenade rigged as a booby trap! Sarah and I looked at each other without either of us drawing a breath. Thank God, the booby trap didn't go off.

"Some friends you keep, Shimon," said Sarah.

V

Next is a Purim story. (Don't worry I'll get to the point about volunteers in a bit).

Purim is a Jewish holiday of the carnival type taken very seriously by the kibbutzniks. Preparation for Purim begins early in January. Groups of members and volunteers combine spontaneously to prepare raucous skits for the Purim night frolic in the main dining hall. They will practice their skits often during the month, generally having more laughs creating the script and rehearsing than they will in the actual production. There is a Purim costume storehouse in an old shed that used to be a sewing room before a newer more comfortable one was built. The storehouse is open every night for the last month before Purim. There you can find a grand mix of clothes, shoes, rags, hats, blankets, heirlooms from Europe, discarded toys and crafts, bawdy posters, horns and other broken down musical instruments, mirrors, make-up kits, and other items of exotic and useless value. Take what you will, and use it for the mirth of the Purim revelers. No one comes without a costume. Children have their own Purim carnival and are not invited to the adult carnival. For the adults there are no limits to the topics of the skits and the design of the costumes. You can be as pristine or as vulgar as you want. You can lampoon the world.

This Purim, I choose to dress up in a tuxedo top (brought to the kibbutz decades ago in some German Jew's trunk), a top hat (donated by a departed, rich uncle of one of our Hungarian members), a cravat (of unknown origin), ankle top black boots (from an box of shoes sent to Palestine by a Czech shoe factory before the war), and a shoddy pair of long underwear (my own). A few days before the party, I receive a note in my post office box, assigning me to do guard duty between the hours of twelve midnight to one in the morning. Our kibbutz defense commander has kindly agreed to break up the guard duties into one-hour stints, instead of the usual eight- hour ones, so that everyone will have a chance to spend part of this favorite holiday with the merrymakers.

My Ruthie and I arrive at the party at 10:00 at night, on the dot. The kids have all been tucked in their beds in the children's houses and it is now time for these serious kibbutzniks to get drunk and make fools of themselves. The dining hall is decorated with plenty of tinsel and colored lights, the walls are covered with posters, many of which parody well-known government officials and religious authorities. Nothing is holy on Purim night. Bottles of beer and hard booze are everywhere and they are emptied faster than the bartending staff can replace them. The bartenders themselves are already smashed. A Spike Jones type band of Cfar Moshe men is blasting away on trumpets, accordions, washtubs, spoons, beer glasses, Purim rattles and an out-of-tune piano. Knowing that I will have to go out to guard duty at midnight, I try to moderate my drinking, but my weak character and the raucous Purim spirit overwhelm me. Bring on the vodka.

The witching hour arrives and my name is called out over the loud speaker informing me of my turn at guard duty. Top hat, tuxedo, long johns, and ankle boots, I head out into the darkness into the silence of the night. The previous guard hands me a Sten gun and I'm sober enough to check the weapon. I take the clip out, pull the bolt back, poke my finger into the back end of the gun barrel, and close the bolt. Then off I go to meander around the kibbutz periphery for an hour. My head is still full of alcohol but it is gradually wearing off and nothing is going to happen on Purim night anyway, right?

While passing by the alfalfa mill, on the West Side of the kibbutz, I hear what sounds like a clip of bullets being fired on the East Side of the Cfar Moshe. Instinctively, I grip the Sten gun in front of my hips and head at full speed toward the direction of firing. I bravely charge through a field of winter wheat, wet with the nighttime dew, and then, as I approach the little fig tree grove near the east gate, I stop and look around. My heart is pounding like a base drum. My underwear has been soaked by the wheat and is beginning to sag. I am an apparition in a Purim costume, crouching behind a fig tree, silent, just waiting for something to move. Now I see a man climbing through a barbed wire fence that stands between the main road and the little pedestrian gate leading into Cfar Moshe. The man carries a small suitcase and carefully, quietly, slips it through the wires. Then, he himself slinks into the kibbutz. I raise the sub-machine gun to my shoulder and carefully draw a bead on him - as much as it is possible with the crude sights of the Sten gun. I figure that he is an infiltrator and my instinct is to open fire before he gets too close with that suitcase. But the rules of sentry duty supersede my instinct.

"Halt," I shout, "password." Very brave of me but I don't even remember the night's password.

He keeps coming. Just a few steps more...I step out from the grove of trees and he sees a Purim costume and a sub-machine gun. He drops the suitcase.

"*Donde esta Cfar Moshe?*" (Where is Cfar Moshe?) He yells in Spanish.

"*Quien es usted?*" (Who are you?) I yell back and slightly lower the Sten.

"*Soy voluntario, busco kibbutz Cfar Moshe. Soy de Argentina. Cuidado con la ametralladora,*" he says with hands raised, "be careful with that machine gun."

I take a closer look at him and, unless the Syrians are getting better at camouflage, the infiltrator is a volunteer from Argentina. But what the hell is he doing crawling through our fence at one in the morning?

Since I have decided not to shoot him, I engage him in conversation. He looks at me as if I am a Martian. This annoys me until I remember that I am dressed in my ridiculous Purim costume. The soggy long underwear probably does not look very soldier-like to this Argentinean. Where he comes from soldiers look like soldiers. He tells me his story, in his strange kind of Spanish. He arrived at the airport and no one was there to greet him; hitched his way to Tel Aviv in the back of a Margarine truck; he managed to hop on the last bus from Tel Aviv to the Galilee; the bus driver had motioned him off the bus in the middle of nowhere at Papyrus Junction (it was almost midnight); he walked alone down the east/west road through the darkness; he was terrified of meeting infiltrators; he bumped his head on the metal struts of the bridge and almost fell down into the Jordan river (at least he knew his geography); he searched for the entrance to the kibbutz but found only barbed wire fences; he spotted the lights of our dining hall and he climbed through the barbed wire and tore his pants and last, but not least, in his unlucky odyssey, he found himself staring into the barrel of a sub-machine gun.

Not quite knowing what to say to this young man whose life had almost ended by my hand, I say, all in Spanish:

"Shalom, welcome to Cfar Moshe. Your name is…?"

"Yankele."

"Yankele," I continue, "let's get you housed and fed. You're just in time for the Purim feast. We should both start with a shot of vodka."

We walked over to the revelries at the dining hall and took care of the vodka, first thing. Nothing like vodka and Purim for two very shook-up people.

Oh yes, the clip of bullets heard during my guard duty? Nothing but the Purim devilment of kibbutz teenagers out on their own holiday adventure, sneaking out of their children's house late at night, and lighting home-made fire crackers made out of gunpowder from loose bullets they found on the nearby hills.

Did they get it from me the next day!

1964: To Serve Our Country

One balmy evening, I join Yitzhak, and Ron for tea, cookies and cigarettes on the porch of our kibbutz coffeehouse. As we watch the peaceful sunset over the hills of Naftali, we are talking about the possible results of the Syrian government's plan to divert the entire Jordan River into the Mediterranean Sea through a canal system. If the diversion plan should succeed, Israel will be left high and dry. Maybe even bone dry. For the three of us, and all of the other residents of the Hulah valley, this is far from a theoretical discussion since, during the daytime, we can easily see the area around the sources of the Jordan—four miles to the north of us—where 7 or 8 yellow Syrian bulldozers have begun their mischievous, malignant work. As usual among many Israelis, we discuss the disturbing possibility by joking about it, the way that teenagers joke about sex before they've had it.

"We could raise camels instead of turkeys," suggests Yitzhak.

"We could drink vodka instead of water," I offer.

"We could import icebergs from Antarctica," is Ron's recommendation.

The three of us have an additional issue in common on this October night in 1964. We each received one of those pink slips in our mailboxes, inviting us to our annual six-week military reserve service. Tomorrow, we and the rest of Battalion 37, will be leaving for parts unknown.

Late October can be a wonderful season in the Galilee. The kibbutz's apple crop is in and the pace of work is slowing. There can be a chill in the air and if you leave your windows open at night you might need to use a blanket. The sky becomes more intensely blue and the shifting colors on the two parallel ridges on either side of the valley take a deeper hue. All this beauty is made even more precious because it is a valley with a long history of danger to its inhabitants; malaria, wars, droughts, flooding and earthquakes have made their mark here. But once you have accepted it as your home, it breaks your heart to leave its splendor.

However, a pink slip in your mailbox stamped **Israel Defense Forces** and dated October 27, 1964, could require you to go away to a military-elsewhere, depending on the luck of the draw or grand army strategy. You never know where you are going to end up. In our previous service, Yitzhak and I went to a special course to learn how to improve our skills in the use of .50 caliber machine guns. Before that, I had mostly been a participant in long and grueling maneuvers in various parts the north of Israel, charging barren hills, firing wooden bullets at cardboard enemies, but mostly swatting flies and mosquitoes.

Early on the morning of the 27th, the three of us take a bus to our regional army supply depot in the kabbalistic city of Safed to receive the equipment and uniforms that will make us look like soldiers. A sullen supply sergeant deals me out a field uniform (thank God it fits this time), an Uzi submachine gun with two magazines and a box of .45 caliber slugs, a mess kit (greasy), a couple of rough blankets, a cartridge belt, a khaki idiot's hat (doesn't fit but I have my own) and a pair of army boots (miraculously they do fit). After carefully cleaning our weapons, we are politely asked to climb onto the back of an army truck to be taken to our still unknown destination. The truck sets off to the west through the northern mountains toward the seacoast. In two hours we are in the port city of Haifa.

"Maybe we're invading Turkey by sea," comments Yitzhak, as we pass the dock area of the city.

"You know what happens to military captives in Turkish prisons," adds Ron, perhaps because he had a sore behind from the bumpy ride across the Galilee or perhaps because he is a Turk himself.

"Maybe we're going on a pleasure cruise to the Greek Islands," I add, hopefully.

But the truck goes on past Haifa port and heads south along the Mediterranean shoreline. After a few more kilometers the truck turns to a dismal army base lodged next to an industrial zone and jerks to a stop. We unload our packs and notice the mix of grease and dust-caked soil in this godforsaken base. The rest of the view is spoiled by a bunch of corrugated iron sheds, some as big as an airplane hanger and some as small as an outhouse. I have a bad feeling about what is about to occur. All that is missing is a sign that proclaims: **Work Makes You Free.**

A hideously fat Moroccan gent, who claims to be our Sergeant for the next six weeks, greets us. We follow him, suspiciously, to one of the larger sheds. He takes out a rusty key and opens up an even rustier padlock. He shoves the sliding corrugated iron door aside and turns on a light switch. In the dim light of a bug spattered light fixture we see a mountain of greasy rifles, machine guns, submachine guns and miscellaneous metallic junk. It is an enormous dump of old weapons that could be of possible use only if the entire country was being overwhelmed by the Soviet Army and we needed to wage a last stand on Masada.

"Your job," commands Sergeant Machluf, "is to sort out these weapons and clean them by the end of six weeks." We look aghast at each other and at the sleaze ball that will be our boss. We sigh a collective sigh of despair.

"You are kibbutzniks, right?" Machluf launches into his drill sergeant *shtick*. "You probably don't know how to clean anything, including your own rooms. Before you go back to your stinking kibbutz, everything here will need to be perfectly clean. For once, you'll have to work hard. I don't want to hear any ideology from you Socialists. Just work. You eat at the army canteen across the road and sleep in the shed here. It will remind you of your life on the kibbutz."

Yitzhak is looking around the shed and its oily contents and I recognize a flash of inspiration and cunning on his face.

"Sergeant Machluf," he says innocently, "I have a proposition to make you."

"What?" he asks as if responding to a dog bark.

"Do you have a family," Yitzhak asks, still very innocently.

"What if I do?" says the sergeant carefully, smelling an insult coming.

"May they all be healthy..." continues Yitzhak. "My idea is that you should go home for six weeks and be with your family."

"What?"

"Look here sergeant," Yitzhak touches him lightly on the elbow, "you're really in luck that we came to work here. We *are* kibbutzniks and we know how to work. And we can finish this job in six weeks. No problem. I do the same kind of work all the time in the kibbutz, cleaning and wiping, (a lie) but you know how we kibbutzniks are. We like to work without a boss around, it's in our ideology, you know...everyone equal. I know it's crazy but it's a break for you. So, let's make an agreement: You come back in six weeks, we cover for you and do all the work. Everything will be shining when you come back and your wife will be happy. How many kids do you have? "

"Five," he murmurs, warding off the evil eye of the kibbutzniks.

"Go see them and give our blessings to your wife and your mother," says Yitzhak, full of a mixture of Middle Eastern submissiveness coupled with a subtlety-implied insult about his mother.

To our surprise, the sergeant buys the idea and within the hour has disappeared for the next six weeks.

After we finish laughing at the sergeant and how we really feel about him and his family, the three of us walk through the shed and look at the mess strewn all over the greasy and piss-smelling floor of the shed. We have a planning meeting to discuss how long it will really take us to clean it out and we come up with a time frame of about a week. That will leave five weeks to enjoy ourselves, doing whatever we liked. And Haifa will be a great city for that purpose. Being good kibbutzniks with a steadfast work ethic, we finish the whole job in four days and nights, everything clean, bright, and operational. Sergeant Machluf will be pleased, and we will have defended the honor of the kibbutz movement. May the sergeant's family be healthy and may he stay away from us forever.

In the meantime, in the Upper Galilee...

Five miles north of the Cfar Moshe, a general of the Israeli army is slowly leading a small group of Centurion and Sherman tanks by night through a forest of dense undergrowth known as *Tel Dan* (the hill of the tribe of Dan). Progress is slow, as the paths through the forest are narrow and crossed by rivulets of water pouring out from one of the sources of the Jordan River. Scouts, waiting at the northern edge of this forest, can view the slopes of Mount Hermon only a few hundred meters away. They can also view the bulldozers and other heavy equipment being used by the Syrian army in their river diversion project. Israeli tank commanders are identifying positions where the tanks can be placed so that they are not visible to the Syrians and where they can quickly move into action. Few people in the army, and few among the population of the Galilee, know that a secret action is in progress.

Back to Haifa...

The three of us are sipping our Goldstar beers in the Victory Café watching the sun go down over Haifa bay. At some point between darkness and light, a chorus of birds begins chirping a celebration mass in the trees of the Arab cemetery across the street. The proprietor is sitting a few tables away counting his morning and afternoon proceeds and the waiter is hanging out on the sidewalk, watching the sunset and listening to the birds as he smokes a cigarette. Tranquility fills the air and we are all silent during this magic moment. Even the proprietor halts his counting and watches the night arrive. I feel like I am in a theater and the curtain has opened with the characters frozen on the stage. It is Act one, Scene one: Shimon, Yitzhak and Ron are drinking beer in the Victory Café. Birds chirp in the Arab cemetery.

Ron, playing himself, unfreezes the scene. "I think I'll have the *kabob* tonight, the *shashlik* was a little tough last night."

Yitzhak fingers a crumpled menu punctuated with grease spots and lines drawn through defunct menu items: "*Schnitzel* for me, with chips."

I say: "I'll have my usual, the *senia* but this time with *tehina* sauce instead of tomato sauce."

Choosing from the menu at this magic hour is really only a rehearsal, since the waiter is busy outside and the proprietor is too far up the Victory's hierarchy to wait on tables. Besides he has become too fat to move around very much.

"What do you think is happening in the kibbutz?" states Ron as the opening gambit for the next discussion.

"Oh, everyone is out in front of their houses having tea, as usual, watching people go by, just like we're doing, and commenting about everybody else. The difference is that we're watching better looking women go by, like that one in the red skirt," observes Yitzhak.

"My neighbor, Yankele, is just getting out of bed from his afternoon nap and letting a fart in the bathroom. By god, our walls are so thin that I know everything that he does by heart," says Ron.

"When does he have sex?" I ask politely.

"Never," answers Ron. "He only farts." We can't help laughing about that one and the proprietor, who's Hebrew is as good as his Arabic, snickers from his lair across the room.

"So it's like this," continues Ron, "my Argentinean neighbors are probably getting ready to have a barbecue, an *asado*, out in back of their apartment. They probably aren't going to invite Sarah and me since we're only Turks and not Argentineans, and pretty soon, if I were home, I'd be smelling their meat. Since it's Friday night and the rest of us will be eating in the dining hall, I would be getting ready to have a bad *schnitzel* full of greasy lumps or some wet chicken with the hairs still sticking out. Instead, here I am in the Victory Café, supposedly defending my country and ready to have another beer before my good *schnitzel* arrives, cooked as it should be cooked, with fat, crispy French fries instead of the skinny, soggy ones on the kibbutz. This is my revenge for all I have suffered in the kibbutz."

"But you do miss your wife and children, don't you?" I remind him.

"No, I don't," says Yitzhak. "But I do miss sleeping in my bed instead of in a cot in our weapons warehouse. It still stinks of rifle oil in there and I don't care much for the mice running around at night. It's the only thing that spoils our vacation here in the beautiful streets of Haifa and in this fine restaurant that is our new home." He becomes increasingly poetic and loud as the beer flows through his Argentinean veins.

Tel Dan...

The plan for the attack on the Syrian bulldozers is divided into two stages. At sunrise, an armored tractor from a nearby kibbutz will begin to plow a field between the forested area and the Syrian military emplacements. The exact border of the field is in dispute and the Israeli farmers have not attempted to work the land, given its dangerous location. The tractor is to start plowing in the area of the field that is not in dispute and then plow closer and closer toward the Syrian lines. When and if the Syrians open fire, as they are expected to do, the tractor will get the hell out of there and the tanks will move up into their firing positions and let the Syrians have it. The major targets will be the bulldozers and the Syrian fortifications protecting the earth-moving equipment. The tank crews are Israel's finest.

Haifa again

The *senia* and two plates of *schnitzel* arrive and are quickly devoured and washed down with another bottle of Goldstar beer. I wipe the bottom of the *senia* bowl with a *pita* and savor the wonderful aftertaste of its contents: fried lamb patties, hot tehina sauce, and pine nuts. All my mouth needs now is the taste of

Turkish coffee with cardamom. The coffee arrives and we sip the thick black liquid out of tiny cups making sure that the proprietor of the Victory hears our grateful slurps. We think of having another beer but then decide to pay our bill and go out for a walk around town to see what we could see. We are in a euphoric mood with only a slight stagger to show that we have had too much beer. After a few blocks, we realize that our next big need will be to find a public toilet or another café with a men's room.

Unfortunately, Haifa, more Germanic than French, has no pisseries and, at this late hour, there aren't any cafés open. What to do? The pressure to solve this problem is growing and will soon be agonizing. This might lead to a loss of control and possible public humiliation. Finally, for lack of an official place to urinate, we find a dark courtyard within an apartment complex and begin to relieve ourselves against a wall with great sighs of relief. Suddenly, in midstream, a light flicks on above us and we hear explosions to the right and left of us, followed by a torrent of curses from above. An old woman leans her head over the balcony and denounces the three off us pissing in the courtyard below her. Her North African accented denunciations include us, personally, our mothers, our grandmothers, the midwives of our grandmothers, the houses we grew up in (may they be burnt!) and the mustaches of our fathers (may they be burnt!). With that, she hurls a third "bomb" down toward us, which turns out to be a paper bag full of reeking garbage. It is impossible to take cover to avoid the bombardment because each of us has at least a half-liter yet to go. Fortunately, she is a bad bombardier and misses us, although the garbage is strewn all over the courtyard. The light goes off among more curses and her ladyship disappears back into the apartment, slamming the door. Evidently, this courtyard is a notorious pissing place for all sorts of male passers-by and the poor woman was just trying to keep the awful male stench to a minimum. All three of us break into uncontrollable laughter as we finish, shake off the last drops and plunge our anatomy back into our pants.

Back out in the street, we thank the God of Israel for the bad aim of our unwilling hostess and vow, as an act of repentance, to go back to the kibbutz for a visit to our families on the first bus tomorrow, hangover or not.

The next day, we get on the first bus from Haifa to the Upper Galilee at six a.m. All three of us sleep heavily during the ride. Yitzhak snores with his mouth open and I dream that I have lost my car in a parking lot in San Diego. I wake up just as the bus heads down to the valley floor around the torturous curves between Safed and Rosh Pinah. It is about 7:45 in the morning and the sun is behind clouds that have blown in from the West.

I can see the entire valley, from Mount Hermon in the north to the Sea of Galilee to the south. At the base of Mt. Hermon, my eye picks up flashes of light, shell trajectories and a line of bonfires among the kibbutzim at the bottom of the mountain. I spot ambulances racing along the same north-south road that the bus will be taking at the next junction. I wake up Yitzhak, sleeping on the seat next to me and Ron sprawled out on the back seat of the bus.

"There's a war on over there," I say. They sit up and I point out the action. The bus reaches the bottom of the Safed road and turns north as more ambulances pass us. The bus driver turns on the 8:00 news and flashes it onto the loudspeakers in the middle and back of the bus. "The Syrians are bombarding the northernmost kibbutzim with unknown numbers of casualties," says a correspondent. The rest of the valley's population, including our own wives and children, is down in the bomb shelters. We hear the whoosh of jet planes above us and catch the silver glint of the Israeli air force coming over to hit the Syrians. The end of the Syrian's Jordan River diversion has begun.

Our vacation is over.

1965: Going Outside

One very early summer morning, just as I finish hosing off the spraying machine and just before I climb onto my bicycle to pedal home to my well-deserved daytime sleep, Stanley, the turkey man, hails me down.

"Hey, Shimon," he yells, "I need to talk to you for a minute."

"What?"

"I hear that you are leaving for a visit to your parents in America," he says, holding on to the handlebars of my bike. "I need you to do me a favor."

"What do you want me to bring you?" I ask, already knowing what's on Stanley's mind."

Stanley is a *chaver* (kibbutz member) who has worked so many years with the turkeys that he is beginning to resemble them. He has a beaked nose, an underdeveloped chin and a frazzle of red hair nesting on the front of his forehead. Although he lacks plumage of his own, his blue cap, work shirt and pants are usually covered with turkey feathers. His big feet are splayed and thus, he walks like a turkey. I've noticed lately that his voice is becoming—you get the picture. Stanley's hobby, after turkey hours, is target shooting. There is a little firing range along the bank of the Jordan

River just south of the living area. Frequently, during the late afternoon, we can hear the pop of the target rifles telling us that Stanley and his fellow marksmen are out there seeking the bull's-eye. The members are willing to put up with this noise because Stanley and his pals are expert shots and habitually carry side arms around with them, affording protection for all of us in case of a surprise attack (not impossible in this part of the Jordan River valley).

"I need a holster for my new pistol," he gobbles. "You can't find one anywhere in this little country of ours, but there *is* a dealer in Los Angeles that carries such holsters. I have an advertisement for it that I tore out of an American magazine in the coffee house."

I yawn and a wall of drowsiness crashes over me. I've been up all night and I want my bed. I want Stanley to let go of my handlebars so I can head home.

"Bring me the ad and I'll see," I say within my trance.

"Bring it over to you now?" he asks enthusiastically.

"No, not now. Bring the ad over late in the afternoon."

I am in my cool bed a few seconds after arrival at our apartment. As I fade out, I hear the faint purr of tractors in the nearby orchard and the soft chatter of turkeys. I sleep soundly without dreams. Late in the afternoon, I awake out of my sleep-pit and gradually figure out where I am—not in San Diego—not in Berkeley—but in Cfar Moshe. I have three children and a wife and my army ID number is 760909.

Next, I put on my bathing suit, take a towel and pedal out to the swimming pool. The cold water of the kibbutz's Olympic-size pool is waiting for me and I crash into its frigid waters. Refreshed, I pull myself out of the pool and head toward my towel. Marta, the head nurse, approaches me in her antediluvian bathing suit and white bathing cap.

"I hear that you are going for a visit to your parents in America," she says firmly.

"Yes."

"Here's what we need: some of those new plastic Band-Aids, several different sizes. The ones we get here from the *Kupat Holim* are useless. I put one on somebody and it falls off in five minutes. Also, we're short on tongue depressors, they cost a fortune here and they're cheap on the 'outside.' Bring us as many boxes as you can."

The 'outside' refers to places outside of the State of Israel, out in that normal world of affluence that we see in the magazines and films. Things that are 'outside' give our pioneers a taste of what life will be like when there are no more wars, no Arab boycotts, or no reserve army stints to keep us in our modest circumstances.

It's useless to say no to Marta. If something serious happens to me, it's Marta that will be in charge of my diagnosis and treatment. She saved my wife's life once by quickly diagnosing a supposed stomachache as acute appendicitis and whisked her off to the hospital in Safed just in time.

On the way back to my apartment, Amos flags me down.

"Don't forget a bottle of *Stolichnaya* and a can of *Benaderet* pipe tobacco for me," he reminds me without ever having asked in the first place. But he is, of course, already on my list.

When I get back to my apartment, I hear gunfire from the direction of the rifle range and find a microscopic ad torn out of an old Popular Mechanics Magazine resting on my unmade bed. Stanley the turkey man has been here and gone.

Ruthie arrives with the kids, five-year- old Galila and the three-year-old twins, Golan and Hermon. I notice that a piece of paper with a long list written upon it rests on top of Ruthie's laundry basket.

"What's the damage?" I ask her, giving her a peck on her tanned cheek and another on the top of her head. I do the tops of the children's heads, too, before they dash out to play with their friends.

"We'll need a freight car to bring back all the stuff that the *chaverim* want," says Ruthie, putting the laundry down. "Look at this list! And it's just from one children's house group."

Ilsa	Nylon stockings, large
Leah K.	Leg razor (for shaving before she visits relatives in Tel Aviv)
Aliza	Jar of Ovaltine, + nylons, large
Bracha	Preparation H for Alberto (her husband)
Chana M.	Holster for Stanley's new pistol
Dvorah Shapira	Carton of Lucky Strikes
Eva B.	4 cartons Lucky Strikes, + Nylons, large
Fayge L.	Two bottles Johnny Walker Black Label (large)

I show her my list. We look at both lists and think about how much of our visit to America will have to be dedicated to shopping for the other *chaverim*. Borrowing a phrase from Chava, our adopted kibbutz mother, we exclaim together:

Jesus, Maria!

II

At Lod Airport, a fierce blonde girl-soldier inspects our baggage with a dedication to thoroughness. Ruthie stands by the suitcases under the merciless gaze of the soldier unwrapping our modest presents for our family in the USA. I am holding Hermon and Golan by gripping their shirt collars so they won't disappear in the crowd. Galila, our beautiful daughter, hangs on to my pant leg observing the strange sights of the "outside" world. What could she be thinking about all this chaos?

These children of ours have only known the simple patterns of life in a remote rural corner of the Galilee, where they are the apples of everyone's eyes, the future of the kibbutz, and the new generation growing up after the holocaust. Everyone on the kibbutz has a stake in providing these children with a happy life, a strong social conscious, and a life of dignified labor on the land. Now they are about to experience the hard world outside of the kibbutz.

I resolve that when we get on the plane, I'll make a list of all the things that our kibbutz-issue kids will be seeing for the first time in their lives.

The blonde soldier waves us through and we do our best to stuff our belongings back in the suitcases. What a mess! People and their baggage are jammed together in front of the ticketing booths like a mashed can of kosher sardines. We try to worm our way through the crowd toward the Air France desk.

"What *Chutzpah*," (nerve) yells an old woman in black with a German accent, as we elbow a passage through the chaos.

"Pardon me," I yell back to her, "I have three kids and two suitcases to handle, Lady."

"There's no order here," she shouts back, waving her hands at the massive crowds of travelers. "Primitive people," she mumbles.

A fat Rumanian couple shove themselves past our kids and both of them clutch the ticket desk as if it is about to fly away. They dump their papers out in front of the attendant, but the attendant shakes her head and points to the Swissair desk clear across the terminal. They snatch their documents and elbow their way back through the rest of us, stepping on Galila's shoe on the way. Now she's crying and I have to put the twins down and hold her in my arms.

Done with the ticket desk, our next hurdle is the security hall, where one by one all the adult passengers are frisked behind a curtain for possible bombs, hand grenades, or Sherman tanks that they might be hiding in their clothing. Then, by God, half-crazy with the confusion, the shoving, the arguing, the smell of undeodorized people, the holding on to scared kids, the fear of losing documents, the lack of lines and order, finally, we find ourselves in the relative quiet of the passenger waiting room. Through the windows of the terminal we see the Air France jet waiting to take us away into the sky. Destinations: Nice, France; Dublin, Ireland; New York and Los Angeles.

III

High up over the Mediterranean, Ruthie and the children are in a merciful sleep after the turmoil and stress of the boarding process. I am sitting in the window seat, food tray pulled down, and sipping a cup of strong French coffee handed to me by the flight attendant. I must really look like I need it. On a notepad, I begin to list things that our innocent Galilee children will likely be seeing for the first time when we get to the United States.

Cities	Money	TV
Forests	Police Cars	Beggars
Christians	Non-Hebrew Speaking Children	Churches
Synagogues	Hamburgers	Tacos
Traffic Jams	County Fairs	Merry Go Rounds
Ferris Wheels	Cracker Jacks	Billboards
Vending Machines	Oriental People	Suits
Ties	High-Heeled Shoes	
Children sleeping in their parents' house	Skunks	Possums
Coyotes	Super Markets	Ice Cream Parlors
Liquor Stores	Stadiums	Crosses
Toy Stores	Used Car Lots	Deodorants
Fashion Shows	Bars	Gas stations
Cigars	Zoos	Drunks
Cigarette Machines	Nail polish	Wedding dresses
Buildings, 4 stories high	Football games	Movie Theatres
Cotton Candy	Native Americans	Domestic Servants
Private Telephones	Escalators	Golf courses
Rattlesnakes	Freeways	Beauty contests
Bacon and Eggs	Black people not from India	Ham steaks
Disneyland		

We are on our way to Ireland so that we can all have a break in the long transatlantic and transcontinental flights that are necessary to get from the Middle East to Southern California. The Irish Republic, we have heard, is the ultimate safe place to take kids. In my mind, it is also a country that has a lot of similarities to our own little country—lots of occupations by foreign powers, a tragic history, the revival of an ancient national language, and the bitter sense of humor of an oppressed people. We hear that it is, unlike Israel, a place where there is always enough water and where everything is green, green, green.

At the Nice airport we transfer to an Irish Aer Lingus jet and make a short stop in Lourdes where pilgrims—the healed, the disappointed and their families, come aboard. The children see their first Catholics and blink at the strange symbols hanging around the pilgrims' necks.

"What is it?" asks Galila in all innocence.

"A cross." I say.

"What's a cross, Abba?"

"It shows that a person is a Christian."

"What's a Christian?" she goes on.

"It's a person who believes in Jesus." I explain.

"Who is Jesus?"

"Fasten your seat belts please," says the freckled long-legged woman in the Aer Lingus uniform. Although saved for the moment by her intervention, I resolve to explain more to the children about Jesus sometime, especially since we are headed for a land where he is so highly regarded.

The plane takes off and levels over the fields of Southern France. I try to explain some of the topography to my daughter.

"What language are your children speaking?" asks a kind grandmother in the seat behind us.

"Hebrew," I tell her.

"Saints alive. I've never heard the Holy language before. And spoken by children as well."

"Are you going to visit Ireland?" asks the young woman sitting next to the grandmother.

"We are," I say. "We will take a car and see as much as we can. But we only have ten days."

"How wonderful," they both say together. "Do you speak English too," the grandma queries Galila.

"A little beet," she responds through the armrest.

"Well, you'll learn," she comforts. "Tell your little girl that English isn't the true language of Ireland anyway. Those of us who know Gaelic, prefer it to English."

I explain this point to Galila.

"Teach me Gaelic word," says my daughter in Hebrew, and I translate her request into English."

"That I will," says the woman. "Say, *Dia Dhui*t. It means God be with ya."

"*Dia Dhuit*," Galila echoes, now leaning over the back of the seat instead of peeking through the armrest hole slot.

Hermon pops his head over the seat back and chirps, "*Dia Dhuit, Dia Dhuit.*"

A few hours later we see the green map of Ireland spreading below us and the children have picked up a few more pleasantries in this strange tongue. They are ready for their first significant encounter with the "outside" world.

IV

We check into O'Reilly's Hotel on Denmark Street, close to the north side of the Liffey River. It is early evening and we are exhausted from the long journey from Israel. We have a small balcony where all five of us stand for a while and look at this strange New World. Cars pass by on the urban street. The swish of their tires hints at an earlier rain. Only a few people can be seen walking down the street, all men, clad in dark overcoats, hurrying on to unknown destinations. Downstairs we hear a little Irish tune start up produced by a fiddle and a flute. We see two well-dressed young couples, arriving on foot at the hotel door. As they enter the lobby we hear the clink of glasses and the hum of conversations. The tune downstairs becomes merrier and the thump of a small drum pours rhythm into the melody. Could we ask for better background music for our welcome to Ireland? Ruthie decides to go downstairs and have a look at what is happening. The children and I remain on the balcony and watch more people, young and old, even a few children, arriving in festive clothes and entering the hotel. Ruthie returns to the room and tells us that a wedding party is in progress.

The children are excited at this news. They have, all three of them, attended our rustic kibbutz weddings. There, the whole community, adults and children, assemble on the lawn in front of the dining hall, the men in white shirts and clean blue work pants, the women in white blouses and simple blue skirts. The bride and groom stand on a stage constructed of bales of hay. The bride has fresh flowers in her hair; the groom stands uncomfortably in his new sandals wearing a blue idiot's cap. Both of them wink at the assembled kibbutzniks as the Rabbi arrives from the neÑrby development town. In his black coat and shaggy white beard, the Rabbi is obviously uncomfortable in this pagan place, forced to be there by Israeli law, but not wanted by the kibbutzniks who regard him as an oppressor. The Rabbi hurriedly unfurls his *Hupa*, the wedding canopy. Four idiot-capped kibbutzniks hold the *Hupa* in place over the heads of the bride and groom. The Rabbi hurries through the blessings and leaves quickly after the groom stomps a glass into oblivion. "Mazal Tov," everyone shouts. The Rabbi flees and the dancing and feasting begins.

Here, in our hotel room in Ireland, the volume of the rousing Irish music from the lounge below increases and we allow the children to come out of the room and peek over the rail of the inside balcony at the wedding festivities. The Irish don't look much like us. Most of the men have a reddish tinge to their faces; they wear modest suits and ties. The women are fashionably, but unpretentiously, dressed. A few couples are out on the dance floor, but most of the people are gathered at the tables, downing large glasses of a dark liquid.

Galila points below and tells her little brothers, "look how many *jinjim* (redheads) there are."

We have only a few of them on the kibbutz but here we look down on a Red Sea.

We take the children back to the hotel room and get them into their pajamas. Ruthie and I are sleepier than they are even though the evening is still young. We have a long day ahead of us in Dublin and in a few minutes, the five of us, children in one bed, Ruthie and me in the other, are fast asleep.

We wake, in the middle of the night, to the sound of screams out in the street in front of the hotel. I grope for the submachine gun under my bed but suddenly remember that we aren't in Cfar Moshe. Poking my head out through the outside balcony door, I see that the street is full of men and women yelling insults at each other. A street lamp illuminates their faces and I see that it is the wedding party itself, last seen inside and now arraigned in two camps facing each other outside. Harsh oaths arise. Suddenly the crowds merge and fists begin to fly. Some of the women are using their purses as weapons, bashing them down on the heads of others. A few people fall down on the sidewalk but then they rise up again flailing at the others with renewed strength. Hats are knocked off and trampled.

I feel little hands gripping my pajama legs and see Golan and Hermon, their eyes as big as poker chips, watching the battle unfolding below. Ruthie joins us.

"Great God," she says in Hebrew.

"Great God," repeat Golan and Hermon.

Men wrestle below and we watch a few barrelhouse punches land on ears and noses.

"Take that!" I hear someone shout.

"You whore!" a woman yells and whacks another female with her heavy purse.

I push the boys back in the bedroom and Ruthie comes off the balcony and locks the door. Galila continues to sleep through all the commotion. The boys are understandably puzzled since they have never seen such violence, unknown in kibbutz life except for the history-making fisticuffs that almost happened once between two chaverim out on the children's farm. But that was in 1962 before the twins were born. Ruthie, always wanting to know the answer to things, gets dressed and heads downstairs to the desk attendant to find out what is happening. She returns with a strange smile on her face.

"What happened?" I ask.

"What happened?" repeat the twins in unison.

"The night clerk said it was nothing," she explains, "The two families just didn't like each other very much. Some of them had too much to drink."

"I'll say." I say.

"What is Guiness?" Ruthie asks.

V

Next morning, we walk over the O'Connell Bridge and peer down at the Liffey River. To the children, used to our little Jordan, the Liffey must look like the widest river in the world. Ruthie and I are a few paces back watching the children explore downtown Dublin and keeping our sharp parental eyes on possible hazards our rural innocents might encounter. We are on our way to Grafton Street to have a look at the wonders of a department store. The weather bodes well, only a few clouds floating swiftly through an azure sky. It seems strange that not many people are out in the streets, after all, it is nine in the morning. In Israeli cities, at this time of the day the streets hum with pedestrians, cars, and buses. People have been at work for at least an hour and a half and it is time for the morning break. Here in Dublin, it seems like only the Irish cats and the pigeons are afoot at this hour.

The department store opens at 10 a.m. and we decided, in the meantime, to sit on a bench in St. Stephens Green, where lawns, gardens and ponds look out at the rows of Georgian houses on the surrounding blocks. Despite the coolness of the morning and the damp, the kids roll in the grass. The grass is unlike the grass they have ever seen in their Jordan Valley home—grass that has no burrs or barbs—grass that is a pillow of green softness, as green as green is allowed to be.

"Where are the other children?" asks Golan, used to seeing children in the morning.

"They are in their parents' houses, getting ready to go to school," explains Ruthie.

"They sleep with their *Abbas* and *Imas*, their Daddies and Mommies, all the time?"

"Yes," says Ruthie, "they get up in the morning and then go off to school."

"What about the little ones?" queries Galila, "the one's like Golan and Hermon? Do they go to school, too?"

"No, they probably stay home with their Mommies or they are put in a nursery school."

"If they stay home with their Mommies, how do the Mommies go to work in the morning?" says our kibbutz-wise daughter.

"Good question," I say.

Passing by a bank, I remind myself that I need to change dollars for Irish pounds, but even the bank is closed until noon.

The doors of the shops begin to open and we head down to Brown-Thomas to show the children the riches of a grand department store.

Ruthie warns, "Hermon, Golan, Galila, stay close to *Abba* and *Ima*. This is a big store and we don't want you to get lost. Don't forget that nobody here speaks Hebrew."

"We can say, *Dia Dhuit*," answers Galila.

"*Dia Dhuit*," echoes Hermon.

"That won't help you very much finding your way back if you wander away," I say, "so stick with us."

The department store is overwhelming for all of us. Ruthie, raised in Beverly Hills, is familiar with such edifices and I have been in them, too, in my other life, but neither one of us has visited one since we arrived in Israel. The children, of course, have never seen such a treasure house. We pass by the jewelry counter where gems sparkle in their plush cases. Their eyes are poker chips again. Then we pass by a candy counter, overflowing with chocolates, pastries, and other unrecognized delights.

"Can I have one?" asks Galila.

"No you can't," says Ruthie.

"Why not?"

"Because it costs money."

"Don't we have any money?"

Ruthie gives me a look and it's time to get some Irish cash.

"*Ima* said no," I explain to Galila. "You can have some candy but you have to wait until I come back. You and your brothers stay with *Ima* and I'll head out to the bank to change some money."

I leave Ruthie and the kids and head out of the department store in search of a bank. I stop a young pedestrian wearing a black business suit.

"Where is the nearest bank?"

He grins, amused by my question. "Have you been long in Ireland?" he asks, as if there is some secret about the bank that I should have known.

"No."

"American?"

"No, Israeli."

"Israeli? Well I guess you're pretty busy with big problems over in your country, maybe you didn't hear the news about our little problem." He grins some more.

"No I haven't. We just got here last night."

"Our banks are closed. There's a bank strike all over the country."

"Yikes, when will they reopen?"

"It's likely to be a long time," says the young Irishman. "The negotiations aren't going too well."

"How long has the strike been on?"

"Two months now." The young man says with another wee little grin.

"Good God! How do you do business with all the banks closed," I ask in amazement.

Even a kibbutznik like me knows that such a strike in Israel would bring on the Bolsheviks. In my mental trivia cabinet, I remember that Roosevelt's bank holiday had only lasted a few days.

"Mostly, we use chits."

I must have looked puzzled.

"Chits are wee scraps of paper that we use instead of money. We promise each other to pay the amount back when the bank strike ends. We've been doing this off and on when the banks are closed and it seems to work out all right."

I'm thinking that this system would never work in either country that I have lived in. He sees the bewilderment on my face.

"Oh, don't worry, most of us are honest people. When the strike is over, everyone will get paid back...but now you undoubtedly need to exchange some money. It's no problem. Just go down the street to the American Express Office two blocks down.

They'll exchange currency for you. As for us local people, we'll just have to rely on our chit system."

Thanking him, I continue on Grafton Street until I see the blue American Express sign. There is a line coming out the door. Americans in their jeans and sweaters are waiting to fork over greenbacks for Irish Pounds. The line moves pretty fast, after all, everyone is there for the same commodity. Just before I reach the counter, I feel a tug on my pant leg. Looking down I see the top of Golan's head.

"*Abba*," he says, "I found you."

"Where are *Ima, Hermon*, and *Galila?*" I ask looking at the door and expecting the rest of my family to come in.

"In the big store."

"How did you get here?" I ask, astonished. After all, the American Express is several blocks from the department store on the busiest street in Ireland.

"Just walked up the street until I found you."

"Oh no," I flushed in disbelief, "you could have gotten lost. Did you tell Ima you were going to do this?"

Golan is beginning to sense that he did something wrong and I see tear drops forming on his big brown eyes.

"I couldn't find *Ima*," he confessed. "I lost her in the big store."

This kid wanders away from his mother, can't find her, heads out the door into the street and smells my trail? He didn't even know where I was going. He doesn't speak English. It's his first day out in any city. Good God! I would lose my temper at this point and probably whack him one but the American Express clerk says "Next client," and it's my turn to change money. I grab Golan by his shirt collar and jam him up against the ticket booth as I count out my dollars. He is crying which only makes things worse.

"Don't move, God damn it," I growl at my three-year-old son. I sound like my father on one of his grumpier days. Five minutes later, the two of us are back in the department store. I've still got him by the collar and he is still sobbing and I am still red in the face with the irrational, frightened anger of a parent who has almost lost his son. Ruthie is sitting on a bench just inside the store entrance with Galila and Hermon and she envelops poor Golan in her arms.

"*Abba* yelled at me," he says, looking at me as if I am a terrorist.

I explain what had happened.

"You scared Abba," she says softly to the boy. "He thought you would get lost. We were worried about you, too. We looked all over the store and the store people are still searching for you."

"And don't you ever do that again," I snap, still angry with the kid. He starts to cry again and my anger begins to melt away. I pick him up, hug him and say, "shhh, OK, OK, you did scare me. But I still love you, very much." With Golan still hanging around my neck, I say to the rest of the family, "*Yallah*, c'mon, let's all of us get some candy."

VI

The rest of the Ireland vacation is a lark. We rent a little Fiat and set out for the Northwest corner of the land. We travel through Navan and Caven, and cross the open border into Northern Ireland. The lush emerald fields and the modest hills soothe us. We have green fields in Israel but none like these.

Going through Strabane it begins to rain and the two-lane road over the mountains to Donegal Town leads through a tunnel of mist. The hedgerow flowers along the side of the road blaze in the foggy drizzle. Passing back into the Irish Republic, we stop at a little inn for a late lunch. There are only a few people eating in the dim dining area. Two old men are seated near us eating what appears to be cabbage and bacon and sipping from two enormous glasses of stout. I order cabbage and bacon—minus the stout—for all of us. We are hungry from the long trip and when the food arrives all five of us dig in. Thanks to the Czech majority in the kibbutz kitchen, we all are accustomed to the idea of eating cooked cabbage at lunchtime but the bacon is a delicious improvement. The children try their first Coca-Cola but soon give up on its inky unfamiliar flavor. Ruthie and I revive ourselves with some strong coffee.

Donegal Town is only another twenty miles down the road. The children are all asleep when we arrive. Ruthie goes into a Bed and Breakfast facing the main street to ask for a room, and I have a moment of silence as I wait in the car looking after the kids.

How tranquil it is here.

I feel a strange burden lifting off my shoulders being outside of Israel. I love Israel, and there are quiet times there as well. There is also the continual presence of tension, not so much, as people might think, from the danger of living in an embattled land, but from the newness, the rawness, the pushing and shoving, the frantic motion, the boiling ethnic soup of people, the bizarreness, the supposed holiness of the damn place. At this moment, in Donegal Town, sitting in a Fiat, watching the mist clouding the windshield, sensing the warmth of my children asleep in the back seat, resting in someone else's country where time moves slower and where there are no claims for holiness, just people living their lives from day to day, not obliged to change the world nor to revenge the past, or create the future, here, in Ireland, I feel an enormous peace.

Weeks later, in San Diego, we heard that the bank strike in Ireland was over and the majority of the chits were bogus.

1965: The Things We Cling To

I

One winter day, I find myself on kibbutz business down in Jerusalem, the Capital City of our Holy Land. I'm staying at the YMCA, and in the evening I decide to take in a classical Arabic music concert over at the Khan Theatre. After listening, entranced, to a few hours of *oud, tabla,* and *nai* musicians, I ask the couple next to me how they enjoyed the concert. He turns out to be an American, about my age, and very Gentile looking. She is comely, with raven hair. Something about her reminds me of the Song of Solomon, although she is actually a nice Jewish girl from South Africa. His name is Donald and she is Anat. We decide to go over to the little restaurant across the street, downstairs in the 'YMCA' and have some *humus,* conversation and coffee.

It turns out that Donald, in the early sixties, had chugged into Jerusalem on a motorcycle and fallen in love with the country for various reasons, not the least of which was Anat, she of the green eyes and a wonderful body. She played oboe in the Jerusalem Philharmonic. Another reason, (as if he needed one) Donald had remained in Jerusalem had to do with his strange belief that

Jerusalem is a holy city no matter what your religion might be. A third reason Donald stayed on was the great job that he found translating Soviet military manuals into English. (Don't ask where the Soviet stuff was coming from and where the English stuff was going.)

We discuss Arabic music, Israeli politics and our personal histories, but we don't quite get to talk about where Donald came from.

Donald and Anat invite me for Sabbath dinner the next night. After a day of poking around the city and visiting a few of my relatives, I drive a short distance out of town to a small village in the Judean hills where Donald and Anat make their home. There is a cold wind blowing from the coastal plain. The inside of their old stone farmhouse is well heated with a couple of paraffin stoves that glow red in the corners of their small dining room. We have good red wine from a nearby Trappist monastery, and we eat the inevitable schnitzel-and-chips Sabbath dinner while comparing notes.

"Where are you from in USA?" I ask Donald.

"San Diego, " he answers.

"Hey, me too," I say with a rush of excitement. "You are the first San Diegan I've met in six years of living in Israel."

"What neighborhood did you grow up in?" he asks, equally excited.

"North Park!"

"Me too," he howls. "This is amazing."

"What elementary school?" I coo. Our sentences are getting shorter and more animated.

"Jefferson" he cackles.

"Me too," I roar.

We are instant brothers. The next few hours are filled with anecdotes from the "old country." We talk about dreaded schoolteachers known by both of us, great San Diego historical events—like the snowfall of 1949—favorite radio programs, favorite hideouts in Balboa Park and other unlimited worlds of San Diego nostalgia. We drink more of the Latrun monks' red.

Suddenly, Donald waves his hands furiously in the air for silence.

"And now, my new friend Shimon, I will show you a treasure from San Diego that I have hidden from all eyes except yours," he announces solemnly, showing signs, like me, of being well under the sacred influence of the wine. "I will now show you the only possession that I've ever asked to be sent from America to this new home of mine. My only un-discardable treasure. Come with me Shimon," he beckons. He leads me, my arm in his arm, down a hallway to a closet door and flings it open with abandon. "*Henai, voila,*" he proclaims in Hebrew and French.

I look into the closet and, behold: a biblical treasure as astounding as the Lost Ark of the Covenant, the Dead Sea Scrolls and the Holy Grail rolled up together. The closet is piled high with old comic books from our childhood days: The Phantom, Captain Marvel, The Black Hawks, Archie and Jughead, Chief Wahoo, Superman and Lois Lane, Plastic Man and Wonder Woman, even Looney Tunes & Merrie Melodies. This entire hoard is hidden in a dark closet only a few miles away from the Temple Mount, the Mosque of Omar and the Holy Sepulcher.

The rest of the evening consists of individual comic book reading while listening to long-playing records of Beethoven symphonies. Anat, being above such things and feeling a little left out, reads her Hebrew translation of Madame Bovary.

II

I didn't bring much along with me when I left the United States to become a farmer in the Upper Galilee. I had one suitcase half full of clothing left over from my Berkeley days, a couple of beloved pipes, a can of Benaderet pipe tobacco, and one small object dating back to my early childhood: my Pinocchio spoon. When I moved into the kibbutz, I received the regular kibbutz issue of a couple pair of workpants, a pair of good trousers for the Sabbath, a belt, work shoes, a pair of sandals, some heavy work socks, a British army-surplus jacket, a conical hat for hot weather and a knitted cap for cold weather. I also received a hard bed, a mattress stuffed with seaweed, two pairs of sheets and a Primus stove for cooking and heating. I could move it all in a small wheelbarrow, and I was happy.

I married, had three kids, moved out of my shack into a nice apartment and added on to my private property: a few more shirts, a raincoat, another pair of shoes, and improved furniture. Before I could bat an eyelash, five years had gone by, and I had acquired enough property to need a tractor and a good size wagon to move to an even better apartment. I still needed nothing from my former life in the United States.

One late spring day, just a few weeks before the holiday of *Shvuot* (Pentecost), I meet my moral demise. I am sitting in my house puffing on one of my old Berkeley pipes and listening to the afternoon concert on my ancient kibbutz-issue radio. My five-year-old daughter, Galila, is off playing Israeli hopscotch with her schoolmates. My wife is working in the dining hall and my twin boys are out playing in a pile of sand left over from some construction work down the sidewalk from us. During the final movement of Beethoven's ninth, little Golan slinks into the house with a very suspicious look on his face. Hermon is peeking around the side of the door. All I can see of him is one eye and his curly hair. I turn Beethoven down.

"What?" I ask.

"You know that pile of sand outside?" says Golan.

"Yes."

"We lost the thing that we were digging with," Golan continues, "It got lost in the sand."

"We looked for it and we couldn't find it," adds Hermon from behind the door.

"Well that's OK," I reassure them, "the workers aren't going to use any of the sand. They're just coming to clean up tomorrow, after the Shabbat. Just get another stick. I want to hear the end of this music."

"The Ode to Joy" is just starting up.

"It isn't a stick," confesses Hermon, he who cannot tell a lie. He comes around the doorpost and stands inside next to his brother. "It isn't a stick at all. It's your spoon."

"The one with the picture of Pinocchio on it?" I ask, my eyes, unexpectedly clouding with tears that I try to hold back.

"The one from your drawer," continues Hermon.

"My Pinocchio spoon," a voice sounds from a secret sepulcher in the depth of my cortex.

"That spoon is all that remains from your childhood," says the voice.

I lose the tear and it slides down the side of my face. I rub my wet cheek, hoping to act like the calm rational parent who values his children's feelings over anything material. But then I lose it and hot anger pours out of the furnace of my eyes.

"You took my spoon to dig in the sand pile and you lost it?"

I jump up and grab both boys by their hair with one hand (a trick fathers of twins have known for centuries). I haul them outside, over the grass, to the small mountain of sand that the damn construction workers have left.

"Now," I say in a cold and threatening voice. "You two find that spoon even if you have to dig all night."

The two frightened boys dare not glance at my angry face and they dig frantically with their hands as I pace back and forth. A half-hour later Pinocchio's silver hat and silver upturned nose appear through the grains of sand. I bend over the boys and grab the spoon out of its grave. It is unharmed.

But the boys have seen the monster of **materialism** within their father.

III

"Maybe it isn't just a matter of materialism," suggests my Saba Yisroel, as we look west toward the apple orchard.

He slouches on a deck chair, one of my new possessions, out on the lawn in front of our apartment. A week has gone by since the Pinocchio spoon incident and the pile of sand is still there, although my boys don't play on it any more (as if it's haunted).

"Maybe it's more a matter of nostalgia," he suggests. "Maybe you are missing your parents and your birthplace more than you are willing to admit."

"No Saba," I deny, "I don't miss my parents very much. They come to the kibbutz for a long visit every year and we have a good time together, but it's quite enough. Your son Zelig gets antsy after a while anyway and heads off for Tel Aviv to see his old cronies.

My mom has more patience for kibbutz life, but after a while I get embarrassed by the muumuus that she wears around the kibbutz, and she gets to missing her friends in Del Mar and wants to go home. As for my birthplace, I don't think that I could handle Capitalism any more. The collective life has a lot of flaws, like the gossip, and the boring jobs that I sometimes have to do. Nobody likes washing dishes for 900 people. But at least here everyone is equal economically. You don't have to kiss anyone's *tuchas* just because they have more dollars than someone else."

"I appreciate that," says my grandfather, "but I see some problems with it too." We can talk about that later. But I was wondering how come you got so angry with my great-grandchildren last week for losing a spoon? Doesn't the kibbutz have enough spoons?"

"Saba, you're seeing the kibbutz as if it's frozen back in the 1920s. We don't wear each other's underwear any more. People want to have some of their own things and to make their own choices about what they need. We're always debating how much private property and how much collective property we want to have. The question is now, how much difference is fair? Should everyone have a car? Should everyone have a phonograph? Should everyone have a TV when TV arrives in Israel? We can work these problems out. Right now no one here wants me to give up my Pinocchio spoon."

"OK, OK," says Saba, "I hope you do work these problems out. But I still think that people are basically greedy, and there will come a time when someone will want a color TV for himself and won't care about the others. And wait until some people have a chance to buy a car. Will they care if the others have one? You're already having problems with who gets what jeep to go out to work in."

"Maybe so, but since we have democratic government on the kibbutz, we have a chance to work things out fairly. I compare that with my life in America, where greed is looked at as a virtue. Rich people, to make themselves look less rapacious, donate a little of their stealings to charity or get their name stuck on a plaque inside a synagogue or a church. Why should I ever want to go back to that kind of hypocrisy?"

"I don't know," sighs Saba. "I just have a premonition that you **will** go back. Maybe life will eventually get too easy for you here. I think that your basic nature is to get into the fight against oppression. Maybe I just can't see you lolling around the kibbutz the rest of your life, playing farmer and smoking your pipe out here on the lawn. I think you'll need more action, one way or the other. For some crazy reason, you have this bug of wanting to be on the barricades.

"What worries me even more is that you'll get yourself in a war over here and you and your family will disappear the way mine did. I've been over on the Syrian side and, believe me, they are up to no good."

I am startled. "How the hell did you get over there?"

"Don't ask," says Saba, finger to his lips. "In fact, don't tell anyone what I just told you. Just get out of here with your wife and kids while you still have time. I don't want to see another generation of this family wait too long and then regret it."

Grandpa, visibly troubled, but trying to keep his cool, gets out the lounge chair and puts on his blue idiot's cap. He, himself, is looking like a typical kibbutz member. Who would believe that he is an Eastern European Jewish ghost just here to help his grandson think his way through life without making any fatal mistakes?

"*L'hitraot,*" he says, "See you later. I'll be around."

He disappears into the orchard just before Galila, Hermon, and Golan, his great-grandchildren, arrive home from their children's houses.

1966: Grapes and Bullets

On a crisp winter day in February, I finally have my opportunity to be a hero again. A strange gathering of kibbutzniks from all parts of the Upper and Lower Galilee assembles in the dining hall of Kibbutz Beit HaKinneret, a kibbutz on the Eastern Shore of the Sea of Galilee. The members have been unable to prune their vineyard due to the trigger-happy Syrian soldiers on the heights above. It seems that the Syrians have the mistaken impression that the vineyard lies in disputed territory.

It is time for a rescue. As every viticulturist knows, it is absolutely crucial to finish the pruning process before the dormant vines begin to seriously sprout. Late pruning will produce a jungle of grapevines but few marketable grapes.

A plan has evolved to bring *all* of the available vineyard workers in the Galilee region to the aid of their brother grape farmers and prune the whole vineyard at once. According to the plan, we will creep into the rows of vines at first light. Before the Syrian soldiers wake up and take their morning constitutionals, we will have the whole job done. Of course, units of the Israeli army will be around just in case the plan doesn't work.

It seems like a good plan to me, but then what do I know? I'm only a beginning viticulturist and a buck private in the Israeli Defense forces, ignorant of the basic elements of grand strategy.

We all assume that the sleeping Syrian military will think that nothing is amiss. The many jeeps and busses full of kibbutzniks that entered the settlement, late in the previous evening were under the guise of merry makers coming to a wedding. Loud Israeli folk dance music has blasted out through the night to keep the Syrians assuming that everything is tikiti boo.

4 a.m., The muddy *botz* coffee jolts us out of our sleepiness, pruning shears are handed out to those who didn't bring their own, and, in the dark, we quietly slip out to the vineyard and sit on the ground waiting for first light. I am sitting next to Sonia, the grandmother of kibbutz vineyard operators in the Galilee. On her own kibbutz, she, at age 70+ still works everyday among the vines, in the heat and in the cold, in the sun and in the rain, doing the things that are necessary to grow grapes. Sonia's face and hands show the lines and wrinkles of a new breed of Hebrew women pioneers: workers on the land, socialists, communitarians, all trained in firearms and equal to any man. No princesses here.

On my other side sits Kobie, the head vineyard operator at Kibbutz Cfar Benesh from the Lower Galilee over by Cfar Tabor. Kobie is a famous fighter from his days in the *Palmach*, the commandos of the War of Independence. After the war, "that Capitalist Ben Gurion," as Kobie calls him, dissolved the Palmach. Kobie felt betrayed and disgruntled. He went to work as a cultural attaché in various Eastern European countries. He lost a son in the Sinai campaign and returned to his kibbutz to quiet his soul in the vineyard. I glow with pride as I sit between these two heroes of the new Jewish State.

At first light, we hear the signal whistle blow and we rise up, shears in hand to start the pruning. Our row is planted with *Dabukki* grapes, a local variety that produces a mildly sweet, green table grape. We snip away at top speed, cutting the remains of last year's long, brittle branches back to two buds. Should we succeed in this valiant operation, in a few weeks, each pair of buds will swell, green will burst forth and this year's crop will be on its way.

About a quarter hour goes by and the rising sun gives us more light. It also gives the Syrians more light and even though we are working fast, we are not working fast enough. A machine gun fires from the heights above and we dive for cover in the dirt between the vines. More bullets fly through the vineyard. I notice a beetle crossing over a dirt clod a few inches away from my nose. "Damn Syrians," says the beetle, as it scurries to a hole under the vine. Another burst from a machine gun and I hear the slugs zipping over my head. Like Mauldin's GI Joe, I'd like to get further down into the ground but "me buttons are in the way."

A brief pause in the rain of lead and we hear two shrieks of a whistle, our signal to **pull out!** We begin a heroic retreat, crawling back down the rows. I'm hoping that there are no scorpions in my path.

In a few minutes, which seem like a few centuries, Kobie, Sonia and I reach relative safety behind a row of chicken houses with no more damage than a face full of grit. The chickens are very silent as they listen seriously to the one-sided battle-taking place. A rooster in the chicken house finally realizes what's happening and gives us a worried *kukuriko* (Hebrew for cock-a-doodle-do). We make a dash for one of the kibbutz bomb shelters only a short distance away and we are safe, underground, in the comforting darkness. The small arms fire continues outside.

Now the back-up troops on our side are letting the Syrians have it with mortar shells and heavy machine gun fire. The Syrians cease-fire and our guys also hold their peace.

Both sides think that they have given each other a message.

We have no casualties, but there will be no pruning in this vineyard, on this particular occasion. All of us viticulturists down in the shelter laugh nervously and sip coffee brought by the kibbutz dining room staff. We try to soothe the glum vineyard workers of Beit HaKinneret who have joined us underground.

"Maybe next year we'll have peace with the Arabs and you'll have a good crop," consoles Kobie.

Oh sure," they mourn, "maybe the Messiah will come next year, too. We'll put him to work in the vineyard."

1966: Why Do They Hate Us?

I

Early in the spring, Ruthie, the twins, and I are taking a walk down the narrow east/west country road that runs from one side of our narrow valley to the other. My daughter Galila is off on a trip to the lower Galilee with the kids from her children's house. Spring has arrived in the Galilee. The almond trees have blossomed and the people of the kibbutz have just celebrated the holiday of Tu B'shvat, the Jewish Arbor Day. Tree planting is an important activity for the Jewish people all over the world. It reminds us that, until recently, the land of Israel had been denuded of its forests by careless farming, hungry goats, Turkish railroad builders and the like. My grandmother (of sainted Socialist memory) back in America never bought her grandchildren toys or games. She bought us certificates with Jewish stars on them, declaring that a tree had been planted in our honor in the Holy Land.

The road west of the kibbutz leads over an old British Bailey bridge to cross a side branch of the Jordan River. Then it becomes a strand of asphalt between a checkerboard of fishponds where the local farmers grow and harvest carp. Most of the carp harvest is marketed in the cities, to the aficionados of the Friday-night gefilte fish cult, rampant among the Polish and Russian Jews of Israel.

A short distance before the junction with the main valley highway, Ruthie and I spot a cluster of Bedouin tents under a small grove of Eucalyptus trees.

"Hmm, what are Bedouins doing this far north?" I ask Ruthie.

"Why don't we ask them?" she says, always seeing the practical side of things.

"O.K."

We walk toward the tents. These are not the semi permanent, black goatskin tents that you see in more thickly settled Bedouin areas in the south of the country. The tents under the eucalyptus trees are constructed with a wooden frame and burlap sacks, designed only for temporary housing. As we approach the little compound, a few dogs—generic yellowish Holy Land variety—come out to ask for the password. Seconds later, a few skinny, dark, Bedouin kids join them. The dogs sniff us from a respectable distance, tails drooping. The dogs discuss the matter among themselves, and then allow us to advance.

The Bedouin kids retreat within the shadows of the eucalyptus trees. Out comes Papa Bedouin to have a look.

"*Ahlan WaSahlen,*" (welcome), he greets us a smile.

He is young and dusky, wears a white *kefia* headdress secured with a black braid. Otherwise, he is dressed pretty much like a kibbutznik, blue work shirt, blue work pants and dust-covered sandals.

"*Ahlan Bik,*" I reply. "*Kif Chalak?*" (How are you)?

"*Hamdelelah*" (Thanks to God, everything is OK.) the Bedouin replies.

The standing part of the welcoming ritual is now over. Papa Bedouin motions us to sit down on a rush mat spread out in front of the family tent. His hospitality is automatic; he can't help himself. Bedouins, like our ancestor Abraham, are at their best in welcoming strangers. It is a religious duty for them and who are we to try and improve them after thousands of years? In fact, it is we Jews who have changed. We have built walls around our communities, locks on our doors, and sometimes iron gates to our heart.

"Where are you from?" the Bedouin inquires politely, in Hebrew.

"Kibbutz Cfar Moshe."

"Ah, kibbutznik," he smiles.

He speaks only to me without looking at Ruthie or the kids who sit behind me on the mat. My two boys shyly turn their heads to peek at the Bedouin boys, who are watching them from a safe distance. I detect motion inside the tent and the wonderful smell of Arabic coffee and cardamom spice heating up.

"*Shu Ismak?*" (What is your name?) I ask, shifting back to the remainder of my Arabic.

"*Ismi Ahmad,*" (My name is Ahmad.) *Wa Inte?* (And yours?)

"*Ismi, Shimon.*"

Now I have totally exhausted my polite Arabic vocabulary. The other words I know would be unmentionable in a civilized conversation. We sit quietly for a few minutes and watch another Bedouin boy approach, prodding a flock of goats ahead of him. Ahmad explains to me, proudly, that he has five sons, the goat herder being the oldest at seven years old and the others are six, five, four and two years of age.

"May they all be healthy." I say, the only acceptable response to such information.

"We have two boys and a girl," I add.

"May they all be healthy," he replies.

If Ahmad has any girls, they are not mentioned on his list. In the meantime, my two boys have gone off with the Bedouin boys to sit on the edge of a carp pond a short distance away.

The next move comes from the tent from which Ahmad's tiny young wife brings out a brass tray with small cups of thick Arabic coffee laced with cardamom. She wears a long rust-colored robe with an embroidered front. Pants worn underneath her robe cover her legs and ankles. Her feet are bare. A white shawl draped down her back covers her head. She gives a small cup of coffee to me, one to her husband, and one to Ruthie. Ruthie smiles at her and gets a gold- toothed smile back. Ahmad does not invite Mama Bedouin to sit with us on the mat. It would not be proper. Male Bedouins, generally, do not drink or eat with their wives. Ruthie falls in the exotic category of Israeli-Jewish women who are sometimes hosted by Bedouins together with their men. Ahmad's wife goes silently back into the tent once the coffee drinking begins. We sip the coffee loudly, to indicate our pleasure.

The Bedouins within the State of Israel's borders are Israeli citizens, but their ways remain separate from the ways of Jewish Israelis and Arab town dwellers. When Jews talk together, the topic usually moves swiftly to politics. When Bedouin Arabs and Jews speak together, sensitive people usually focus on the weather, crops, goats, sheep and the cost of living. Let the politicians, generals and God try to work out the heavier problems and let us try to be civil to each other.

Ahmad says that he is camped in the Upper Galilee because the winter has been dry further south and the non-irrigated grain crops of the Bedouin have not done well. He thinks that the conditions in the far north of the country might be better for grazing his goats and sheep.

"I heard that you had troubles with the Syrians last week," he says.

"Not too bad," I reply.

"Anybody hurt?" he inquires.

"No, just a few mortar shells on the kibbutz down the road."

"Nothing on your kibbutz?"

"No, we're O.K."

We talk some more about the weather and the goats.

I stand up and thank Ahmad for the coffee and ask his permission to leave his tents.

"Need to get back to the kibbutz. My kids have to go to a birthday party," I lie.

"Come to our village sometime and visit," he offers.

"I would like to."

"Maasalame," (Go in peace)

"Maasalame," I reply.

Ruthie and I collect our boys and we head back to the road. We walk quietly back toward the kibbutz. I think about why I felt compelled to lie to Ahmad about leaving his camp. After all, many men in his village serve in the Israeli army as scouts. They have been loyal Israeli citizens since Independence was declared in 1948. But I have adopted the way of most Jewish-Israelis, to be suspicious when any outsider asks questions related to military security. You never know where such information might end up. When I get back to the kibbutz I will talk to Pinhas, our Security Director, and let him know about the Bedouins in the area. Pinhas will check to see if they have a permit to be in our valley and the military intelligence officers will probably pay Ahmad a visit. You never know.

II

A few weeks later, I find myself, on an oven-hot day, lugging a rifle around on maneuvers in the hills of the lower Galilee. I am not alone in my suffering in this blistering *Hamsin* (dry wind from the East). The rest of my buddies in the 34th battalion are with me, tongues hanging out, feigning attacks on barren hillsides and thinking of how many cold beers we will drink when maneuvers are over. This time, our generals have decided that we need to rehearse the possibility that some day, enemy jets may dive upon us with their bombs and machine guns. We are instructed to jump into ditches when we hear planes coming and to bravely fire our blanks at them as they roar over. Of course the particular planes will be ours and, if all is coordinated correctly, they will not try to rain death upon us. It's only a play attack. So they say.

As we anticipate, the planes fail to arrive on time and we are now sitting by the side of the road, in full battle dress, in the heat of the day, waiting, and waiting. Down the road from us there is an Arab village, with its stone, box-like houses and a nice white minaret painted blue at its tip. Fields of wheat and olive groves surround it. Goats and sheep graze in the distance looking like part of a Christmas crèche albeit in the middle of summer. We can hear the clucking of chickens and barking of the village's dogs. By now our canteens are empty and we chew on the dryness of our mouths. Finally, we hear the thunder of jets approaching from the south. Mabsut, our Moroccan light machine gunner, draws his bolt back and points it upward at the approaching noise.

"I hope you don't have real bullets in that thing," I say to Mabsut. "Each plane costs 30 million liras."

"Don't worry, all my bullets are wooden just like your rifle bullets and your head," he assures me.

The planes arrive. They come in low and fast. I barely see them as they thunderclap by, trailing a confusing and terrifying cyclone of wind after them. Fire bullets at them, my ass. I crawl back out of the ditch without remembering how I jumped into it. Mabsut is still standing on the road firing off a clip of wooden bullets but the jets are far away by now making a U-turn so that they won't go into Lebanese air space. Mabsut must think that he's the Israeli John Wayne after this brave, single-handed encounter with the Israeli Air Force.

Now that we have learned to fight off an air assault, we are ordered to march north toward the Arab village. We drag our feet, hoping against hope that we will make a pit stop in the village for a bottle of orange soda or something. There are probably a few kiosks along the road. Maybe we could even find some ripe peaches and apricots to buy. We stop in the village but only because the road is jammed full of hopping mad Arab citizens of Israel. Some of them are holding dead chickens in one hand and shaking their fists at our officers with the other.

"Our chickens, our chickens," they scream in Arabic and Hebrew. "Your planes killed our chickens."

This sounds implausible to us, since the jets had not bombed or strafed any of the barnyard animals or human beings. This is play war and the enemy is only a play enemy. But the villagers persist, blocking the road and waving dead chickens.

Mabsut says to me, "Crazy Arabs, they made us suffer in Morocco and now they want to sabotage our maneuvers. They killed their own chickens, the bastards. I know them."

Avner, our battalion commander, arrives in a jeep, hops out and faces the angry villagers with his hands on his hips.

"What's the problem?" he yells back at the crowd.

They wave their chickens at him.

"Show me," says Avner, a stocky and tough private farmer from Metulla.

Avner chooses a squad of soldiers, including Mabsut and me, to accompany him on his investigation. The Mukhtar (village chief) leads us through the village to a cluster of chicken houses that look like they have been built recently with the latest technology. Hundreds of chickens are dead on their backs in their wire cages.

"Your soldiers did this," says the Mukhtar, almost in tears. "These are our new chicken houses, our hope for the future of the village. Your planes killed the chickens,"

"How?" asked Avner, looking at the dead birds in wonder.

"The jets, the jets," exclaimed the Mukhtar. "The noise of the jets. They flew too low. The chickens died from shock. Don't you understand? Chickens die when they are that frightened."

Silence.

"What are you going to do about this?" groans the Mukhtar. "Perhaps you can take your war somewhere else and leave our village alone."

Avner thinks silently for a moment.

"Look, I'm a farmer, too. I'll make sure the army investigates this incident but you have to clear your people out of the road. I have a lot of soldiers here with a lot of weapons. God forbid that some hot-head does something stupid. It's bad enough that your chickens are dead. Let's not have any of your people or my people get hurt."

"Oh sure," replies the Mukhtar, "the army is going to investigate, just like they investigated who tore up our new olive grove last year. We didn't get a lira in damages. What are you going to destroy next?"

The Mukhtar turns his back on us and with his companions, strides out. We are left in the chicken house with the feathered future of the village's economy lying deceased in their brand new cages.

"They're right," says the battalion commander, "I'll make out a report and nothing will happen. Then we'll wonder why these villagers hate us. When will this all end?"

We followed Avner back down to the road. The villagers have disappeared into their homes to mourn their chickens. And we move on to practice our military art in the hills of Lower Galilee.

III

In the early autumn, most of the orchard crew is either on holiday or picking grapes under the watchful eye of Zalman the boss of the vineyard. Zalman is an Uruguayan, eternally fat from a childhood diet of beef and beef followed by beef. No matter what size work shirt Zalman has chosen in the kibbutz clothing warehouse, its buttons play tug of war over his hairy chest and stomach. His *tuches* looks like an enormous map of Uruguay. He arrived in the kibbutz in the mid-nineteen fifties as part of a South American Zionist youth group, leaving his country of birth behind to be a pioneer and to build the Jewish homeland. He married one of the local Moroccan girls from Kiryat Shmonah. Within a few years, he had become the father of three look-alike swarthy, hairy, fat kibbutz boys and two pretty, thin girls with their mother's blue eyes and kinky black hair.

We are Zalman's slaves, for the month or so that it will take until the grapes are all packed and sent off to the market.

I hate stoop labor, so I volunteer to work on the loading crew. It is our job to stack the heavy boxes of grapes high onto the trucks that arrive from all over the two Galilee's, Upper and Lower. The trucks are there to haul the fruit of our labors down to produce markets in Tel Aviv, Haifa, Jerusalem and other minor destinations in the Holy Land. An added benefit of being on the loading crew is that its work begins much later in the morning than that of the pickers…*they* have to be up at first light. *We* can show up at eight o'clock. What a pleasure, even though when the pickers have gone home, we are still, several hours later, loading grapes onto the trucks! This particular job is also good for building muscles since the stacking is by manual labor, box to truck–no forklifts available in the vineyard. It is also a wonderful job for tanning purposes, since the truck isn't parked under a roof and the sun is merciless.

Once or twice a week, during the grape harvest, my friend Muhammed shows up in his decrepit old truck with its eternally bad brakes. He buys muscat grapes from the kibbutz and hauls them around to the Arab villages and Arab town markets. The Arabs and I share a preference for the sweet tang of the maroon colored muscats, as humble as they might seem to connoisseurs of good French varietal grapes. Muhammed is not a full time trucker. He does this job during the summer. The rest of the time he is hard at work on his Bachelor's Degree in Islamic Studies at the Hebrew University in Jerusalem. After he parks the truck next to our loading ramp, he doesn't much have to do until the vehicle is fully loaded. When we have finished our task, it's his job to tighten the ropes that will hold his cargo steady for the bumpy ride around the narrow Galilee roads. Then off he and his truck go to sell the grapes to his fellow Arabs.

While we are heaving the boxes onto the truck, sweating gallons of Zionist sweat, Muhammad stands to one side, watching us load and engaging us in conversation. We listen more than we talk, saving our breath for lifting the heavy wooden boxes of fruit. His main topics are 1) Middle East politics and 2) great looking Israeli women he has seen and liked. The two of us, Muhammed and I, are not far apart politically. The little splinter group that I like to vote for in Israeli elections had, at one period of its history, before the 1948 War of Independence, advocated a bi-national Arab and Jewish State, instead of the present difficult arrangement. On the issue of Israeli girls, Muhammed seems to prefer hefty, almost porky blondes while I like to look at thin

Mediterranean lasses with black ropy hair. Especially if they are in uniform. Don't ask me why. I'm a married man, after all!

During one hot afternoon of bantering while loading grapes, Muhammed brings up the subject of economics.

"You *Yehudim* (Jewish people) have crazy economic habits," he says. "Why do you always get yourselves in debt?"

"What do you do when you need to buy something?" I grunt, and heave a box of muscats onto the truck.

"In my family, we save our money until we can afford to buy what we need to buy."

"That's your family, but how about the rest of the Palestinian people?" I query.

"Why do you include all the Jews as one group," yells Doron, another loader who is also a University student during the school semester but just another of Zalman's slaves during the summer.

"Jews *are* all the same for economic purposes," Muhammed replies in a friendly manner.

"Is that what your economics teacher told you down at the University?" I puff, lifting box number 999 of the day. I wish I could be in an air-conditioned library down at the University instead of loading grapes.

"Now I understand why you drive around in this old pile of rust instead of a decent truck," says Doron. "You haven't got enough money stuffed into your mattress yet?"

This comment hits a nerve in Muhammed; Doron has now insulted his beloved truck.

"Your mother..." says Muhammed.

"Your mother's midwife," says Doron completing the insult protocol.

A few weeks later, toward the end of the grape harvest, Muhammed shows up for more grapes and more bantering.

"Guess what, Shimon," he begins, enjoying our sweating and swearing as we load his damn truck. "I took my first step to become a Jew."

"You're crazy," I respond, mistakenly thinking that he was telling me the truth.

"Why am I crazy?" he continues his game. "If you can't beat them, join them."

"You're crazy because your family and the whole village would shove a sharp pole up your *tabun* even if you mentioned becoming a Jew."

"All the same, I took the first step."

"Nu?" I said, giving our new convert his first Yiddish word.

"You want to hear what the first step was?

"OK, lets hear it."

Muhammed grins and slaps me on the back, almost making me drop the 1000th box of grapes that I am loading on this hellish day.

"I'm buying a new truck on the installment plan," he proclaims.

"Welcome to the Jewish people," I say and we all have our best laugh of the day.

Several months later, I pay Muhammed and his family a condolence call. His father has died. We are sitting in the courtyard of his father's house situated in a village perched on a low ridge in the Central Galilee. We watch the setting sun repaint the mountains from brown to ochre. The death of a patriarch is always a big event in our little Holy Land. Muhammed's grief is deep. We sip a special strong and acidic tea, brewed during the mourning period, to emphasize the bitterness of death. I have asked my Arab friend to tell me about his father's life.

"My father," Muhammed recounts, "like his father, was born in this village and spent all his life here until the year 1948. In that year, the war came. At that time, my grandfather, Abu Salem, was the Mukhtar of the village. Most of the people living here wanted to live in peace with the Jews, but of course there were a few hotheads who wanted to fight. One day a Jewish brigade occupied the village. There were no shots fired and the hotheads hid their guns away. The commander of the Jewish brigade, Colonel Motti, knew my grandfather. He went to my grandfather's house and promised him that no one in the village would be harmed. It was as he said. My grandfather and the rest of the villagers kept the peace and so did the Israeli soldiers. My father was only a teenager at that time. A few weeks went by and Colonel Motti's soldiers had to leave the village to fight on another front. Another brigade of soldiers occupied the village. Their commander did not know or care about the previous arrangements. The soldiers searched the houses of many of our people and in a few houses they found the weapons that had been hidden. They were only a few pistols and old rifles from the Turkish days. The Jewish commander ordered all of the men of the village to stand in the central square, over there next to the mosque. He chose five young men and took them out to that field that you see by the road. Then, by his orders, the five men were executed by a firing squad."

"Jesus," I blurt out.

"The new Jewish commander told the rest of the men in the square, including my father, to pack their bags. Then, they were taken by bus to the Jordanian border and pushed across at gunpoint. My grandfather stayed in the village and died of a broken spirit not long afterward. All the people that were left in the village were old men, women and young children."

As Muhammed speaks, I find myself weighing out my own personal guilt, if any, for his family's bitter tragedy. Muhammed senses my confusion and pours me some of the bitter tea, as if to say, 'but we're friends, you know. We understand these matters. If everyone was like us it would have been different.' Maybe.

Muhammed continues: "My father lived in a tent camp on the outskirts of Amman for about two years. He met my mother, there, another Palestinian refugee, and they married. Soon after that, they moved to the South of Lebanon. My father always had in his mind that he would return, someday, to his village.

"In Lebanon, he found out that a few Palestinian men had managed to infiltrate back into what was now Israel, to see their families who had remained behind. My father decided that it was worth a try. By night, he crept past the border past the Israeli guards, and wandered through the Galilee Mountains until he reached our village.

"During this visit, he learned that his father had died. He helped my grandmother harvest the family grain crop and then stole back into Lebanon, to bring my mother back to our native village. At that time, my mother was already pregnant with me. My father decided that his child would not be born in exile. He guided my mother back over the border, through the mountains, past the Israeli border police, past the Israeli army patrols, back to our home in the Galilee. Once home again, he found a way to talk to the Israeli brigade commander, Colonel Motti—the friend of my grandfather—who was now a high officer in the army, and somehow my father talked him into approving our return to his village. From then until now, my father lived a quiet life here. He never owned a gun. He never oppressed anyone else. He never knowingly harmed anyone. He lived in peace. Now, here we are, nine brothers and sisters, and twenty grandchildren mourning his death."

"Tell me about your father's life, Shimon."

I sigh and begin the story of my family's odyssey: "My father was born in a Polish town named Ostrolenka. He immigrated to Mexico in 1927, and eventually he made his way to the United States. His parents(my grandparents), remained behind in Poland. At the beginning of World War II, my grandparents and the rest of the Jews of the town were driven out of Ostrolenka by the Nazis and became refugees in a small village in Byelorussia. In 1941, when Germany invaded Russia, they..."

Something tells me to stop my narrative. I feel like I am approaching the edge of a cliff. I feel a sense of whirling history. A confusing wind. A mistake about to be made. An abyss or a pit in the forest. This is Mohammed's day to mourn, my rational self interjects. I'll tell him about my family some other time when he has room for someone else's grief.

1966: The University of the Vineyard, Part 1

I

I'm sitting in front of my kibbutz apartment watching the local dogs cooperatively biting, snapping, frolicking, and humping each other on the lawn. My daughter Galila is playing *Princesses and Queens* under our walnut tree with the girls from her children's house. Amos saunters by and unexpectedly plunks himself down into the lawn chair beside me. He seems in better spirits than his usual grumpy and aloof self. Perhaps he is looking forward to a good apple crop in the coming harvest season. More likely, he wants something from me.

"Shimon, how long have you worked with us on the orchard staff?" he asks.

"Let me think," I calculate, "including smuggling operations, I guess about four years?"

"And how many times have we sent you down to the Agricultural Institute to learn how to be a scientific farmer?" he continues his line of questioning.

"Twice, once to the Pomology course and once to the pesticide spraying course," I reply gratefully, but suspiciously.

"Very good," he says, beads of sweat beginning to show under his blue idiot's cap. "You've really come a long way in your work, but I'll bet that you could use a rest from spraying pesticides on the 9 p.m. to 5 a.m. shift. Doesn't your wife miss having you in bed beside her at night?" remarks Amos with a hint of friendly lechery in his voice.

"I don't know. You could ask Ruthie about our romantic life when she comes back from the baby house. It's her turn to bring the twins home this afternoon."

"Well my thinking is this..." says Amos almost inaudibly clearing his throat.

"I really don't want to take over the vineyard, Amos," I state bluntly, having suspected in advance what he was up to.

News travels in subtle ways in the kibbutz community.

"Why not?" he asks, his classic red flush of temper beginning to show on his face. He pulls out a wrinkled pack of the deadly Daphne Brand kibbutz-issue cigarettes and lights one of the stinking things up. I chew upon my reply.

"Look, Amos, I know about Zalman (the vineyard manager) leaving the kibbutz and I know that you're looking for a replacement. I also know that you've asked Avraham and then Yaakov to take the job. They both refused and now you come to me because you know that I have never refused to take on a responsibility."

His intentions disclosed, Amos braces himself for the coming confrontation.

I continue, "You are playing on my thing about not wanting to appear as a spoiled American plutocrat. Good old Shimon. A real kibbutznik. Always willing to take on a job. I also know that the work in the vineyard is mostly stoop labor. As a kibbutz business, it has the lowest priority, since it doesn't make much money. Zalman was always begging you for tractors and equipment and he was always short-handed for workers. When you *did* give him workers, they were usually Danish girl volunteers who were out there to get a suntan instead of putting in a day's work. Why would you think I would take on a headache like the vineyard?"

"But Shimon," bargains Amos, "if you take over the vineyard, I'll give you a new tractor plus the two hired employees from town that already work there plus two full- time guys, Doron and Yankele."

"Sure," I smirk, "the two workers from Kiryat Shmonah work in the packinghouse during the harvest season when they are needed the most in the vineyard. Doron goes to the Hebrew University most of the year and Yankele is a new immigrant who has no experience in agriculture. Thanks Amos, you're very persuasive, but the answer is no. I'd rather continue to spray Cyclon-B or DDT in the orchard. Ruthie and I can make love when I get home at five in the morning."

Amos smiles a little, beginning to enjoy the chess game that goes on when kibbutz members are bargaining and already have anticipated all of the possibilities. By our rules, you can't be forced to do any particular type of work, and all work earns the same pay.

"OK, Shimon, I know you'll come around to this new proposal. You're a good fellow, always pulling your share of the yoke," Amos gets up to continue on his way, he smells a possible victory. "You always do what is right since you are a good kibbutznik, for an American, that is. *L'hitraot* (see you later)."

Galila and her little troop of girls come dancing out of their imaginary castle under the walnut tree. She sits on the grass in front of me and proclaims proudly to her friends, "My *Abba* is going to be the new head of the vineyard!"

My goose is cooked.

1967: The University of the Vineyard, Part 2

To my surprise, the vineyard turns out to be not such a bad place to work. I get a bright, new, red, Ferguson tractor and, as promised, I get Yankele and Doron when they are available. The two employees from Kiryat Shmonah are good workers. Amos also keeps me well supplied with Scandinavian volunteers. During the first year of operation we have a great crop of table grapes to send off to the markets in Tel Aviv, Haifa and Jerusalem.

We even figure out how to get more work out of the Scandinavian volunteer girls. We learn to request only Norwegian girls for work in our vineyard; the Swedes and Danes could go to the apple orchard. Our ethnically chosen Norwegians are just as beautiful as the others, but also genetically programmed with a work ethic. There *is* a God.

Early in May, we are hard at work tying the long branches of each vine to the cordon wires. The purpose of this activity is to train the vines so that they will be more accessible for the next phases of work: spraying, irrigating and weeding. Then, our bright red, narrow-bodied tractor will be able to pass through the rows without damaging the crop. We are working our way down each row, and the conversations drift over the dusty grape leaves.

Massaud, a Moroccan man from Kiryat Shmonah, is trying to convince us that scorpions have eight eyes. All the rest of us insist that there are only six eyes per scorpion. No scorpions are available in the vineyard today, thank God, so none of us can prove our point. But we can bet. I put up a bottle of 100-proof *Arak* as the prize. Doron, the university student, is assigned the task of researching the truth about scorpions' eyes.

The topic of the likelihood of a war comes up next. Yankele, our new immigrant from Argentina, is good at making political analyses, a skill learned in his Zionist youth movement days in Buenos Aires.

Yankele says, "There will be a war, for sure. The Egyptian army is camped in Sinai. The United Nations troops, standing between our army and the Egyptians, are going to pull out. Our outlet to the Red Sea has been blocked. We'll have to go to war."

I say, "I don't agree. According to my view of grand strategy, the Egyptians will back down. After all, the American 6th fleet will come to our aid and our air force can finish off all the Arab air forces. We just shot down six Migs over the Galilee last month without even one of our planes damaged. We saw the battle with our own eyes, didn't we?"

Doron adds, "I don't think that we can predict if there will be a war, too many unknown variables. But the Syrians seem quiet enough. How come there haven't been any incidents since the air battle? Palestinians, not Syrians, did the attack near Rosh Pina last month. If there is going to be a war, it doesn't look like the Syrians or the Jordanians are getting ready for it."

Massaud replies, "Never trust the Arabs. Look what they did to us in Morocco!" He spits to emphasize his point.

Saadia, a Tunisian worker from Kiryat Shmonah remarks, "Never trust the Arabs. They used to sic their dogs on me when I was a kid in Tunisia."

Astrid, a beautiful Norwegian volunteer girl says with disdain, "How about doing some work? Look how far I am ahead of the rest of you. All you do is talk politics."

The next day, the old Rabbi from Rosh Pina shows up for his yearly inspection of the vineyard. In order to get a kosher stamp on our grapes, we kibbutz socialists are obliged to honor certain religious laws of agriculture.

These all date back to the period of the *Mishnah*, 2000 years ago. According to the *Mishnah*, you are not allowed to harvest grapes from vines less than three years of age. You may not grow any other crops between the rows of the vineyard. You must leave all the grapes around the periphery of the vineyard unharvested so that the poor can gather them.

We need the kosher stamp since otherwise the Israelis, who are religious Jews won't buy our grapes. The problem is that we grow sweet peas between the rows of the vineyard after the autumn harvest to replenish the nitrogen in the soil. We also harvest the grapes that grow on the periphery, although it is OK with us when people from town come to pick the clusters that we have missed during our harvest operations.

You might think that all of these sinful practices could get us into trouble with the local Rabbi, but no, the great rabbinical scholars of Rosh Pina and the humble vineyard workers of Cfar Moshe have discovered a solution. It works like this: On his yearly visit, the old Chief Rabbi of Rosh Pina has his son drive him to our vineyard in a pick-up truck. Aided by his son (who every one knows is a notorious smuggler of various items of trade over the Lebanese border) the Rabbi shuffles over to our vineyard shed and shakes hands all around. We load two big boxes of his favorite Muscat grapes into the back of the pickup. Next, an envelope with 100 Israeli Liras passes from my hand to the son's hands and with heartfelt *shaloms* the Rabbi returns with his gleanings to Rosh Pina. We hear that the Rabbi's wife makes great wine out of the muscats. The kosher stamp is ours. The wine is his. And the only losers in the game are the sages of the Mishnah.

We reach the middle of May and the long green vines are all neatly tied. It is time to irrigate. The aluminum irrigation pipes are brought out to the vineyard to be hooked together between the rows of grapevines. This will be oppressive and sweaty work. The pipes become hellishly hot to handle and our shoulders and hands will be blistered by the time we are done.

Doron, in the meantime, has completed his scorpion research: It would seem that scorpions have from six to twelve eyes depending on the species. None of us can claim the prize, so we toast each other *l'chaim* (to life) until we drain the bottle of *Arak*.

Before we can deploy the irrigation pipes, a fleet of buses fans out to the towns and settlements in the Galilee and all over the rest of our tiny country to pick up the thousands of reserve soldiers of the

Israeli army. War clouds are gathering. The busses enter Rosh Pina, Kiryat Shmonah and the kibbutzim, and we bid farewell to our families. Most of the foreign volunteers leave the country for safety including Astrid. Doron, Massaud, Saadia, and I are called into our reserve army units and poor Yankele, the immigrant from Argentina, becomes the lone worker in the vineyard. He has not yet served in the army. Thus, he gets to do the irrigation pipes all by himself or with whomever Amos gives him to finish the job. The problem is that Amos has gone to the army too.

1967: Those Heroic Days

I

As I leave the kibbutz with my emergency army pack over one shoulder, I stop by the dental clinic to see if Shmuel, the kibbutz dentist, has finished the repairs on my bridgework. He hasn't, and I have to go off to the army with a gap between my front teeth.

Generally, the army gives us a month's notification before a call-up, but these are tense times and we are forewarned only a few hours before the military buses roll into the kibbutz to haul us away to our supply base, a short distance away. At the supply base, I receive my uniform and a 128 pound .50 caliber machine gun to play with. After that, I go to talk to Lieutenant Gelb, a kibbutznik from Cfar Baruch who wields some power in our unit.

I ask for a short leave to go back to my kibbutz and get my tooth back from the dentist. After all, I don't want to go off to war looking like the "what me worry guy" in *Mad Magazine*.

The Lieutenant looks up at me from his desk and smiles weakly.

"Sure, Shimon," he says, "I'll look into getting you a pass as soon as I can."

I get back onto the bus with the machine gun, a tripod, four boxes of .50 caliber bullets, one cleaning kit, a camouflage net, a broom and trenching tools, and four soldiers. Their job is to help me dig emplacements and to help lug the gun around and set it up, as needed.

The bus driver, who has been taken into the army along with his bus, heads south along the main valley highway and then turns west onto a bumpy dirt road between rows of dusty Cyprus trees. He curses every bump and pothole that his beloved vehicle encounters and a cloud of dust blows in on us through the open windows. We arrive at a small wheat field surrounded by basalt rock fences about five miles from the Syrian border. Our lieutenant explains that the wheat field will be our new home for a while, and he commands us to set up our tents along the edges of the field and to prepare to act like soldiers. Then we sit in front of our tents and talk grand strategy, waiting for the sun to go down so that the flies and gnats will leave us alone.

The first night we sleep, but on the second night we are sent off to prepare machine gun emplacements along the Israeli bank of the Jordan River. The river is due east of us where an old iron and wood Bailey bridge, left over from British Mandate times, crosses the biblical stream. The river officially marks the boundary between Israel and Syria and fortifying our side of it is an ominous sign meaning that the little war we have been fighting, off and on, for the past decade might explode into a big war.

I think about Lieutenant Gelb's promise to get me a pass to go home and finish my dental work. Six years of reserve duty in this backwater unit of the Israeli army have taught me what *that* kind of a promise means. How pleasantly surprised I am a week later, to be called into the Lieutenant's tent and handed a pink colored pass to go back to Cfar Moshe for a period of not more than twenty-four hours.

"Give my regards to Ruthie, and call my wife and tell her that everything's O.K. here," says the Lieutenant.

Cfar Moshe is only a half-hour's ride north from the blasted wheat field—with its malicious insects. I head down to the main highway and within a few minutes hitch a ride north with an ammunition truck driver. Who wouldn't pick up a soldier in uniform during these heroic days?

I arrive back in the kibbutz in my dirty uniform and seek out my wife who is working in one of the children's houses.

"What a pleasant surprise," she grins, looking really good in her dark skin, her blue apron and white shorts.

"Good to see you, too. Can you get some time off?" I ask suggestively.

"Sure," she says with an even wider grin, "I'll be home in a half hour."

I run over to the dental clinic and luckily find the dentist drilling an older member's tooth. The dentist is courteous enough to leave the other guy in the dental chair and slip the repaired bridgework into my mouth. What people won't do for a soldier in uniform! Fully toothed, I head home, throw the cat out, take a delicious shower, wait for my wife and make love with her shortly after she arrives in her apron and shorts. There is nothing like army duty away from her and a threat of war to fan my passion.

"My mother is still here," she reminds me as she slips her work shorts back on. "She's thinking of shortening her visit and going back to the USA. She's worried about a war breaking out. She got a telephone call from the American Embassy advising her to leave. What to you think I should do?"

"Ruthie," I say, "I think you ought to send your mom home. She's an old lady and she'll just get in the way if things get any worse around here. There are still planes leaving from the Rosh Pina airport to Tel Aviv. You ought to see if she can get on one."

"What do you think is going to happen?" she asks.

"Look Ruthie," I patiently explain, "I think that everything's going to be all right and there won't be a war. But just in case there is one, to be honest, my unit is in a location that is not so great for one's health. Be optimistic." I pat her on her head paternally, with a big knot in my throat.

I drop by the telephone booth and call Lieutenant Gelb's wife. I tell her that everything is all right. So far I'm not lying.

I walk on over to the children's houses where my daughter and my twin sons are bouncing around with all the other kids their age. I give each of them a hug and hang around for a while watching the boys play war and the girls play dolls. Everything is normal. There are no questions from the kids about military strategy, the Syrian army, or the future of the Galilee.

Then I walk over to the laundry house and ask Max, the boss of the laundry if he might be willing to do a quick job on my uniform...God knows that it needs cleaning. "No problem, it'll be ready in the morning," he says. Several of the laundry staff ladies ask me about their husbands, who are in my unit and I tell them that everything is O.K.

The next morning, in a clean uniform with the big lump still in my throat, I say goodbye to my wife, my kids and my cat and I hitch a ride back to my unit.

To my pleasant surprise, I find that we have been moved from the wheat field to a better location in an apple orchard right next to the little airport in Rosh Pina. There are fewer insects around to torment us, and lots of shade for our afternoon naps. The negative side is that we are a lot closer to the border with Syria. Every night, we walk the mile or so down the road to work on the machine gun emplacements overlooking the bridge and the river. Then, we return to the apple orchard before sunrise and take a long snooze. In the afternoon we clean our weapons and discuss the rumors of the day. The latest one being tossed around is that since there are so few Israeli units along the Syrian border, our brilliant and all-knowing generals are not planning a serious war along this front. If we go to war, it will undoubtedly be against the Egyptians who are busy concentrating their armies in the South.

Other great military thinkers among us hold the opinion that the entire Middle East will march against us and we shall all be slaughtered. Others think that we will destroy the entire Arab armies in short shrift just like Moses did to the Amalikites. Still others predict a world war quickly escalating to a nuclear cataclysm. Then there are those who, irrationally, surmise that the Israeli army will cut through the Syrians, the Jordanians and the Egyptians like a knife through butter and occupy Sinai, the West Bank and the Golan Heights. Whatever happens, I figure, at least I have my tooth back from the dentist.

A few days later, I am sitting under an apple tree cleaning my weapon and watching the goings-on at the tiny civilian airport just beyond the orchard. I see a plane loading up with passengers, mostly civilians, and my mother-in-law appears with her big purple hat getting on with the others. Chaim, the kibbutz driver is helping her negotiate the ladder leading up into the plane. She stands in the plane's doorway for a second, waves to Chaim and disappears into the cabin. I am too far away to call out to her but I wave to the plane as it taxies up the little runway and roars off for Tel Aviv. At least *she* is out of danger. The sight of the plane heading south has a strange plunging effect on my optimism: about how this will all turn out and, for a second, I wish that I was on the plane, too.

June 7, 1967: Of Bombs and Mules

A few hours later:

Syrian shells by the hundreds are raining around me. I've lived thirty-two years and I'm about to die. I throw my body behind a concrete porch leading up to the front door of a little farmhouse. I ponder my fate as time slows down. Just a matter of a few moments left. The houses up and down the street are blasting apart. Only the mule and I are alive, the one stupidly standing in the field in front of the house, the other groveling for cover under the house.

Roaring, death-dealing explosions shake the earth. Does this mule know that it will die too? The two of us together? Mule and man about to meet their makers. The mule is still eating. For him it is probably the Last Supper but he grazes as if the shrapnel was not whizzing by. I'm not hungry.

One shell hits the back part of the house and I hear the water pipes bursting inside. I'm still alive, but not for long because no one can survive in this bombardment. No God can save me. No man can rescue me. The air is full of jagged metal. No respite. Maybe God is protecting the mule and at least I am under the porch. A Katyusha rocket slams into the back of the house and part of the roof flies off and crashes into a field. The mule doesn't care. It chomps. Won't die hungry.

Time to think of my family. Three children about to be orphans. Wife about to be widowed. Try some prayers. No, no, too early for that. That's for the dying seconds like in the *Sands of Iwo Jima*. Now I'm in my own movie. But I'm not John Wayne at all. Meantime, watch mule, count bombs, think of family. Never wanted to be a hero. Bombs are dumb. No heroism here. Just stupid blind chance. Me and the mule. Shrapnel clattering against the wall of this half-ruined house.

How does the engineer in the Russian bomb factory feel? I mean the man who designed these bombs to break up into razor-sharp shrapnel. Jagged things. His bombs postmarked to me, an Israeli soldier, and no hero, lying in the mud underneath a farmhouse in a dusty Galilee village.

Sudden vision: My college girlfriend Carol appears to me. She's in her apartment on top of a hill in San Francisco, looking out at the sunset. She's alone in the house and thinking of me, knowing that the war has broken out, but not knowing that it has broken directly on me. Wondering if I am alive. And the vision passes.

Others appear: Mr. Elkins, my Hebrew teacher. My grandfather. Harry S. Truman. Ben Gurion. The Lone Ranger. Fred C. Dobbs. Attila the Hun. Porky Pig. Old McDonald. Pete Seeger. Elijah the Prophet. My cat Shunra. The bombardment goes on. I've already seen this movie. Stop the music.

I don't know what to do now, just like the mule, I'll do what I do best. Read my book. I feel it in my back pocket. Pull it out and open it to where I left off. Chicken feather bookmark. A *Simenon* detective novel. "Who done it?" The Syrian artillery? No, they're busy doing me. Will I have time to get to the end of this book before I get to my end? Ten more pages. No way. But it's something to do when there's nothing I can do. Takes my mind off impossible prayer and thinking about other people. I want to think of me. I want to be me. I want to know "who done it?" I don't want to die.

An astonishing silence. The bombardment is over. The mule lives. I live. I listen to myself breathing. I wait for a few more minutes and then crawl out from under the smoldering house. I slowly walk over to the bomb shelter that I couldn't reach when the shells began to fall. The door of the shelter is shut. I knock on the door. It opens with the squeak of its rusted hinges.

The dusty face of Sergeant Buzaglo peers out. "Shimon, you're alive. You lived through that?"

June 9, 1967: I Thought the War Was Over

Friday night and we hear that the war is over. A transistor radio tells us that Egypt, Jordan and Syria have asked for a cease-fire. First reactions: now we can sleep for the first time in five days. After brief mutual congratulations on surviving the war, I curl up in a foxhole, not too far from the bank of the Jordan River and plunge into the deep, trance of a dreamless sleep. Around three in the morning, Sergeant Buzaglo wakes me up with a rough hand on my shoulder.

"Shimon, wake up, the war is on again." He says in a much too quiet voice.

"I thought it was over," I complain as sleep fades gradually and I realize where I am.

"Dayan wants us to take the Golan"

"Just you and me, or is the rest of the army going with us?"

"Be at the road in ten minutes," says Buzaglo, like a line in a 'B' cowboy movie.

A one-lane road runs parallel to the Jordan a short distance west of the river. We gather silently, in the darkness, on the side of the road. The cooks have prepared our gourmet breakfast. They have sliced some bread and opened cans of olives and tins of strawberry jam. Some tins of sardines have also arrived. Coffee heated up from last night tastes like the cook's boot. Our Last Supper? I figure that it will be for some of us. Then it is time to prepare our weapons of war. Since we aren't lugging the machine guns with us in our charge-to-be up the heights, I'm handed an Uzi sub-machine gun. Sergeant Buzaglo hands me a pamphlet barely readable in the predawn light. It is a message from the chief military rabbi promising us that God will be on our side during the coming battle against the enemies of Israel. Such an encouraging message! I nudge my friend Gabi's arm as he frantically cleans his rifle. Gabi is a kibbutznik from Cfar Baruch, trained to be a machine gunner but now, for some unexplained reason, toting a bazooka.

"Gabi, look at this. We're in God's army now."

"Tell him that his cooks are for shit," mutters Gabi, even more of an unbeliever than I am.

Nothing happens for an hour. We sit around on the edge of the road patiently waiting to be sent to our death and, as usual, being told nothing.

Now we all know that our time has come.

At first light of day all hell breaks loose, but not on our side of the River. The Israel Air Force shows up and begins to rain bullets, bombs and napalm on the Syrian fortresses. We haven't seen much of our planes for the last five days. They have been busy causing havoc in Egypt and Jordan. Now they are unleashed on the Syrians. We watch with gaping mouths as napalm bombs slam into the hills opposite us bursting into sticky red fire balls.

My Prayer: War is war, better them than me. No, no, those are people burning inside their emplacements. But why are they in their emplacements? Because they want to kill me. But do they want to kill me? Yes, they're under orders to kill me. And I'm under orders to kill them, and I'll do it, but I'm glad that it's the pilots doing the dirty work. The napalm stinks even from here. Hope they get 'em all. Above all, I want to live. Better them than me. Better anybody than me. Amen.

Then, to the north of us, we hear the sound of volcanoes erupting above the roar of the airplanes and their bombs. It sounds like an avalanche, thunder, and an earthquake combined. We look, but the lines of eucalyptus trees along the road mask our view. Above the treetops we see clouds of dense smoke laced with flashes of lightning. Opposite us on the Heights, the Syrian fortresses are as quiet as we are. Our sector becomes a silent spectator to the terrible but invisible struggle as Israel's elite Brigades begin their assault to break through the Syrian Maginot line. We sit by the side of the road. Our radio sets are silent. No orders for us. I thank our new commander, God, that we are a second line unit of no fighting prowess. We inhale our cigarettes and watch the smoke and dust pile higher and higher into the northern sky. It seems as if dusk is falling up there while we, in the south part of the front, are in broad daylight. We sit humbly in our soiled, dusty uniforms and think of the people who are dying in the hand-to-hand combat in Syrian trenches above our Hulah valley. The same valley where we all live and work as civilians, where our families are now crouched in bomb shelters. Hours pass and gradually, the roar of battle recedes. The war has gone east.

Around noon, we receive our orders to proceed across the bridge into Syrian territory. "Resistance will be light," we are promised. "Sure," we scoff.

We trudge down to the bluff overlooking the Jordan, stopping at the Israeli police station on our side of the river. We halt for a last check of our fighting gear. A policeman is lounging on a folding chair set against the back wall of the bullet-pocketed edifice, facing the Golan Heights.

"What's going on?" we ask, somewhat surprised at the policeman's brazen exposure to the Syrian snipers on the other side of the river.

"Trust me, the Syrians are gone," he says. "I've worked in this building for ten years and this is the first time I've ever been around the back side of this station. If I'm sitting here you can believe me. They're all gone."

We cross the little bridge into enemy territory. On the other side of the Jordan we pass a ruined Syrian customs house and then cautiously move forward up the side of the Syrian Heights.

I can't help thinking—despite the assurances of the policeman—what if enemy soldiers are waiting for us, just beyond that wall over there, squinting at us through their machine gun sights, their officers waiting to give the command to fire?

And it's such a beautiful day.

June 10, 1967: A Walk Up the Golan

A half hour's walk in the sun, past the old customs house, past a Syrian bunker and on up the winding road to the top of the heights, brings us to the scene of a brief battle that was fought only a few hours ago. There are a few dead Syrian soldiers stretched out on the ground. A burial squad is digging their graves a few yards away. The Syrian soldiers, we are told, met their death defending a fort abandoned by their officers.

My eyes photograph the corpses but, to my own surprise, my emotions are flat. They are young boys, maybe 17 or 18 years old. Not far away, we see the first Syrian prisoners crouched on the earth with an Israeli soldier standing guard, holding an Uzi submachine gun. The prisoners are also very young, dressed in light khaki uniforms. They are frightened, hugging their knees and trying not to look at what is going on around them. They are silent. A guard tells us that these troops were commanded by the Syrian officers to fight to the finish because the Israelis always kill their prisoners. Good reason to be scared even if it isn't true.

In the past few days, I have continually surprised myself by my lack of affect. Commanded to obey orders that might end in my being killed or wounded—no reaction. Discovering that my combat death was, after all, unlikely—no reaction. Seeing dead Syrian boys—no reaction. Getting my first face-to-face look at the enemy prisoners—no reaction. Is this a temporary dulling of my compassion, along with fear? Or have I lost something coming into this war?

Entering the enemy fort through its backside, we move carefully past bunkers and entrenchments until we reach a point with a view from the heights down to our valley. We can see the Jordan River and the bridge we have come across. There, in the valley below, is the police station with the Israeli policeman still sitting in his folding chair staring up at us. Through the eucalyptus trees, we see the road, in Israel, where we waited to go into battle. To the north, we see Mt. Hermon and the Hulah valley. I can't quite make out Cfar Moshe through the haze. Closer to us, we can see the kibbutzim in the south of the valley, Gadot, Mahanaim, Hulata. Across the valley we make out the red roofs of the towns of Rosh Pina and Hatzor, seemingly intact, as if there hasn't been much of a war at all. We sit on the edge of a Syrian bunker and wonder at the view below us and think about the enemy soldiers who had watched this same view not so many hours ago. How much detail there is to see! They could track every move that we made and spot everything we were doing. What targets we were. But again, I feel flat, emotionless, distracted.

A few minutes later, Sergeant Buzaglo posts Gabi and me as sentries by the entrance of the fortress near where the Syrian prisoners are guarded. Some of our soldiers are offering the prisoners canteen cups of water and cigarettes. The prisoners accept the water and light up the cigarettes. Gabi and I pull two chairs out of the ex-Syrian guard box and sit down by the side of the road to observe the military vehicles coming from the valley.

Two jeeps arrive filled with our cooks, their pots and pans and some boxes of rations. The cooks are a tough lot. They talk rough and look like pirates. Even worse, they don't know how to cook. Several of them are soldiers that have had bad service records. A few of them were liberated from army jails at the beginning of the war and sent to the front to do something for the war effort, whether they wanted to or not. Some of them are deserters from other units. We wave them into the entrance to the fort and they get their gear out of the jeeps to cook something up for the rest of us.

Two of the cooks, spying the Syrian prisoners sitting on the ground nearby, scowl and walk over to them. Both of them pull the heavy magazines of bullets out of their rifles and, before anyone can do anything about it, use them to land some heavy blows on the heads of the captured prisoners. The guard, distracted for a minute, quickly cocks the bolt on his Uzi and points it toward the cooks. To my own amazement, I also find myself grabbing my weapon and aiming it at the cooks. The cooks freeze.

I hear the guard say: "Hit one of the prisoners again and I'll shoot."

My heart is pounding. I hate what the two cooks have tried to do. I hate it more than the whole war itself.

Lieutenant Gelb appears and arrests the two cooks. He looks over toward the guard and me and says, "O.K., take it easy, no one is going to hurt the prisoners."

I lower the weapon slowly and so does the guard. I look at him and he looks at me and as our eyes meet, we nod.

Something instinctive has happened between the guard and me. During our basic training and all through our years of service, we have learned a code of behaviors known as *the purity of the weapon*. These are spelled out to all new recruits in boot camp with great solemnity as if they were a part of the Ten Commandments: Thou shall not harm prisoners. Thou shall take no plunder. Thou shall not harm civilians. Do not desecrate civilian property. I took this code very seriously and so did most of the other soldiers.

I go back to sitting by the road with Gabi and his useless bazooka to watch the Israeli military traffic coming up to Syria. A long obsolete Sherman tank lumbers up the hill. The tank stops and the driver pops his head out of the turret.

"Shimon, Gabi, what are you two doing up here?"

It is Yosef, another member of our kibbutz who in normal times sorts apples in the packinghouse.

"Invading Syria," I say, "what news from home?"

"I hear everyone's OK, I'm also invading Syria. Got any cigarettes?" Gabi throws him a pack of *Daphnes* and the turret pops down. Yosef and his museum piece move on.

Next comes a long convoy: jeeps, command cars, recoilless rifle vehicles and armored personnel carriers moving past our fort headed north. Many of the vehicles sport captured, framed portraits of various leaders of the Arab world lashed onto their front bumpers. I see a picture of King Hussein and several Abdul Nassers go by. The convoy seems endless. The drivers wave at us as they go by. Then, the convoy slows down and halts for a few minutes. Gabi and I walk over to one of the command cars. The driver is wearing an Australian-like campaign hat and sports a dusty red beard.

"What *is* this convoy?" we inquire.

"Reinforcements from the Jordanian and Egyptian fronts," says red-beard.

"Where's the end of this convoy?"

"God knows, probably still down in Egypt. The whole army is coming north."

He pulls a chocolate bar out of a box on the seat next to him and hands it to Gabi.

"Here, you look like you could use this. It's Egyptian." The convoy starts up again.

"See you in Damascus," he calls back.

I look over at my buddy Gabi and say, "I guess we're not alone up here anymore."

June 10: 1967: Thou Shall Not Plunder

There is nothing much more to do at the Syrian fort. The burial squad has finished its work. The prisoners have been taken down to Israel for incarceration and eventual exchange and someone has thought up some new orders for our battalion. They load us on trucks with all our gear and send us north to Nafakh, a large Syrian base six miles up the road. We're not sure about what might be waiting at our destination, perhaps more war, more prisoners, more food, more work or more nothing.

In fact, what we will find waiting for us at Nafakh will be the beginning of a new period in our history. Soon we learn what it means to be an army of occupation.

Nafakh has been taken without much trouble by better units than ours. Most of the Syrian soldiers have fled toward Damascus; their lunch is still on the table. Our job is to tour the barracks, mess halls, officer's quarters, and storehouses to make sure that there is no lingering enemy around to cause us any harm.

Gabi, Moshe Buzaglo and I poke around in a row of barracks assigned to us for inspection. The beds are neatly made and pin-ups are plastered all over the walls. I note, anthropologically, that Syrian soldiers seem to like well-padded blonde women for their pinups. There is a map of the Middle East tacked up with a blank space where the State of Israel has been rumored to exist. Gabi decides that it would make a good souvenir and he carefully takes it off the wall, rolls it up and sticks it into his cartridge belt. I see a great looking green beret hanging on a peg with a metal Syrian badge on it and into my back pocket it goes. Moshe Buzaglo gives us a disapproving look dating back from biblical injunctions about plundering, but we assure him that these are just token souvenirs that God wouldn't care about. Finally, Moshe succumbs and helps himself to a picture of someone's wife and three kids that has been tacked above one of the army beds.

"I'll just keep this and return it to the Syrian's wife when we get to Damascus," he explains.

"Oh, listen to the great conqueror" Gabi says. "Maybe his wife has a sister too?"

"Maybe you have a sister too." he retorts gruffly, like a true native of Tiberius,
and we have a good chauvinist laugh. Part of our laughter relates to the spookiness of being in another army's barracks. Who were the men who had been sitting on these beds a few hours ago, griping their own Arabic gripes and telling their own Arabic jokes? But now the language of gripes and jokes is Hebrew.

Back outside, we run into some other soldiers from our units who have been checking out other barracks. One guy, a kibbutznik from Cfar Giladi, has a burlap sack over his shoulders loaded with a heavy object.

"Hey, Shlomo, what'd you find?" I ask, feeling a growing party mood.

"Television set," he answers. "There's a bunch of them in the officers quarters. These Syrian bastards were living it up here like they were in America."

(Finding a TV is especially impressive since there are only a few TV sets in Israel and no TV stations.)

By now, every soldier we run into bears a gift from the Syrian army. A few have managed to find the ultimate souvenirs: a Syrian flag or pictures of the President of Syria. Within a short period of time, bartering begins and there are already a few arguments among our heroic soldiers as to the ownership of booty and its price. Behold the free market cometh.

Into the middle of this economic process, one of the young lieutenants, Gad, enters upon the scene. Gad is a good friend of mine and a member of our kibbutz. He was my drill instructor during basic training and fancies himself a tough officer in the British tradition.

Gad's feathers are up as he sees what is happening with our souvenir hunt. He doesn't say anything, just does an about face, muttering, and stalks off to talk to the other officers.

A few minutes later our entire battalion is ordered to form ranks on the Syrian parade ground with all of our gear. The parade ground has several of the green and red, wooden, triumphal arches that the Syrians like to erect in public places. There is a great view of the Hulah valley down in Israel, from whence we all came. The platoon commanders line everybody up and order us to put our weapons, packs and baggage on the ground in front of us. Then we are ordered to strip naked and lay out our uniforms along side of the rest of our stuff. Across the parade ground we can see another platoon divesting itself of its baggage and clothes and they too stand naked against the setting sun.

At first, I figure that we were going to be deloused but within a few minutes I notice the officers going from soldier to soldier, taking away the packages of war booty and rifling through our stinking army pants, shirts, squalid underwear, cartridge belts and packs. In a short amount of time, they have all the booty that we have collected and are making a big pile of it in one corner of the parade ground.

A couple of the cooks are put to work dumping gasoline on the pile and then before anyone can say anything, one of the officers tosses a match into the mountain of booty. It erupts into a fierce blaze. The Syrian flags go up in smoke and the TV sets shatter inside the burlap sacks. We all curse the officers inwardly and outwardly. All that work gone to waste, and all our trophies going up in smoke. The feared Battalion Commander appears before us as the sun dips below the mountains of the Galilee.

"What in hell did you men think you were going to do with all this stuff? Take it to the next battle with you? Take it home and give it to your kids? How do you know that this war is over or ever will be over? What kind of soldiers of Israel are you? Do you remember anything from your basic training? Do you remember how to clean your rifles and tie your shoes and wipe your noses? Do you remember our *purity of the weapon code*? Do you remember what our Bible says about plunder and what oaths you took when you joined this army? This plundering is a disgrace and you're lucky that the only thing we burned was your stealings! We should have burned your mustaches too. Any more of this and we'll be giving long jail sentences in this unit instead of passes to go home."

Silence on the Syrian parade ground at Nafakh.

"And, incidentally," he said in a slightly lower voice. The war *is* over. The cease fire began ten minutes ago."

As if by a signal, in the gathering dusk in the valley below us after six long days of total blackout, the lights of the towns and the kibbutzim suddenly go back on as if thrown by one gigantic switch. We look down from the heights toward our homes. Something biblical has happened. The army of Israel has defeated its enemies on all sides, against all odds. For a second, I think about the pamphlet from the Army Rabbinate that had been put into my hand as we went forth to battle. Maybe there was something in what they said about God being on our side.

...No, no, this is too easy, there is no God of Israel on this battlefield, only a pantheon of the pagan gods: the god of randomness, the god of good and bad luck, the god of stupidity, the god of dirty underwear, and the gods of cruelty, plunder, slaughter, bad jokes, greed, napalm, terror, fatalism, fake bravery, and bad food. All of these gods are wandering the battlefield, taking a life here, taking a life there, but mainly just causing havoc and making human beings less than human.

I shake off my biblical and philosophical thoughts and begin to put my filthy uniform back on. As I stuff my leg into the pant leg,

I feel a lump of cloth and the coolness of metal. It is the green Syrian beret, my own plunder. I push my other leg into its pant leg, pull the pants up, button the fly and cinch my belt. This parade and the Six-Day War are over.

And do you think that I gave the damn officers back my Syrian beret?

1967: The Aftermath

I

A few days after the war, I become a civilian again. I hand my army gear back to the quartermasters and hitch a ride in the Cfar Moshe shoe factory van all the way from our base in Rosh Pina to the kibbutz. Rudolf, the driver, and his green van are also returning from the war. The vehicle, just like us soldiers, had been called up to the army to fight for Israel. It's still driveable but there are a lot of bullet holes that will have to be plugged up to make it presentable again.

Rudolf lets me off in front of the dining hall. I need to see my wife and children first and then to get a bite to eat. Then, I'll head home for a shower and much needed sleep.

The entire civilian population of the kibbutz had been in the bomb shelters during the six days of warfare and the people passing by still seem bleary eyed and tired. There is a big, two-column chart tacked to the bulletin board in front of the dining hall. The names of all the members of the kibbutz who were called up to the army are in the first column and a status report for each soldier is in the second column. There are many blank spaces in the status column next to names of soldiers who haven't reported in yet. There are a few soldiers listed as wounded but none killed. So-far-so-good. I notice that, for some unknown reason, I am listed as being wounded. So much for accuracy in reporting, since, physically, I am fine except for mosquito bites, crud under my fingernails, and some rib pain from bumping into an angle-iron during one of the bombardments.

I go over to the children's house where Ruthie works and she gives me a tight hug that banishes my deep fatigue—temporarily at least. After a few more hugs, a layer of dust remains onto her blue apron from my filthy uniform.

"You better go shower and get that smelly uniform off," she recommends, "I'll be home around four."

I drop by the children's house and receive some more hugs from my Galila, my Hermon, and my Golan. Galila explains proudly that her class stood by the side of the road on the last day of the war when the tanks passed by on their way to the battle of the Golan Heights. They handed out Cfar Moshe apples to the soldiers—alas, many of who were never to return. My boys seemed unaware that anything unusual had happened. It somehow was like a game for them hiding down in the bomb shelter for all six days.

Golan tells me that Shunra our cat disappeared.

I walk down the path to the south end of the kibbutz where we live in our wooden prefab. Things seem strangely normal. No parades. No hoisting up heroes on people's shoulders. No speeches. No medals. It is the best kind of homecoming, quiet, normal, uneventful. Perhaps because every one of us: soldiers, wives, kids, had taken some part in the war effort. Every one of us had heard the artillery shells crashing into our valley and seen the warplanes loaded with bombs and napalm zooming over to rain death on the enemy. Now we desperately want to get back to a sane life again. Maybe later we will delve into our deeper feelings, fears of our own death, fears for the children and our community. For now we postpone these hidden war wounds. Everything's O.K. C'mon, let's get back to work.

On my way back to our cabin by the orchard, it seems to me that the gardens and lawns of the kibbutz look greener than ever. The turtledoves in the trees are cooing a welcome-back concert for me. Instead of going directly home, I turn off onto the path that leads to the little branch of the Jordan River, down to the narrow beach where we used to swim before the kibbutz swimming pool was built. The water looks so inviting and I feel so foul after six days of dodging bullets, jumping into foxholes, eating dust, sleeping in the dirt, and chasing after the enemy, that I just plunge into the muddy, cold water, uniform and all. A couple of kids fishing off the riverbank look at me like I am crazy and I wave as I backstroke past them. I return to the beach, splashing around and laughing like a madman and then walk back home in my soaking uniform. All I can think of is: "I am alive!"

II

Later, at home, while the kids are playing around in the sand pile outside, Ruthie explains to me the astonishing circumstances of her mother's exodus from the Galilee:

"The same day that you left the kibbutz, Mom got a telegram from the American ambassador in Tel Aviv, ordering all American citizens immediately out of the country. As soon as she got the telegram, she tried to convince me to take the kids and go with her back to the U.S. She said that she just knew that there was going to be a war and that we were in great danger. When I said that I wouldn't go, those big blue eyes of hers teared up. I've never seen her look so pitiful. Anyway, she said, 'at least let me take the kids.' She was really pleading and I had to think about it for a bit. So I went for a long walk around the kibbutz and then came back to the room where she was staying. I had made up my mind.

'Mom,' I said, 'our kids were born here just like the rest of the kids. We are truly one big family here and I really can't go with you or send our three children with you. What about the rest of the children of the kibbutz? Where would they go? They don't have rich grandparents in America. Whatever our fate will be here, our kids will share it. Now let's get you packed up to go to the airport.' I arranged for Chaim, the driver, to take her down to the airfield in Rosh Pina. And that was it."

I look at this brave woman and for the first time in a long time I allowed myself to cry tears of joy. We are alive!

The next day, *Shunra* the cat, returns from the wars.

III

For the first few days, I practice an exercise that many returning soldiers do, called in Hebrew, *gav-betten* (in English: back-belly). This is accomplished in the following manner: you get into your pajamas, lie down on your *gav* (back) in bed, cover yourself with a blanket or two depending on the weather, and go to sleep. When you wake up, you turn over in bed and lie on your *betten* (belly). Then you continue the exercise for as long as you can until all the fatigue, pain, shock, sorrow, madness, lack of sleep, and misery of war have purged themselves from your body.

I awake from my *gav- betten* and see my deceased grandfather Yisroel Chmiel, sitting on a chair next to my bed. He himself seems to be deep in thought and hasn't observed that I have drifted out of my sleep.

"*Boker tov Saba,*" I mumble.

"It's not morning, *boytchik*" he replies softly, "It's seven o'clock in the evening."

"Where is everybody?"

"Your wife and children are in the dining hall eating," he explains, "and your cat is with you underneath your blanket."

I peek under the blanket. Sure enough, Shunra is there, still doing a *gav-betten* of her own.

Saba Yisroel pulls the chair closer to my bed and peers into my eyes.

"So what was it like?" he whispers.

"What?"

"The war."

I think about his question for a bit and then try this on him:

"It's too early to tell."

"Give it a try, anyway. I want to know," says *Saba*.

"What is it like? It's like a lot of waiting, a lot of talking, a lot of griping, a lot of bad food, a lot of feeling sick to your stomach, and a lot of wishing that it was all over. A lot of dirt, and a lot of fear that you can't tell anyone else about. We told jokes to each other. We talked about sports. But after the first day of the war, no one told jokes any more. We were too busy keeping our heads down."

"Did you think that you were going to get killed?"

"Yes, up to the last day and up to the last minute. Even when we saw that the Syrians had surrendered, I worried that I would die in a road accident, or, let's say, a bullet fired by mistake by our own men, or a mine tripped off—all the stupid things that might have ended my chances of living through this war."

"Did you think of running away? Of deserting?"

"Many times, Saba, many times. But I was too much of a coward to do it. What would my fellow soldiers say? What would my family say? What would my kibbutz say? What would you say? I wanted to live. I would have done almost anything not to get killed. Once, I even prayed to God that someone else would die instead of me. With all of that, I kept doing everything that I was supposed to do. Like a machine, I kept my weapon clean, followed orders, went into battle, and fired at the Syrians. Right now I'm still confused about this whole thing. Maybe later I'll have some clear ideas about what it all meant."

"Did you see people die?" asks my grandfather, leaning even closer to my face.

"I don't want to talk about that," I answer.

"Still, I'm proud of your bravery, even if you say you were a coward," says Saba.

I feel anger rising at this remark.

"Saba, you don't understand. War is murder. I hate the whole idea of bravery. I just wanted to get home alive so that my life wouldn't be stolen away from me—so that I would know my kids and grandchildren. So that I wouldn't be taken away too early like you and grandma were, and my uncles, aunts, cousins were- killed for nothing in the middle of a forest!"

Grandfather is silent during this outburst. For the first time, he seems not to know what to say.

"Maybe you should take a shower before Ruthie and the kids come back from the dining hall," he advises.

Now I know where my avoidance of sensitive questions comes from.

In the shower, I turn up the hot water full blast and scrub my body from head to toe with the rough, yellow kibbutz–issue soap. Steam creeps out a crack in the shower room window and into the crisp evening air of the Galilee. By the time that I dry myself with a coarse towel, put on clean underwear and open the shower room door, I see that Saba Yisroel has gone and Shunra, my heroic and imperious cat, is curled up in the warmth of Saba's chair.

IV

Whether I think that there is glory in war or not, the glory industry is running full blast in the international media and in the Israel press. In July, I get a free gift from my backwater battalion, a signed copy of an album of sketches drawn by a well-known Israeli caricaturist who accompanied the army into battle. The sketches capture the reality of the war better than a photograph. The text is factual and low-key. It makes me feel pride in the miniscule role I had played in this military affair, now known as the Six-Day War.

Later in July, the more commercial and popular picture albums appear in the stores and I buy one from the traveling book salesman that frequents kibbutzim in the area. I look through the album. Something sticks in my throat.

"Did you see this?" I ask Yigal and Chava, my adopted parents in Cfar Moshe, showing them the cover of the album I bought.

Yigal puts his glasses on and squints at the khaki tinted cover.

"Ah, our generals," he sighs and gives me a wink. "Here's Dayan, Yoffe and Rabin marching to the Western Wall. What next?"

He flips through the album to a picture of our president, Zalman Shazar, kissing the Wall with an old, flat British helmet on his head.

"He'll break his nose if he kisses it any harder," quips Chava.

How I love their sweet sarcasm, their Czech humor, their *Schwikien* mischief. I'm feeling better already.

Chava flips a few more pages of the album over and confronts a photograph of the Chief Military Rabbi blowing a blast on a *shofar*, a ritual ram's horn, in front of the Wall."

"Jesus, Maria," she detonates. "Is this what we went to war for?"

V

Every summer, David, a prominent right wing politician who is on the city council of Jerusalem, and who is a second cousin to my wife, pops by the kibbutz for a few hours to pay his respects to Ruthie and me. He is happy to see us and we are happy to see him. He is a nice man in spite of his reactionary ideologies. This time we have plenty to talk about in the aftermath of our latest war.

"Nu, David, what now?" I ask my cousin-in-law as we sit in our lawn chairs and watch the sun set over the hills of Naftali. "This time last year you were a city councilman of a Jewish Jerusalem. This year you are a councilman of a Jewish, Moslem and Christian Jerusalem."

David replies, "Shimon, maybe you haven't heard the news up here on your kibbutz in the Galilee, but there has always been only one real Jerusalem, and it is called *The Capital of the Jewish People.*

He strokes his little red goatee and waits for my clever and sardonic reply—we both love this little game.

"And what are you going to do with this Holy Wall thing, cousin. Are we going to rebuild the Holy Temple, too? If so, our kibbutz could do some business selling chickens and goats to your priests for sacrifice. We don't have any bulls for you but you could buy some from our neighbors in Cfar Baruch. We have some hogs, too, but we wouldn't think of sacrificing them."

"Save your hogs for yourself and the rest of your kibbutzniks," smirks David. "As for rebuilding the Holy Temple, for the time being we have a mosque where the Temple stood and it's really too nice to tear down."

"I'm relieved to hear that," I counter. But, despite the joking nature of this discussion my arm hairs are tingling from the looming seriousness of our subject matter.

"Seriously," I ask, "what are your plans for the Muslim population?"

"Seriously?" he answers question with question, an old Jewish custom.

"Seriously."

"Our plans, at this point, are to convert them to Judaism," he says quietly, and I realize that he is not joking.

"David," I continue, very, very seriously. "Do you know what it means for a Muslim to convert to another religion, even of his own free will? After conquering these people you want them to be Jews? Have you ever spoken to a Muslim? Converting ten of them to Judaism, even if they are begging to become Jews, would cause a *Jihad*, a Holy War. We would be fighting against every country from here to Indonesia. They would march on us: the armies of Pakistan, Afghanistan, Iraq, Iran, Saudi Arabia, Oman, Yemen, Egypt, Jordan and Syria again and all the rest of North Africa not to speak of Chad, Senegal, Tanzania and God knows who else. Maybe even the Christians will join in, too, not to speak of the Communist World! Won't it be fun to fight a big war against all of these people?"

Silence.

A sigh. "Don't worry, Shimon, we *have* a plan, but I can't tell you the details," he whispers. "I wouldn't worry about fighting a war with anybody. Look what we just did to the Arab armies, all three of them."

Avoiding further politics, my head spinning, we move inside for some *humus*, bread, and goat cheese that Ruthie has prepared. Then we part, still cousins and still friends. But my cousin, his capital city, and our government, I fear, are heading for difficult times.

1968: The Outhouse War

I

Only seven months have passed since the Six-Day War and the victorious Israeli Defense Forces now possess the same basalt heights that had so recently been the bastion of the Syrian army. The Syrians have retreated toward Damascus leaving a junkyard of ruined weapons, vehicles and lives. The Israelis have stopped short of occupying the capital city, Damascus, and are scurrying to build fortifications and infrastructure for the occupation of this sad and treeless plateau.

Early in January of 1968, Aleph company of the 34th battalion of the Israeli army, the backwater reserve unit that I serve in, is plunked down in a previously owned Syrian fortress by the side of the road to Damascus, a mere fifty miles away. The fortress consists of a single barrack, tastelessly furnished with the original rows of Syrian army beds, blankets and mattresses. Next to the barrack is a small shed for cooking and dining purposes. A solid earthen wall surrounds the fortress with niches for weapons of defense. However, due to bad planning by the enemy, the existing niches point in the wrong direction, west toward Israel instead of East toward Syria.

Bet Company of the 35th battalion of the Israeli army has been encamped in the fortress during the previous month and is now going home. For the next sixty days, it will be our unit's responsibility to hold the line against the demoralized Syrian army. That enemy army is parked five or six kilometers away to the Northeast.

We spend the first hours in our new fortress, going through the laborious procedure of signing over weapons and equipment from the 35th battalion to our own unit. Abutbul, the head of 35th battalion's .50 caliber machine gun squad, walks me over to where the weapon is stashed in the north east corner of the fortress wall. He tries to get me to take over ownership of the gun and its equipment without inspection. Of course I refuse and make him unpack all the paraphernalia that comes with this particular piece of military hardware, just in case something is missing. To his further dismay, I insist that he take the machine gun apart, to make sure that it is ready for action. Naturally, I complain about the lack of cleanliness of the barrel but in a magnanimous moment, I offer to clean it myself, especially since he is beginning to get that impatient look. He is probably thinking of getting back to Mazal, his pretty Moroccan wife in Kiryat Shmonah and would have done a bad job of cleaning the barrel anyway. I sign for the damn thing and let him go on his way.

"Enjoy yourself and name it after me," I yell at him as he scurries across the fortress ground and climbs up on one of the departing trucks.

As we poke around our new home, we find, to our amazement, that the fortress has no toilet facilities. The 35th battalion had halfheartedly dug slit trenches outside of the west wall of the fortress and the whole area still reeks from their droppings. We are not surprised, since the 35th is notorious for its bad hygiene, but why hadn't the Syrians, through all their years of service in this fortress, installed toilets?

Various admittedly prejudicial theories are heard among us, about this lack of basic facilities:

"The Syrians are worse than animals. They crap in their own nests."

"The Syrians crap into buckets and ship it all back to Damascus for fertilizer."

"Lacking adequate mine fields, the Syrians do their thing outside of the fortress wall for strategic purposes."

"The Syrians' food is so bad that they don't need to defecate."

My first task for the day is to prepare a better home for the .50 caliber machine gun. Abutbul and his crew, in my estimation, had done a half-ass job. The weapon is too visible from the outside and doesn't have enough protection around it. Several hours of work and many sandbags later, my crew and I stand back and admire the elegant, well-camouflaged gun emplacement we have created. We hardly notice that the sky has turned steel grey and that a cold wind has blown in from the northwest. When I finally do notice the weather change, I quickly pull a tarpaulin over the machine gun, its ammunition boxes and the miscellaneous pieces of equipment that came with the weapon.

Leaving Private Mizrachi, one of my crew, with the machine gun, the rest of us saunter over to the barracks to enjoy a cup of hot coffee. The sky darkens and the temperature drops rapidly. By the time I carry out a cup of coffee to Mizrahi, tiny flakes of snow are falling on the epaulets of our army shirts

"Snow," says Mizrachi, and points up toward the heavens.

"Have you seen it before?" I ask him.

"In Morocco, I used to see it on the mountains. Here, I've seen it on the Hermon, but I've never been where it was falling. What about you?" he asks and sips his steaming coffee.

"In California, where I lived, I could see snow on the mountains, just like you did. Once in a while my family would drive up to the mountains after a snowfall, so that we could play and build a snowman. But I've never been in it when it was falling either. Look, your whole shirt is covered with flakes."

"The snow is beautiful," Mizrachi comments, brushing snowflakes off his army shirt, "but it's going to be dog-cold on guard duty tonight." (Dog-cold is as cold as it can get in the Hebrew language).

"Dog-cold, it will be," I add and realize that none of us have coats. The Israeli quartermaster corps, in its great wisdom, probably has not anticipated what winter would be like on the Golan Heights.

"We can't plan for everything," they would say in their warm bunks down in Israel.

But for once, the supply officers move fast and within a few hours, after a frantic exchange of radio messages with the supply depot, a jeep-load of greatcoats arrives. They are heavy coats with big buttons on them so cold hands can push them through the buttonholes. They smell of mothballs and have been probably stashed somewhere at our supply center for years.

"Where do you think these coats came from?" I ask Gideon, the fortress commander, sitting on his bed in the dim light of the barracks.

"Probably left over from the British Army or the Turks," he answers. He has his stocking feet on the metal bar at the foot of his bed and his head propped up on a blue and yellow flowered pillow that he always brings from his apartment back on the kibbutz.

"And look how generous the Syrians were. They have given us all these wonderful things. The stove over in the corner to keep us warm, these nice wool blankets on our bed, my AK-47 rifle, all this just for fighting a little war with them…and we didn't have to give *them* anything at all."

"How about all that lead we sent them during the war?"

Gideon thinks about that for a few seconds and then retorts. "I guess you're right about that. Don't you think we broke even?"

"I just hope that we don't get our lead back during the time that we have to be in this fortress. Even with a hero like you here in command, I don't feel very safe. How do you think our tanks are going to get up here to support us if the snow blocks the road?"

"Grand strategy as usual, Shimon. I'm surprised you never made it to be a general. How about leaving all that up to the guy with the patch over his eye?" he smirks. "In the meantime, make sure that you have someone sit up all night with that machine gun of yours. It's cold out there so we better change the guard every two hours instead of every four hours. Even that way we're going to freeze our balls off, as you crazy Americans say." Captain Gideon yawns. He'd had a hard day trying to get his new command in order and is now ready for his afternoon nap.

"That's what we crazy Americans say, all right," I humor his stereotype. "What are the chances of getting some long underwear sent up here from your friends down in the supply depot?"

Looking out the barrack window I see that the sky is now the color of an ammunition box and snow is floating down, thickly covering the entire reddish-black dirt courtyard of our lonely fortress on the Golan.

"Freeze our balls off..." murmurs our fortress commander, in English, as he falls asleep on his yellow and blue pillow.

That night, I dream that I am back in San Diego.

It is my birthday and there is a big party going on at my home on Dale Street. I wander from crowded room to crowded room seeing people I haven't seen for many years. Snug and Albert, my friends from Jefferson Elementary School are there, wanting to talk about old times. Albert is wearing his Cub Scout uniform. I pass down a hallway and notice that my Grandmother's bedroom door is open. Grandma isn't here, probably out to one of her Socialist meetings, but the odor of glycerin and rose water is still in the room. So is the map of Israel, still on the wall along with the pins that show where new Jewish settlements have been established. So is the blue and white coin box where we all put our nickels and dimes for the purchase of trees in the Holy Land.

My Aunt Gertrude is sitting out on the porch with her boyfriend talking about the bombing of Pearl Harbor. My dog Swifty's bowl is out on the porch as well. But Swifty is nowhere to be seen. Our old crank-powered phonograph is playing a scratchy version of Blue Skies. I can't find my parents. Maybe they have gone to LA to see Uncle Abe. Then I suddenly remember that I have left my car in downtown San Diego, but where? I look down at myself and realize that I am naked. It starts to rain and the party guests stand by the windows and watch the downpour. I decide to find my raincoat and go out and play in the rain—or do I need to go out to guard duty instead?

Confusion, loss, dislocation, shame. I wake up in a barrack on the Golan Heights. It is still snowing, and it is my turn to guard the machine gun.

A few weeks later we are still knee-deep in snow as more storms swoop in from the north. The Hermon is completely white. Looking over toward the Syrian defense line, only a few basalt boulders break the arctic-looking view. Our long underwear, made in Syria, arrives in a timely fashion and although it is itchy, it serves the purpose.

Life in the fortress has normalized except for a few minor incidents. One incident occurs when a Syrian camel that can't read the posted warnings about minefields, gets himself blown up. Another more serious incident involves our two cooks, one a Moroccan and the other a Rumanian who don't like each other personally or ethnically. They finally have it out in our kitchen shack with butcher knives, frying pans, and the butt of an Uzi. They are rewarded with a trip back down to Israel to the military jail for trying to kill each other.

The good side of the latter incident is that we acquire a great cook: Yehezkiel, our garrison medic and kosher inspector. He is a Yemenite from Moshav Elifelet and treats us daily to *shakshuka*, *schug* and other Yemenite delicacies. He gets three assistants from the recoilless rifle team whose jeeps aren't driveable, given the deep snow cover. They have nothing to do except prepare great food for us.

The Syrians remain quiet and we almost forget that they are in the neighborhood.

I spend my days hanging around the machine gun emplacement and shooting the breeze with my crew or with off-duty soldiers who feel the need for conversation. Every day, one of us cleans the gun and once in a while we add a few more sandbags to improve our defenses. As far as sanitary facilities are concerned, we have discovered that snow banks make excellent toilets.

One Saturday night, our radioman receives a communication from headquarters down in Kuneitra. The Battalion Commander himself will be visiting our fortress tomorrow to perform a garrison inspection. Mere mention of the Battalion Commander puts the fear of *Elohim* into all of us. We work most of the night, scrubbing the floor, shining our shoes, making our beds and cleaning our weapons. We know from bitter past experience, that clean weapons are the most important item in the eyes of this particular Battalion Commander. Being caught, by him, with a dirty rifle is as terrifying as war itself. After a few hours of furtive sleep, we greet the dawn and head outside to pick up any *shmutz* around our fortress. I take my crew over to the .50 caliber machine gun. We carefully disassemble the weapon down to its tiniest parts, clean them all so not a grain of dirt remains inside it or outside of it and cover the weapon with the tarpaulin. Just as we finish the job, the Battalion Commander arrives with his bevy of subordinate officers.

We line up in the snow and shout our names off as the commander scowls and mutters at us. He inspects the barracks and comes out and scowls some more. He orders me and my crew out of line, marches us over to the machine gun emplacement, removes the canvas blanket and looks over the gun with his x-ray eyes. In my dread-filled imagination I fancy the commander crawling down the barrel of the machine gun with a microscope, searching for any molecules of dirt. In reality, he only gives a quick glance at the exquisitely clean gun, replaces the canvas and strides off to ruin someone else's morning. The entire Syrian army, across the way, hears our sighs of relief.

The Battalion Commander heads for the recoilless rifle jeeps behind the barracks. A few minutes pass, and we hear the commander yelling at the top of his voice. We can't quite make out his words but they aren't complimentary for the recoilless rifle crew. Later, we hear that the worst has happened. The jeeps, having been out in the snow for the first time in their mechanical lives, have developed a few rust spots. Just a few, but enough for the commander to threaten to send part of the crew to jail and cancel all leave for the rest of them.

He also points out to Gideon, our garrison commander, that the Israeli Defense Forces do not solve their sanitation problems by crapping in the snow and waiting for the big spring melt. Miraculously, he doesn't sentence the entire fortress garrison to death but advises us that he will send some portable outhouses out tomorrow and if they are not installed quickly, he will turn us over to the torture department of the Mossad. Inspection completed, the Battalion Commander and his boys climb into the jeep. He scowls at his driver and takes off down the road to Kuneitra. Simultaneously, we hear a roll of biblical thunder from the black clouds over Mt. Hermon.

Probably not by coincidence.

II

The next day, as promised, three gigantic outhouses arrive on the back of a semi-trailer. Most of the brave soldiers of our fort, except those on special duty, are digging deep holes, down through the snow, deep down into the reddish and stony earth of the Golan Heights. As for me, it is my good fortune to be snuggled up against the .50 caliber machine gun, just in case another war breaks out while we are installing our outhouses. The entire digging process takes several hours and the diggers find that they have no need for their greatcoats despite the cold weather. Now that the holes are at the proper depth, the truck drivers back their precious cargo of giant privies over the pits that will be the solution to our sanitation problems.

In the meantime, I have been amusing myself by watching the Syrian fortifications to the east of us through a set of binoculars. I spot a couple of Syrian officers staring through their own binoculars at all the commotion produced by our outhouse operation.

Perhaps they are impressed with the functional beauty of our Israeli built super-crappers. With their shiny silver paint and massive construction, they are certainly superior to anything the Syrians could make—if the Syrians were at all interested in sanitary facilities. Who could imagine that national pride could be instilled through anything as prosaic as an outhouse?

Carried away by my patriotism and my curiosity to see how these massive structures are going to be unloaded from the truck beds, I shout to Private Mizrachi to kindly take my place in the machine gun nest. Mizrachi complies and I walk over to the snow-bank to view the next step in this great architectural accomplishment.

I squat on a snow-free basalt rock next to Yohanan Vilenski, a member of Kibbutz Gadot and part of the recoilless rifle crew that had somehow survived yesterday's castigation. He is busy cleaning his rifle and getting ready to oil the barrel with a square piece of flannel patch, a pull through cord, and an open can of rifle oil.

Bullets suddenly whiz by me like swift deadly birds in the air. Motions freeze. Mouths open without sound. Then, the soldiers of Aleph Company hit the dirt, just as they learned in boot camp. More lead birds whistle over us and swish into the snow. Motion resumes and we are up and running for our defense positions along the fortress wall. I head for the machine gun position. Yohanan is running in front of me with the can of rifle oil still in his hand. The oil spills over the edge of the can and I cartwheel onto the snow with a ripping noise and a sharp pain somewhere south of my knee. On my back, I see several more soldiers down on the snow, all victims of Yohanan's spilled rifle oil. More bullets fly by. I can't move my leg. I watch the still running soldiers squirming into their positions along the fortress wall. I hear the familiar bark of the .50 caliber machine gun. My machine-gun, without me! Private Mizrachi is returning fire. I hear the radioman inside the barrack shouting code numbers to Battalion headquarters. Everyone is in place except for us downed soldiers and we are flat on our front or backsides depending on how we fell. The firing has stopped, for no particular reason, and our Yemenite chef and kosher inspector, Yehezkiel, appears, now resorting to his role as medic.

"Looks like your leg might be broken," he proclaims in his wonderful Yemenite accent. "No wounds. Crazy American, slipping on rifle oil!"

"Your mother," I curse, as he diddles with my broken leg.

"Your mother's midwife," he answers politely, before he moves on to the next casualty.

The Syrians start up again. The bullets are hot but the snow I am stretched out on is dog cold. The sky has turned ugly again and another snowfall is in the cards. No sense in trying to move the wounded. Yehezkiel reappears out of the barrack bravely crawling past the flying bullets. He has four bottles of a light brown liquid clasped in his arms. He sits down next to me and hands me a bottle.

"What's this, holy water?" I scowl.

"Cognac, stupid!" he says impatiently, and leaves me to suffer in the snow with my bottle.

I look at the label. "Medicinal cognac, *kosher for Pesach*," it says.

"Well, what do you want for nothing?" I say to myself, "Courvoisier?" I unscrew the cap and begin nursing my bottle. My leg hurts less after every swig.

III

The Outhouse House War is over after about an hour. The United Nations troops down the road from us have managed to establish radio contact between the two sides and all of us Semitic cousins agree to hold off shooting at each other before any real damage is done. It turns out that our Syrian neighbors opened fire only because they thought that we were installing nuclear missals instead of outhouses. In spite of these glad tidings, my leg is still broken and needs medical attention. The other four soldiers have less serious sprains and bruises, and get to stay at the fortress to be tended by corpsman Yehezkiel. All five of us are in great spirits, especially since we are deep under the influence of the kosher medicinal cognac.

An ambulance arrives to take me down to the former Syrian military hospital in Kuneitra. I don't mind the ride at all since I am busy singing a selection of bawdy ballads in English and Hebrew at the top of my lungs.

"*Uncle Bud, Uncle Bud, Uncle Bud, Bud, Bud.
One foot on the floor and one foot on the table,
Her xxxxx stretched out from her xxx to her xxxx,*" I serenade the driver, pounding the rhythm onto the dashboard with the flat of my hand.

He smiles even though he is Kurdish and doesn't know a word of English. I give him *"Moonlight Bay," "Hatikvah,"* and the *"California Drinking Song,"* until we arrive at the hospital. An Israeli nurse unpacks me from the ambulance into a wheel chair and rolls me down a corridor. She seems to be enjoying my singing, although for some reason, she slaps me on the hand. Later, she tells me that I pinched her in a sensitive spot. Still full of good cheer, I am lifted up and gently deposited in a bed. An army physician comes in to have a look at my leg. He asks me for my army ID number and I shout it out to him, along with my American Social Security number and my locker combination from Roosevelt Junior High School. I hear one of the nurses explaining to the doctor that I have arrived inebriated from the battlefield.

"Send him down to the hospital in Safed," I hear the doctor order. "He has a broken leg and a big mouth. By the time he gets down there he'll be sober enough for an X-ray and treatment. I'm not running an alcohol rehabilitation ward here."

Back to the ambulance we go. I'm lifted into the front seat and find that a Georgian driver, who seems to be having a hard time getting the vehicle into first gear, has replaced the Kurd. *"Yop Tfi Yu Mat,"* he curses and grinds the gears.

"Does your mother know that you say things like that about her?" I ask him with false innocence.

Finally he gets the ambulance into gear and lurches onto the road leading out of occupied Syria, heading for the State of Israel. The cognac begins to wear off. I offer Sergei or whatever the hell his name is, a Daphne cigarette. He mutters the word "kibbutznik" as if it is an obscenity and pulls out a pack of his own city brand weeds. He lights up. The road down the Heights is narrow and bumpy and my leg starts hurting again. The driver can barely see where he is going since night has come and a blackout is in effect. The headlights are masked with blue paint. I slip into a nice sleep interrupted only by the rumble of the ambulance as it crosses the wooden boards of the Bailey bridge over the River Jordan.

I dream again.

I am living the United States but visiting the kibbutz. Everyone is happy to see me. I bump into Ron and Yitzhak in front of the dining hall. "Where to?" they ask.

"Just looking around to see what's new?" I reply.

"Hey, come with us, we're going to Kiryat Shmonah for a 34th Battalion reunion."

"I don't have too much time before I have to catch my plane to America."

"Oh come on," they insist. "We won't be there very long. All the guys are going to be there, Gideon, Vilenski, Yehezkiel...They'll want to see you. Come along for old times sake."

We take the Egged bus to Kiryat Shmonah and the whole gang is there to greet us. I notice that everyone is getting into uniform, just for old time's sake, of course.

"*Shimon,*" says Vilenski, "*don't be such an American. Put one of these uniforms on, too. Just like in the old days.*"

"*Why not.*" *I put on the uniform. It fits just right, for once.*

Then we all get up on a bus and head for the picnic area near Kibbutz HaGoshrim. Getting off the bus, I notice that each one of us is being handed a weapon. I'm get an Uzi and I feel much relieved that I don't have to mess with the .50 caliber machine gun and all its paraphernalia. Gideon, who is now a general, orders us forward into some trenches that have been dug. To my horror, I realize that this is all for real and that we are about to go to war with the Syrians again. I don't want to be here. I don't belong here. My home is back in America. The Syrians are coming and we're all going to be killed. I don't belong here. I don't want to be in this damn outhouse war.

I wake up on the crisp sheets of a hospital bed. It is morning. Just to check on my whereabouts and to separate my dream from reality, I sit up and look out a nearby window. I see two bearded *Chasids* in black fedoras and black coats smoking their cigarettes on a bench. The sky is a crisp blue, a color that only appears at heavenly elevations. I spot an old British Taggert fort on a nearby hill. I see the old Turkish maternity hospital where my twin boys were born on separate days. Yes, I'm in Safed. The ancient home of the Kabbalah, and a good place to get a schnitzel and french-fries. Yes, I'm hungry. But first, I need to get out of the hospital.

A few hours later a trio of doctors arrive in their lab coats to survey the damage to my leg.

"Your leg will be good," says one of them in ungrammatical Hebrew and an American accent that sets my teeth on edge.

"Where are you from?" I ask in my best English, already detecting the answer to my question.

"Brooklyn," says the white coat. "And you?"

"San Diego. How long will it take you guys to get me out of here, back to my unit?" I say, for some reason wanting to play the role of a man of valor for this American doctor.

"We'll get a cast on it today but we're sending you home. You're going to be laid up for six or seven weeks and you won't be able to move around very much. Waste of time to send you back to Syria. We've already called your kibbutz and they're sending someone to pick you up this afternoon. You can be a hero in bed at home."

In the early afternoon, Chaim, the kibbutz driver, picks up the plaster cast and me. He tenderly hoists me into the shoe factory van.

"How come that idiot spilled rifle oil on the snow? I heard that four other soldiers were hurt at the same time. Thank God you only had a simple fracture, you can get back to work in time for pruning season."

"How do you know all this, Chaim? It just happened yesterday."

"You know how fast news travels around the Galilee, Shimon. Everyone knows everything before it happens. For instance," Chaim continues, "I know that you want to eat a schnitzel plate at Kaufmanns's restaurant in Safed, before we go back to the kibbutz."

"Bulls eye," I say.

"I know you, Shimon," winks Chaim.

IV

Chaim returns me to Cfar Moshe, gently helping me climb out of the car. He carries me to the apartment and gently places me in bed. An hour or so later, Marta, the head kibbutz nurse visits me and warns me to stay in a prone position until otherwise notified.

A few days later she visits me again.

"You are a terrible patient," scolds Marta,

"Why?" I say in fake wonder, looking up at her stern face from my bed.

"You were told to stay in bed. Don't you want your broken leg to heal?"

"I did stay in bed." I lied.

"Then what were you doing on your crutches at the packinghouse. You know that there are no secrets in the kibbutz. We find out about such things."

"OK," I confess, "I was just drinking a cup of coffee with the packinghouse crew and sorting a few apples. I'll go crazy if I just have to stay in bed and not work. The vineyard-pruning season is starting up in a few days. What am I going to do?"

"Stay in bed. You're useless to the kibbutz for the time being. Get better and then prune the vineyard."

"O.K., O.K., *B'Seder...*"

Marta leaves. I wait a few moments and go on with my disobedient plan.

After making sure that the nurse is not hanging around outside to see if I am a compliant patient, I pull my crutches out from under the bed and head for the shoe factory. Fortune is with me, and even though it rained yesterday, the path is dry all the way to the industrial wing of the kibbutz. I enter the shoe factory the back way so that I will not tip off Marta's spies working on the assembly line. I slither into Gad's office without being seen. Gad is seated behind on old scratched up desk, picking his nose with one hand and sifting away at an enormous clutter of papers, invoices, bills, and memos, with the other.

"What the hell are you doing here?" he growls in his very foul English. He had spent his early childhood in Nigeria, thus his spicy English. His Sephardic-Jewish parents were killed in a car crash, and one of our kibbutz members, who was the ambassador to Nigeria, shipped Gad off to be raised by the kibbutz.

"Just came to watch your nose picking," I reply.

"You're supposed to be in bed," he scolded. "Incidentally, couldn't you find a better way to get out of reserve duty than breaking your leg? Why didn't you get gonorrhea or something, at least you could have gone back to your work in the vineyard?"

"That's what I came to talk to you about."

"Gonorrhea?" he smiled.

"No, going back to work in the vineyard."

The foreplay now over with, I lay out my plan to Gad.

"I want you to make me a special water-proof boot that I can pull over the plaster cast on my leg. Then I can get out to the vineyard in time for pruning. I can't expect Yankele and Saadia to do the job by themselves and the rest of the crew is away in the army. If we don't finish the pruning in time, the vineyard will be a mess."

"Now I know for sure that you're an idiot, Shimon. It's too wet out there. You'll just break your leg again and cost the kibbutz more money."

"Do it," I insist, "or I'll tell your wife everything I know about your sadistic behavior in boot camp."

"OK, you crazy American. I'll make the boot for you, but don't expect me to visit you in the hospital. Go to hell." Gad blesses me and I salute him, giving him the finger at the same time.

Two days later, Gad shows up at my apartment, with the boot. We exchange insults and I slip a thank you in and then another insult. I hide the boot in the closet.

The next day is Shabbat and I enjoy Israel's single day of rest with my family. My kids play outside with their gang of future kibbutz members and my wife and I read through the thick, meaty Friday newspaper and listen to our favorite radio programs: the weekly news review, the bible quiz, and the Israeli Philharmonic concert. Marta drops by, supposedly to visit but actually to make sure that I was dutifully in bed.

Sunday it rains again, but I am determined to go to work. I wait for the rain to stop, pull the boot up over my cast, grab the crutches and head out for the vineyard. I hitch a jeep ride with Chaim, who is taking lunch out to the orchard workers. When I get off at the vineyard. Yankele and Saadia look up from their pruning work and together slap their foreheads in dismay.

"What the hell are you doing out here?" they say in unison.

I clump over to them and gripe, "Just making sure that you aren't ruining the vineyard."

Yankele says, "Wait till the nurses find out about this."

"Sure, call the police. Call the fire department. Call the nurses. But I'm here anyway," I say with much bravado.

"We should really call the *Beit Meshugaim* (the nut house)," says Yankele in his singsong Argentinean accent.

"Maybe we ought to talk about this over a cup of coffee," I say.

"OK," says Yankele, "we just happen to have some brewing in the tool shack."

I cautiously follow them on the muddy track to the corrugated iron tool shed. My boot is getting muddy but the cast seems to be dry inside. This system may work after all. Just before we reach the door to the shed we hear a familiar Galilee noise far in the distance. It is the war starting up again deep into the Golan, part of the strange war of attrition that breaks out for no particular reason and stops for other unknown reasons.

Boom Boom...(muffled and far away).

A hollow thud follows as mortar shells seek their targets in the distance. We are ten or twelve miles away by the sound of the explosions, and given the informal limitations of this war, we, down in the valley, are not at immediate risk.

Silence,

Boom Boom Boom (closer but still muffled).

"There goes the concert again," says Yankele. "I hope they get this war over before I get called up."

We sit around the table in the dimly lit tool shed. The coffee heats on the little Primus stove and Yankele produces plastic coffee cups from a paper bag.

Boom Boom (a little closer).

"Looks like the pruning is moving along without me," I say. "I should be O.K. in a week or so, and I don't think you two will ruin the vineyard. But I will need to go to the nut house if I stay in bed. I'll hang around here anyway. Maybe I can stick labels on the grape boxes or something."

"Maybe, if you don't fall down on your ass and break your leg again," advises Saadia.

Boom Boom Boom (further away again).

After coffee, I step outside the tool shed with my two comrades. I accompany them to a row of dormant vines. The view from the vineyard is spectacular. The air is crisp. I am out of bed and ready to be productive again.

Boom Boom (far away).

I think about how Yehezkiel, Mizrahi, Gideon, Valenski and the others from the 34th Battalion. How are they doing in the bombardment? Maybe the Syrians are trying their weapons out on one of the other forts. If I weren't an unbeliever, I would pray for them. Maybe I'll do it anyway...nah.

V

With all this dramatic and heroic bravado, I step, cast-foot first, into a mud puddle. Down I go into the muck. I don't hear the snap, but, from the sharp pain, I know I've broken my leg again.

Boom, (Rumble, barely audible).

VI

This time, Marta shows up at my apartment with Ron, the work coordinator. His major role in the kibbutz is to place members and volunteers who are between jobs into new work slots. Over the years, most of us graduate into more or less permanent occupations but there are always those that for various reasons can be plugged into wherever they are needed. Ron's job is inevitably stressful in this great Social Democratic experiment, because work is the religion of the kibbutz, and because placement is almost always fraught with arguments, deals, politics and heartburn.

Ron, Marta and I begin our debate.

Marta, frowning severely: "I told you so."

Ron: "You're completely out of your mind."

Shimon: "O.K., O.K., I was just trying to do a little work. That's what I'm here for, right? *Avodah, Zot Hayainu* (work is our life), isn't that what Tolstoy said? Or maybe it was A.D. Gordon"

Ron: "Tolstoy and Gordon are both dead."

Marta: "Ron, find this maniac some work. I know him. He's stubborn and stupid. Don't pay any attention to what he says. He won't stay in bed. Give him something to do! Maybe he can change diapers in the baby house"

Shimon: "Yeah, give him something to do. But no diapers."

Ron: "Yeah, give him something to do, something for the crazy American. I'll think about it."

The next day, Ron pulls up in a kibbutz jeep.

"Are you ready?" he shouts.

"For what?" I say.

"I have a job for you. Put your magic boot on and let's go."

I put the boot on and gimp my way over to the jeep. Ron heads out to the main road at a furious speed, makes a right, crosses the bridge over the Jordan and then turns north.

"Where to?" I ask.

"Cfar Baruch," Ron replies.

"I don't work with cows," I remind him, referring to Cfar Baruch's main business.

"No cows—kids"

"Kids?"

"What kids?"

"High School kids."

We pass through the gate of the regional kibbutz high school, newly built by the side of the Jordan River. Ron helps me out of the jeep and into the office of Jacob Perkal, the principal of the high school.

"Blessed be your coming," says Perkal. "You're taking Rina's job as teacher of the slow English class."

"But I'm not a teacher," I protest. "I'm a vineyard operator."

"These children are your new vineyard," announces Jacob and, shoving a stack of books and papers toward me, he turns to other priorities.

1968-73: To School and Back

I

A year passes by. I survive the school year in Cfar Baruch. The slow class kids like my low-keyed style and some of them even learn to speak some English.

On the last day of the school semester, Perkal, the Principal of the Valley Regional High school in Cfar Baruch, is enjoying his late afternoon cigar. Cigars are not included in the modest kibbutz budget but he has a good connection with a certain tobacco merchant in Providence, Rhode Island. Even a kibbutznik needs a little luxury. Perkal looks out the window of his office and sees Mt. Hermon and the Golan Heights, now safely within the borders of Israel. He takes a long draw on the cigar and thinks about the upcoming pleasures awaiting him during the coming three-month summer vacation. He will go to concerts in Tel Aviv, visit relatives in Jerusalem, and perhaps even take a trip to the Island of Cyprus to get a little breather from this beloved, but intense little country. Towards the end of the summer, he may do some curriculum writing and organizational work, but not now.

"Cyprus, good idea. Maybe in August, when it gets so damn hot in this valley."

He blows a smoke ring—an art learned in his Rhode Island youth. A knock on the office door disturbs his daydream.

"Who's there?"

"Shimon, from Cfar Moshe," I answer, "I've come for my cigar."

"Come in Shimon, but I warn you, I'm just finishing the last one. You'll have to wait for the next shipment."

I laugh as I enter Perkal's den. He knows I would never deign to puff on a rum-soaked cigar.

We have a nice relationship, Perkal and I, both of us being crazy Americans who gave up a life of plenty for the simple joys of kibbutz life.

"So you want to go back to school? Yes, I think it's a good idea, especially since you've shown such promise in your first semester here. How did it go with the special education class? Did they learn any English from you?"

"Maybe a little. I think I have a long way to go before I can give myself an "A".

"Well, after all, as I remember, you were kidnapped by Cfar Moshe's work coordinator. They brought you over here in a cast without any teaching background and I tossed you into the lion's den with the slow learners. I guess you're doing pretty well. I heard one of your students say a whole English phrase during recess a few weeks back. 'Kiss my ass,' I believe it was. You must be doing something right."

"Seriously, Perkal," I say, getting down to brass tacks, "I don't really know a thing about teaching although I winged it this year. I want the school to send me to the Kibbutz Teacher's Seminary in Tel Aviv next semester and I need your recommendation."

"You've got it, Shimon. Sure we'll miss you around here until you finish your coursework. I'll type the recommendation out for you in a few days. Yes, we have to invest in our teachers. You may have one of my kids in your classroom some day. I'll type it out soon."

"Just do it before you go on your vacation to Cyprus," I added gruffly.

There are no secrets in this valley.

II

For the summer, I rejoin my kibbutz's vineyard crew and spend the time tying up the long light-green shoots springing out of last year's buds with raffia. We haul irrigation pipes, murder the rats living in the bamboo windbreaks, and talk philosophy. The veterans of previous years, Yankele, Massaud, Doron and Saadia are all here but Astrid, the Norwegian girl has departed for Oslo. Now we have Ingrid, from Bergen, as her replacement. Ingrid is not quite as beautiful as Astrid but makes up for her deficiency by working twice as hard as any of us kibbutzniks. God Save Norway!

Toward the middle of August, I complete my registration at the Kibbutz Teacher's Seminar and prepare to leave Cfar Moshe for the secular and sinful city of Tel Aviv. Thus far in my life, my higher education experience has been limited to "Beer Drinking 1A" at UCLA, "Socialist Politics and Sorority Girl Chasing 1B" at Berkeley and a few courses in pesticide application at the Agricultural Institute near the fly-infested town of Hadera. At age thirty-two, I am finally ready for some serious academic work. Of course I will miss Ruthie and the kids, but thanks to the miniscule size of our nation, I will be home every weekend. I look forward to a new professional start in life.

However, a week before my studies are to begin I receive a little pink slip in my mailbox. The Israeli military machine needs my military skills for a period of not less than 42 days, beginning the first of September. I try to get past this obstacle by visiting our company headquarters in Rosh Pina and pleading for a delay, but the Lieutenant on duty denies my request.

"Don't you know that there's a war on?" he inquires.

"There's always a war on," I grumble.

So, it's off to the Golan Heights again to refresh myself in the cool breezes and bleak basalt vistas of the front line. Back to dirty socks, lousy food, night guard duty, machine gun cleaning, and unexpected visits and humiliation by the brass. By the time that we are dumped back in the State of Israel, it is too late to start my studies at the Kibbutz Teacher's Seminar. Maybe next year.

I do my best for another year teaching at the Regional High School without any pedagogic training and somehow the students and I survive. The following summer I'm back in the vineyard. Doron has finished his degree in marketing, Yankele's wife is pregnant, my kids are flourishing, Massaud has a pair of twins, Saadia is the Gabai (Sexton) of the Tunisian synagogue, and Astrid is back from Oslo. To complete the yearly cycle, I get a pink slip again for army duty beginning on the first day of September, the same day that I am supposed to begin my studies in the seminary. This time, I'm really pissed. I find my way up the chain of command to the Battalion Commander's office in Safed.

It is a clear day in Safed and my hopes are high. How can they be so merciless to do this to me twice in a row? The battalion commander's office is in a small grove of pine trees in part of the old British police station, still pockmarked with bullet holes from the 1948 War of Independence. A *Chayelet* (a girl soldier) is sitting at a desk doing her nails.

"Private Chamiel, 760909," I introduce myself. "I have an appointment with the Battalion commander."

Unimpressed, she waves me toward the half-opened door in the back of the room where I see the big guy's feet protruding out from under a vintage desk.

"What can I do for you, Private Chamiel?" he asks in a flinty manner.

"Haven't I been a good soldier for you for the last seven years?" I say to the major, a kibbutznik from south of Rosh Pina along the Jordanian border. I want to get right to the point.

"You have been a good soldier," he replies. "At least you've never been in the stockade, according to our records."

"Didn't I willingly report for duty last September, even though it meant putting off my studies at Kibbutz Teachers Seminary?"

"Yes," he stated pleasantly, thumbing through my fat military record on his desk.

"And did I try to pull any strings with a certain general that lives on our kibbutz, to get excused from duty?" (At least now he knows that I have some strings to pull).

"What is it that you want?"

"Last year I got a pink slip just before I was supposed to start my studies. This year, I want to you to do without me for a few months so that I can get going on my course work. You can take me in January or February. I'll figure out how to keep up with my readings and tests while I'm mobilized."

As an afterthought, feeling very brave I add: "Better yet, why don't you just do without me for the year? I'm sure the army will survive."

"Can't do it, Shimon," he smiles and then frowns. "I've had some of the same problems you are having. Here I am, supposed to be the manager of my kibbutz's garage and they take me away four months of every year, much more than your six weeks. The Battalion is short on manpower and it looks like we may be sitting on the Golan for the next hundred years until the Syrians decide to make peace with us. There was a guy in here yesterday, a private farmer from *Mishmar HaYarden* who wanted to stay home to finish his apple harvest. His wife is crippled and his kids are too young to do the harvest on their own. You know what I had to do. I had to turn him down. You want me to let you go? How can I excuse you if I can't excuse the farmer from *Mishmar HaYarden?*"

"OK, I get the point, but how am I ever going to be a good teacher for my students if you keep calling me up? Can you guarantee that this won't happen next year again?"

"No, can you guarantee me that there won't be a war next year? Can you guarantee that the Syrians won't try a surprise attack?"

I felt a knot in my throat, a thick bud of anger, frustration and sorrow. No, I can't cry in front of the Battalion commander, and I certainly can't punch him out. But I feel like doing both.

"Tell you what," softens the commander, obviously noticing my knot. "Look, there is a way out of this for the both of us. This may seem crazy to you but it's true. If you can get your kibbutz to send you abroad to study, then I would have to let you go. Do you know anyone in the exile, outside of Israel, that might sponsor you?"

A picture of my parents back in San Diego flashes before my eyes.

Why not?

III

Three years later, our family returns from San Diego to Cfar Moshe. Ruthie and I move into a new apartment on the East Side of the kibbutz. The children now are fluent speakers of English, and I have a Master's Degree in Health Education from San Diego State University. Galila, Golan and Hermon are back in their children's houses as if they never left. Ruthie, on the other hand, would have preferred staying in the USA.

In the meantime, a new and spacious dining hall proudly fills the empty space in the middle of the broad green lawn between the Kibbutz Office and the first line of wooden cabins. Lots of babies have been born and three more groups of 18-year-olds have entered army service. I haven't missed any big wars but there have been plenty of small border incidents to take their place. As in the past, it is still a rare night without the sound of small arms fire somewhere just beyond the Golan Heights or up on the Hills of Naftali.

"What else is new?" I ask my kibbutz father, Yigal.

"Well, you know that your vineyard has been torn up. After you left, Yankele decided that he wanted to go to school too and be a professor just like you. There was no one to take his place and the price of grapes was way down anyway. Sharik decided that he would grow alfalfa out there instead."

The vineyard gone! The death of an old friend.

"What else?"

Yigal went on, "We are now in the plastic-making business. You probably noticed the big building over by the turkey sheds. Go in there sometime and you'll see a lot of your friends standing by the assembly line making big grain bags of out polyethylene. They tried to get me to work in there, too, but I can't stand working inside. I'll stick to poisoning rodents."

"Sounds pretty toxic to me," I say.

"You think so?"

"I'll check it out."

"What is this health education thing that you're going to be teaching in the high school?"

"Oh, it's a combination of things: nutrition, ecology, sex education, drug education, hygiene, traffic safety and I'm especially interested in the pesticide spraying problem."

"How did you get into that? I thought you were going to be an English teacher."

"I changed my major study during the first semester of my work at San Diego State. One of my teachers told me that there were probably enough English teachers in Israel already. Then she talked me into becoming a Health Educator."

"You better watch out on the pesticide issue," warns Yigal. "Now that Avraham is the new boss of the orchard, I tried to talk to him about using some natural methods for getting rid of pests but all he could do is scream at me. He thinks that if we cut down on our spraying we're going to lose a lot of our crop. You should see how he turns red in the face if you even try to talk to him about it. Just now he's come back from a marketing course down at the Agricultural Institute. Making a profit is the new bottom line."

"OK, I don't want to start a revolution right off the bat, especially with Avraham and his temper. I'll just pick apples quietly until school opens. But eventually we've got to do something about this problem. We've been ignoring the effects of these poisons for years. Next thing you know, there'll be a lot of cancer patients in the kibbutz."

"Where are you going to work, Shimon?"

"I'm like you, Yigal, I didn't come here to work on a factory assembly line. I have a month before school starts over in Cfar Baruch. They want me to teach Health Education there and I'm real excited by the idea. I guess I'll work in the orchard until then. How's politics?"

"Very bad, as usual" sighs Yigal. "The Labor Party still has a majority in the Knesset, but our United Worker's Party has lost a lot of ground. Instead of trying to make peace with the Arabs after our victory in the Six-Day War, our leaders are busy fortifying the Suez Canal and appropriating land on the West Bank. I think there's going to be another war."

"That's a grim thought."

The next morning at six o'clock I show up at the orchard committee shed in full apple-picking uniform. I learn that that I'll be assigned to supervise the Arab villagers picking Golden Delicious over in *Gimmel* orchard. But first I have a cup of coffee with some of my old buddies.

Ziggi has continued his traditional task of brewing coffee so that we can get the morning started with a buzz. He still sports a full mustache but I see streaks of gray in it just like on an old dog's snout. We joke around while the tractor motors warm up. There is still some lingering early morning fog drifting over the mountains and the last thin traces of chill seep out of the nearby orchards. In another hour we will have discarded our khaki jackets to begin our long day wrestling with the heat.

"Hey, Professor Shimon!" scoffs Ziggi, as he pours me a cup of caffeine out of a battered kettle, "I'm surprised that you're here. Are you going to teach us philosophy while we pick our apples?"

"No, I'm just here to tell you that your coffee tastes like ink."

"Oh ho, my American friend," Ziggi salutes me, "now you have more refined tastes. Would you like an espresso?"

"Would you like a coffee enema?" I retort.

"Not from you, but maybe from your wife," he snickers.

"And how's your wife?" I say, implying a whole host of ribald images.

Avraham, the new boss of the orchard crew, arrives on his bicycle. He looks grouchy with his new responsibilities as the leader of the orchard workers. For some reason, even in the heat of the summer, he wears an old knitted stocking hat all the time. Must be getting bald.

"Professor Shimon, looking for work are you?"

"No, I've heard that you can do it all yourself now that you've been to Agricultural School. I'm only here to study the Sociology of Arab Farm Workers."

As soon as I say it, I regret this snide remark referring to the controversial new practice of hiring outside labor, at minimum wages, to do the dirty work in the orchard.

"Easy to say," Avraham retorts with a smile.

I don't have to strain my imagination to understand the implied message that hovers over me like a secret fart. Avraham is referring to my three years of absence over in the California fleshpots.

I swallow hard and remember my vows about not making a revolution.

"O.K., Avraham," I say apologetically, "just tell me what you need me to do. I'm your slave until school starts up next month."

Coffee ritual completed, I head out on my bike to *Gimmel* where the Arab workers and their foreman are already busy at work. The workers are Arab-Israelis from a village in the hills of the central Galilee. Most of them are kids earning a few *liras* before school starts.

I'm elated at the chance to get back to some physical labor. Ahmad, the Arab foreman, seems to be well in control of supervising his village boys and girls and I decide to just do some picking. I put on a picking harness, fastening the shoulder strap and open up the cloth waist bag. I poke my ladder into a tree and ascend to the top step to begin pulling off the yellowish green Golden Delicious apples.

I love standing on the highest step of the ladder, picking the most unreachable apples, and enjoying the warm rays of the Galilee sun on my head. The apples grow heavier in my picking bag. I need this physical work after sitting so many hours in classrooms, taking tests, writing papers, reading textbooks, and studying in libraries remote from the sun and the sweet smell of ripening apples in the Galilee. There will be plenty of time to be a professor when the school year starts.

Suddenly, I hear the buzz of a small airplane flying low over the orchard. I feel little droplets of a sweet smelling liquid on my nose and hands. Spots appear on the lenses of my sunglasses. A spray plane banks over the rows of Golden Delicious, gains altitude, circles over Cfar Baruch—our neighboring kibbutz—then makes another pass over *Gimmel* Orchard. Again, a familiar sweet smell and its accompanying droplets drift down upon the Arab workers and me. I know that smell.

"Malathion."

Five minutes later I march into the orchard committee shed, right into Avraham's face. Avraham is sitting at his scarred desk doodling market strategies on a wrinkled piece of graph paper.

"What happened?" he asks, looking at my scowling countenance.

"What was that plane spraying out in *Gimmel* Orchard?"

Avraham, taken by surprise, holds his answers, as the wheels in his thick head spin out evasive strategies.

"Moth bait," he answers.

"Moth bait?"

"Yeah, it's a new thing that we started doing a few years ago. You must have been in America when we started it. So what?"

"Please cut the bullshit, it was Malathion wasn't it?"

"So it was," says Avraham. "We're doing so much spraying by air now that I can't keep track of it all. It beats sitting on a spraying machine all night long like you used to do, right Shimon? Don't worry about the workers, that little amount of Malathion is harmless. Would you rather have the fruit flies eat up the orchard?"

"You know Avraham, maybe you're right. A little Malathion won't hurt us apple pickers. I always wondered why our government has a law against spraying pesticides on people. (Avraham winces). Oh, I'm not angry with that. What's a little Malathion among friends? But the thing is, I'm just a little upset that you didn't ask my permission to get sprayed. Of course, it doesn't matter that all the Arab boys and girls got sprayed too. But they don't count."

Avraham loses his cool. "Welcome back from America, Shimon. Are you trying to make a revolution already? Maybe you should do a little work like the rest of us instead of being a professor of Malathion. Maybe the orchard isn't quite ready for your advice. Maybe we're just a bunch of primitive people trying to make our living from growing apples."

"Don't be angry, I just don't like being sprayed without my permission. Maybe I'm selfish. Maybe I'm spoiled. Let's just say that I like to be kissed before I'm fucked."

Avraham swallows hard and walks out on me, shrugging his hands as if he had just been talking to raving maniac.

"You spray the workers once more and I'll have the Ministry of Health up here you bastard," I yell at his fat, retreating behind.

I believe that I have won this round. But in the intense world of kibbutz human relations I've made myself an enemy. Sooner or later he'll pay me back the compliment.

1973: Yom Kippur

"So Shimon, how does it feel to be back in Cfar Moshe?" asks Yitzhak as we sit on the grassy mound overlooking the swimming pool. "Are you a capitalist now?"

"Of course," I humor him, "I spent three years in the USA learning how to invest in the Stock Market just so I could buy up the kibbutz and evict all of you Socialist maniacs. Soon, I'll have this Olympic-size swimming pool all to myself."

"And what's this I hear about you getting a degree in Sex Education? Any tips for me and my wife?"

"I hear that you and your wife have made two babies since I've been gone and you're asking me for advice? How many more Argentineans do we need around here? Besides, my degree is in Health Education."

"How is that going to grow more apples in the orchard?" Yitzhak taunts.

"You're the orchard man now," I point out. "While Avraham makes you sweat out there, I'll be teaching over at the air-conditioned high school educating your kids to stay away from the pesticides that he's been spraying on the fruit."

We both chuckle and clap each other on the arm. I've missed this old bantering. Three years is a long time to be away from friends.

We watch one of the older grannies in the kibbutz sidestroke down the pool, a real tough old Hungarian bird. The kids call her "Grandma Crab" because the sidestroke is her forte. I have missed her, too, and all the rest of other strange characters who populate Cfar Moshe. People behave in strange ways when they are all equal to each other.

Giora Leahman is the only other swimmer in the pool right now. He is a famous general here in the Galilee and he commands a reserve-armored division. Giora swims with a powerful crawl stroke.

October is a good month for the kibbutz. The apple and pear harvests are over, and only the grape harvest remains—but I don't work with grapes anymore. *Rosh HaShanah*, the New Year has passed, but we freethinking Democratic-Socialists mark the occasion by having a big picnic. After all, we are not seeking repentance, at least of the religious kind. In fact, this very day is *Yom Kippur* and while most of the Jewish people around the world are in synagogues beating their breasts in fear of heavenly wrath, we, kibbutzniks are lolling in the sun next to our swimming pool. Sweet secular mischief!

Yitzhak and I lie back on the lush grass and watch a helicopter, high above us glinting in the flawless blue sky, circling like a metallic gnat. Maybe the pilots are watching old Grandma Crab do her sidestroke or maybe they are having a peek at the Syrian army over on the far ranges of the Lebanese Mountains. "Ah yes, here it comes," I yawn to myself, "I'm about to slip into nap mode on this sunny Galilee late morning."

"Shimon, the helicopter is landing. Looks like he may come down in the alfalfa field," says Yitzhak.

End of my nap.

I sit up and sure enough the helicopter has touched down in Cfar Moshe. A few minutes later two military officers run to the side of the pool and motion General Giora to come out of the water. He stands with them, dripping wet, across the pool from us, and a quiet but obviously serious little conference takes place. Giora collects his towel and the three men disappear in the direction of the helicopter. Obviously something is up. Instinctively smelling trouble, most of the other people at the swimming pool pick their towels up and head to their apartments. As I leave through the gate of the pool complex I see that Grandma Crab, unintimidated, is continuing her sideways strokes.

Ruthie is standing on the porch of our new upstairs apartment on the East Side of the living area. She smells trouble, too.

"What's going on?" she asks as I make my way up the stairs.

"Don't know, let's turn on the radio."

We turn on *Kol Yisrael* (the voice of Israel) and hear Beethoven's "Eroica Symphony" instead of the usual Saturday morning quiz show. Now we know that something serious is happening.

Next, the children come home, unexpectedly, from their play areas around the kibbutz.

"What's going on?" I ask Galila, as she comes up the stairs.

"Don't know, our teachers told us to go right to our parents' house. I saw Avraham and Yankele opening up the shelter doors."

Golan and Hermon appear. They had been down at the soccer field watching Cfar Moshe playing the Rosh Pina B team.

"They told us all to go home," complains Golan. "We were ahead by two goals."

Next we hear the sirens go off, at first our own, and then those of the neighboring settlements down the road, a symphony of wailing bad news for the people of our valley. But none of us know what kind of bad news. A few more minutes and members of the education staff of the kibbutz fan out between the apartments ordering the children to report to their assigned bomb shelters. Our three kids head down the stairs to join the others.

This is all very strange. We are used to this type of drill when there are infiltrators in the valley, but why would the national radio station cancel its regular programming? And why Beethoven now?

All of a sudden, Ruthie and I feel the house shaking, a slight trembling noise that gradually increases its volume. A far away giant, clumps and rumbles his way somewhere beyond the Golan Heights. *Og,* the King of Bashan, has broken out of the earth and is stumbling toward us. The bumping increases and Beethoven and the radio are suddenly drowned in static. Ruthie and I are sitting on the couch, saying nothing, waiting to know, wanting to be told, our minds trying to minimize what might be happening. The radio clicks back on, solemnly chanting:

"Red Sky."

"Bright gates."

"Southern Star."

"Running Antelope."

"Old Violet."

"Crooked Finger."

Now we know. Code names of military units are being called, mobilizing men and women to their battle stations. Time passes while Ruthie and I still sit in silence, listening to the breath of war, the rumbling continues on the Golan. Then, we hear the rolling noise of buses driving down the east\west roads of the valley coming to pick up reserve soldiers to take them away. Young men in civilian clothes and daypacks, board the buses, silently, as if they are going home after a lost soccer game. But we all know that this is no soccer ball game.

1973: Blackout

Even though we can hear the far off thump of artillery shells falling to the east of the Syrian Heights, the valley is strangely quiet and peaceful. The war has moved off toward Damascus. I have no specific part in it. My unit had been called up but only for a few days since there is little use for infantry in this particular conflict.

There isn't much to do around the kibbutz. The latest shipment of turkeys has been sent off to the market. The shoe factory is running on a skeleton staff. Israel is in the final phase of the Yom Kippur War. In peacetime, this is the season of the year when people take their autumn vacations, going off to Eilat to bask on the shores of the Red Sea, or to visit relatives in the city. But we are far from being in peacetime.

Cfar Moshe is in a somber mood. We have lost three young men in the tank battles on the Golan Heights and in the Sinai desert during the first hectic days of battle. In the initial chaotic hours of the war, we had been faced with the possibility that the Syrian tanks would break into our narrow valley and overrun its meager defenses. All we had were a few heavy machine guns. Some shoulder launched anti-tank missiles and a store of obsolete rifles and submachine guns—no match for the massive armor of the enemy. Fortunately, with the help of our General Giora, our outnumbered troops up on the Golan manage to slow the Syrian advance long enough for reinforcements to climb the heights and push the invaders back.

Even though the war has moved to the east, we maintain tight security. There is still the possibility of raids by Syrian paratroopers or from the Palestinian Liberation Army, based on the Lebanese border only a few miles to the west. The children are still down in the bomb shelters and most of the men and some of the women are taking turns doing long shifts of guard duty along the periphery of the settlement.

My job during much of the day is to climb a ladder to the top of the alfalfa silo, the highest point of the kibbutz, to keep my eye out for possible infiltrators, Syrian helicopters, or suspicious movements of any kind. I have a pair of field glasses, a thermos jug of lemonade and a Soviet-made assault rifle to keep me company.

Half way through my four-hour stint on the top of the silo, I see Moshe Lamed, the manager of the shoe factory, approaching on his bicycle. He parks at the bottom of the access ladder and yells up to me.

"Shimon, having a good vacation up there?"

"Not so great," I yell back, "I'm getting hungry. Could you send your wife up here with a steak dinner and a bottle of wine?"

"Sorry," he yells back, "she's busy with the war effort and has no time for lazy guys sitting around sunbathing. But I do have some good news for you."

"Don't tell me that the Syrian paratroops have landed."

"You'd know it if they had," Moshe Lamed bellows. "The good news is that you get to do the second shift of guard duty with me tonight."

"Oh sure, great news" I yell back from the top of the silo, "I don't need to sleep anyway. Maybe we can discuss grand military strategy while we tour the outer fence and then send our conclusions to Moshe Dayan."

"See you at midnight." He waves and bicycles away.

Two hours later, half-fried in the sun, I trade places with the next silo guard, Yankele, my former co-worker in the now uprooted vineyard. He climbs up the ladder with his *Klachnikov*, his thermos, and his grumpy attitude. I pass him the field glasses and retire down the ladder to my bicycle. I head for a long awaited swim in the kibbutz swimming pool followed by a long afternoon's nap in my cool bed. What a way to fight a war.

When I awake from a well-earned and heavy sleep, my wife and I listen to the five o'clock news to make sure that no one we know has been killed during today's fighting. Then we walk over to the dining hall. During the war we eat earlier than usual since there is a total blackout at night. We finish dinner and sit outside on the grass next to the dining hall with the other parents, waiting for the kids to come up out of the bomb shelters for a short break in their otherwise underground day. The children and the stars come out around the same time. We watch the children by starlight, playing their games on the lawn, enjoying their brief freedom from the confines of the shelters. The little girls play five stones, a jacks-like game involving scooping up and balancing tiny plastic cubes on the palms and backs of their hands. The little boys are roughhousing or playing their special game of shooting little paper balls up in the air with rubber bands and watching the bats fly out of the trees to snatch the paper missiles. I am never sure if the bats know that they are playing a game or just following their bug hunting instincts. After an hour or so the kids retreat back down into their missile-proof shelters and their parents step carefully along the dark sidewalks to their homes to sleep or, like Moshe Lamed and me, to guard the periphery of the kibbutz.

At midnight, I meet Moshe in front of the tractor shed. Yitzhak and Ziggi, the eight to twelve o'clock guard shift, are happily waiting to pass their weapons over to us and to go home to their beds. During peacetime, the night watch is a pleasant night's walk around the kibbutz with good jokes, lots of cups of coffee in the little guard booth at the front gate, and long conversations about political and kibbutz matters. However, in late October 1973, we are still at war and not *that* far from the front. We take our work seriously. I accept the Uzi from Yitzhak and go through the ritual of pulling the clip out, opening the bolt, feeling the back end of the barrel to make sure no bullets remain inside, closing the bolt, putting the clip of bullets back in and making sure the safety is on. Moshe Lamed does the same dance with Ziggi, and we begin our four-hour stroll in the dark.

With the full blackout, no moon, and the need for silence there is nothing more to do than to walk and listen to the night. We couldn't see a Syrian soldier ten paces away in this moonless night. Once or twice during the first hour we hear artillery falling in the far distance but otherwise a heavy stillness settles over the kibbutz, broken only by a few peeps from the night birds, by the hum of a generator, by the gentle whoosh from a steam pipe, by the faint rustle of the doomed turkey chicks in their pens, and by our own footsteps along the periphery road.

Just beyond the children's farm and the horse barn, Moshe Lamed whispers to me that he needs to heed the call of nature in a most serious way. We are about fifty dark yards away from the nearest outdoor toilet. Rather than waiting for him to finish and come back to search for me in the dark, I propose that I keep moving along the road and meet him over next to the alfalfa silo where the metallic glint of its sidings could be seen in the starlight. I am concerned that trying to find each other in the darkness without a clear marker might be dangerous. Moshe Lamed takes himself to the outhouse and I move along through the void toward the alfalfa silo.

Unexpectedly, I hear heavy booted steps on the dark road behind me. I stop and listen. Utter stillness. I take a few breaths and then move on. The heavy steps behind me begin again. Moshe Lamed is busy in the crapper and no one else should be on this road. Why fool around? Quietly, I bend down, stretch out in the dust of the road, with my head in the direction of whoever, is following me. As silently as possible, I slip the Uzi's safety catch off, and try to slow down my breathing. I cradle the stock and quietly pull back the bolt. Then, in as firm a voice as I can muster, I challenge the unknown stalker.

"Password!"

Another heavy step, then silence again.

If I'm smart I'll shoot, I try to convince myself. They may be drawing a bead on me right now or be pulling the pin of a grenade.

I wait another few seconds and think about it again. *If* I shoot and there's nothing there at all, I'll have the entire kibbutz awake, piling out here like maniacs, maybe shooting Moshe Lamed on the crapper and making me look like a idiot.

Against my better judgement I find myself rising up out of the dust of the road and ever so slowly moving toward the unknown being in the dark. I take one, two, three, four, five paces, Uzi at hip level ready to fire off the clip. I bump into a cold nose with two white-rimmed eyes above it. It's Konga, my favorite kibbutz mule, out of the barn and on the road to pay me a visit.

As my pulse drops somewhere down to twice its normal rate, I say the first crazy thing that pops into my head.

"Konga, damn it, you almost made an ass out of me."

1973: Ruthie

With the outbreak of the Yom Kippur war, a cloud gathers over Ruthie's spirit. During previous military conflicts—the Six-Day War and the War of Attrition—she had been as steady as a rock. Underground, during the long days and nights in the dimly lit bomb shelters, she had tended the kibbutz children, soothed their fears, helped them write letters to their fathers at the battlefronts, taught and played games, and lullabied them to sleep in their stacked wooden bunks. But something has changed within her during this latest of our wars. She does her work in the bomb shelters, but hesitates to come above ground, even when the all-clear siren sounds. When the war recedes deep into Syria and it is safe to bring the children up from the shelters, Ruthie and I bed together in our new apartment, but she has trouble falling asleep. She looks dazed.

I am of little help in recognizing and helping her with what turns out to be a collapse of her fortitude. This is the first time during a war that I have been posted inside the kibbutz instead of on a battlefield. My time is taken up with long stints of guard duty and long days of work trying to get the apple harvest in with a much-reduced work force.

Like most of our people, I have automatically adopted the stiff upper lip attitude that has carried us all through the wars. I assume that Ruthie has her stiff upper lip, too, and, alas, I am blind to her suffering. Our marriage has not been doing well for a long time——I, stupidly assume that our relationship is "all right," just not very passionate. She, being more honest and insightful, knows that it isn't all right.

One night, sleeping in our new bed with mortar fire thumping far to the east, I awake to find Ruthie gone. She has heard the dim war-noise on the Golan and has fled, by herself, to the safety of the bomb shelter, sitting there, underground, all night, alone. She returns only in the morning without saying a word. It is so pitiful; she is so frightened, dashing out of our apartment like that, without even waking me up from my deep, unthinking sleep. She continues on with her work and mothers our children, but she never seems to smile. Sometimes she just sits in her chair and looks out the window toward the Golan Heights.

One twilight, standing on our balcony at sunset watching the colors darken on the surrounding ridges, she says, "I feel like those mountains are closing in on me."

It is clear to both of us that she needs to go back to America.

1973-1975: Of Personal, Local and National Depression

After the Yom Kippur War, the whole country goes into a state of depression. As in the past, we have survived as a country. We have won a military victory of sorts, but many of our soldiers have been killed. Too many. A whole new generation of war widows begins to mourn their losses, not to speak of the parallel grief on the other side of the border. The kibbutz has lost its good luck charm. Whereas in the previous wars there had been no serious casualties, this time, three young men have joined the big kibbutz in the sky: Baruch, the Turk, blown up by a Syrian shell; Clarita's husband Hillel, burnt up in a tank on the shore of the Suez Canal; and Doron, the University student and vineyard worker, killed by a mortar shell in Egypt. What to do? What to think? Our world turned upside down.

There have been so many combat losses in so short a time. The dead are quickly buried in temporary cemeteries far from their families, far from their mourners. I drive Clarita down to a military burial ground near Ashkelon, in the South of the country. She manages a stiff upper lip on the four-hour drive but loses it as we approach the cemetery gate. The earth is so raw; the graves are so new. What remains of her husband is buried in the red earth of the coastal plain instead of the dark soil of Cfar Moshe. I cry, too. Hillel and I had been working together in the packinghouse just a few days before this sad war broke upon us.

Ruthie, tired of wars and tired of me, leaves to go back to the United States. By mutual agreement the children will remain with me in Cfar Moshe. I end up driving her down to Ben-Gurion airport, again trying to maintain that same kibbutz stiff upper-lip so common among kibbutzniks. When Ruthie mounts the stairs to the departing passenger terminal, my eyes cloud with tears and then the tears spill over. Ruthie, as if she is shell shocked, can't cry at all, so I cry for her.

After a mournful drive alone back to the kibbutz I ponder what to do about my disintegrating life. Overwhelmed by the idea of being a single father, I decide to bring another woman into my life, my old high school love Deborah. Perhaps she can fill my hollowness. Deborah and I dated when we were young in San Diego. We had both married other people and both experienced the death of love. We had reconnected and kindled our ancient fires while I was earning my degree.

A few months later, Deborah brings her own three children all the way from San Diego to Cfar Moshe. I receive her with love and relief. She is so practical, so competent. She rescues me from my confusion and depression. The kibbutz is scandalized with my behavior—one wife disappears and another takes her place—but it fits in well with the general craziness of the times. I'm nuts. The country is nuts, and the world as a whole is not doing much better.

Amidst all this dislocation, the Regional High School semester begins, albeit a month late because of the war. Too many of the students' fathers and older brothers have been killed and wounded for any of us to have great joy at the beginning of classes. There are still armed soldiers patrolling the roof of the school building. We all ask each other, students and teachers, how did this happen? How were we so unprepared for the war? Why were there so many deaths? When will the next war begin?

One answer to our questions comes from the younger members of the teaching staff who have returned from the battlefield. These are tough men, raised since birth in the kibbutzim, used to defeating the Arabs with relative ease, convinced that they are morally superior to our enemies, and angry with the nation's leaders. They aren't mixed up and they know what to do. Or at least they think they do.

"We've been stabbed in the back," one of them says, "the government is full of old men and women that are out of touch with reality. We need to clean house and find out who or what betrayed us."

"Yes, we've become too soft," another says, "We have to get rid of our old leaders. We need new blood. Dangerous ideas have come to us from the outside world. Our people think that the Six-Day-War fixed everything and all we have to do is hide behind our defenses. People have become too Americanized, too comfortable, too consumer oriented, too corrupt, too permissive, too flabby. Yes, creeping Americanism is the problem. Now we are back from the front and we're going to set things straight."

These earnest men believe it's too late to fix the older generation, but they'll lay down the law to the young. And they'll start with our high school.

My professional life goes on, and it's time to begin teaching. My war trauma and my marital trauma are healing, at least on the surface. I let myself enjoy teaching my first Health Education classes. It's a great experiment, testing the methods and subject matter that I have learned in the USA. I carefully plan my pedagogical approach.

"Let's start modestly," I preach to myself. "Stay away from controversial subjects, teach about disease prevention, nutrition, physical fitness and save the ecology, sex education and drug education for later when I have a better feel for the attitudes of the teachers and students at the high school."

The plan immediately stumbles. The first week of school, three tenth graders are caught smoking marijuana in Kibbutz Cfar Baruch. The Vice-Principal expels them from school. A few weeks later, an eleventh grader, one of the top students from another kibbutz in the valley, runs through the communal dining hall, yelling obscenities. A search is made of his bedroom and rumor has it that LSD has been found.

Perkal, the Principal, invites me to organize a drug education workshop for the teaching staff of the high school.

"Why not?" I say to him in all humility. "I'm not the world's expert on drugs but I think I can teach the staff a few things."

I had planned to teach about drugs later in the semester but, given the present emergency, why not take advantage of the opportunity to show my stuff?

"Let's do it," smiles Perkal. "After all, what did we send you away to college for?

"If you say so."

Why do I have the feeling that I am about to put my foot into a bear trap?

II

The day of my drug workshop for the faculty of the Regional High School has arrived. The school building is as quiet as a monastery in the absence of the students. The teachers relax in their chairs, light up cigarettes, joke around, gossip, put tired feet up on chairs, sip tea and prepare to sum up the events of the past six days of work.

Shlomo, the Vice-Principal, begins by describing the incidents that have taken place since the beginning of the school year. He is kibbutz-born, in his early 30s, dedicated to shaping the younger generation to be morally strong, rooted in their motherland, loyal to the kibbutz movement, and elite defenders of our troubled borders. Shlomo was one of the last teachers who returned from the battlefields to resume his job at the Regional School. He had fought in the tank battles of the 7th Brigade on the Golan Heights, that same unit which had, in the words of the Israeli High Command, "Saved the People of Israel."

Shlomo is in a fighting mood over the drug issue. And to my complete surprise, he has decided that I am the enemy.

"Students have been telling me how much they enjoy Shimon's Drug Education class. I asked one of the 11th graders from my kibbutz, what he had learned so far, and this is more or less what he said (looking at his notes). 'Shimon taught us that all drugs could be harmful. He said that this is true of both legal and illegal drugs. He listed the worst drugs on the blackboard. Along with heroin and marijuana, he included nicotine and alcohol' "

Raising his handsome head from the notes he states, "My own opinion is that the use of drugs is not an educational problem at all. It is a discipline problem. Our school code requires us to immediately expel any drug user. The expulsion is supposed to be permanent. This is the only way that we will be able to control the drug problem. Shimon's permissiveness is wrong and I call upon him to not teach this subject any more. He should go back to teaching English."

Daphna, the head of the counseling department, puts her cigarette into an ashtray, stands up and faces me.

"Are you really telling the children that heroin is the same as cigarettes?"

Asher, a history teacher, addresses Perkal: "Why are those three students here who were permanently expelled for using drugs. Why did you allow them to come back? Why are we exposing our learners to narcomaniacs? We have to draw the line somewhere, otherwise this problem will only get worse."

Perkal himself seems dazed at this unexpected outburst.

"Well," the principal says in a low voice, "we granted them an amnesty because of the good work that they did during the war. The kibbutz psychologist felt that the boys were not mentally disturbed. They are all very bright students."

"Then they should have known what the consequences would be if they were caught." Shlomo retorts. "We have to be tough on this matter. I also think that Shimon should go back to teaching English and leave drug problems to the Vice-Principal. He's much too permissive about these matters."

The workshop turns out to be a debacle. It's a declaration of war instead of my inauguration as a health education specialist. I see a long battle looming up with me being the fall guy. Later I find out that Shlomo has been collecting espionage reports from selected kids in my classroom. I can smell a witch-hunt on its way.

After thinking about the matter for a few days, walking down the banks of the Jordan, cursing the war, cursing my own stupidity, cursing my own arrogance, I decide that I don't want to waste my energy on a pedagogical battle that I can't win. Shlomo is a hero and his combat experience might well have contributed to saving my life, too. He will have plenty of friends to back him up. I am stereotyped as a hippie American, a flesh-potter, a wife swapper, and a non-combatant in this our latest war. Wounded but not defeated, I decide to not fight this battle.

Fortunately, up my professional sleeve, I have a job offer from the Ministry of Health in Jerusalem—five days of Health Education curriculum planning per week down in Jerusalem our

Holy City. Sooner or later the Regional High School folks will realize that I was right and they were wrong. And you know what they can do to themselves in the meantime. End of round one, I'm off for Jerusalem. See you all on the weekends!

III

"See you on weekends? Oh yeah, that's real great for you!" is Deborah's reaction to the good news about my job in Jerusalem. "You want to leave me here punching holes in shoe straps and taking care of six kids for five days of the week. You must be out of your gourd. I'm not even sure that I want to live in this crazy commune!"

I wince at the 'crazy commune' remark.

"O.K. I'll find a way to cut it down to three days a week in Jerusalem. Maybe I can teach in our elementary school the rest of the time."

A stormy silence ensues as Deborah's well-greased wheels turn. She is a woman who doesn't mince her words. She is the last person on earth to play a subservient role to her husband, to the kibbutz, or to the whole damn State of Israel. She is here for me and not for ideology.

"I'll agree to two days a week. I can do without you for a couple of days, but I don't know what I'm going to do about this miserable job. I wasn't raised to be a slave in a shoe factory. The managers don't know what the hell they're doing anyway."

"Why do you say that?"

"I've only been there a week and I see how they throw half the leather away when they make a sandal. I talked to your pal Gad, who claims he manages the place. I showed him all the stuff that he could make out of the leather scraps. But he wasn't interested. What kind of businessman is that? Isn't he interested in making money?"

Look out Cfar Moshe!

I make an arrangement with my new employer in Jerusalem to fly down just twice a week and take my work with me back to the kibbutz. Besides being in love with this person, I have no desire to go to war with her. She just might win.

A year goes by and the Ministry of Health offers me a chance to be in charge of Health Education for the entire Galilee. I've made it. Now I don't have to go down to Jerusalem to work—except for the grand occasions when I will report on my achievements to the Ministry officials. My ego inflates almost to the point of forgiving my enemies who did me wrong at the Regional High School. With a few years of excellent work in the Galilee I will undoubtedly be ready to do a Ph.D. and become an internationally recognized figure. I see trips to conferences in Buenos Aires, London, Paris, Tokyo and the other great capitals in the near future. Big man!

In the meantime, Deborah has made her way out of the shoe factory, into a more respectable position in the kibbutz kitchen. She now cooks all of the dietary food for the aging members of Cfar Moshe. Is she happy in her work? Not really. She's used to making a good living managing her family jewelry stores in San Diego. Naively, I figure that she is so in love with me that she will eventually be content.

You bet.

An even bigger threat to my new career comes from Avraham, formerly the boss of the orchard and now the economic Czar of Cfar Moshe. Avraham has some serious occupational problems of his own. The kibbutz has bet its economic chips on a plastic factory. Everyone looks forward to seeing the profits from this enterprise, but few people volunteer to work in this sordid jungle of machinery. After all, you weren't going to make any more money as a robot on the assembly line than you would make zipping along on a tractor out in the field crop department with a view of Mt. Hermon. What glory could there be working an eight-hour day in a pile of polyethylene?

One lovely Galilee day in 1975, Avraham stops by our apartment and asks to talk to me. We sit out on the lawn chairs in front of the house. Avraham looks quite uncomfortable; we haven't said three words to each other since he sprayed me, and the rest of the workers with Malathion, two years ago.

"Look Shimon," he begins awkwardly, "I need you in the plastic factory."

"You must be joking."

"It's not a joke; we're really short of working hands."

"Don't you know that I'm working for the Ministry of Health?"

"Of course I know that. But this is a real emergency. We're asking the members who work outside the kibbutz to come back and put their shoulders toward making the plastic factory a success."

"Who else have you asked?"

"You're the first one. You've been working outside the least amount of time."

A wall of anger crashes down on me. What nerve this idiot has!

"Hey, I'm just getting myself established in my professional work. Why don't you ask some of the old timers who have been working outside for decades?"

"We have to start somewhere."

"Not with me, you don't," I hear myself saying coldly. I want to murder this guy, and Avraham senses my anger. He shakes his head and grits his teeth.

"You think about it, Shimon; we may have to do something drastic."

"Go drink some Malathion," I propose to Avraham.

A few months later, I have my next go-around with Avraham. The Ministry of Health is willing to give me a car to travel the wilds of the Galilee in my new job. Up to now I've been using the Egged bus system to take myself around to the villages, kibbutzim and small farms in the north. A car could make my work a lot more efficient. But the kibbutz would have to pay for the upkeep of the vehicle. To make a long, sad story short, there is no way that the kibbutz is going to do this for me. Not with Avraham and his cronies in charge. This time he wins.

I tell Deborah about my dilemma and, after many long discussions, we decide to take our kids and leave the kibbutz. I have been a member for thirteen years, my children have been raised here, a piece of my heart will be here forever, but it's time to move on. We try to figure how much it would cost to live in Jerusalem or Tel Aviv with six kids. Impossible. The next best alternative is to move back to San Diego where we both can find jobs and live in a decent house, albeit 10,000 miles away from the country I love.

The die is cast. The arrangements are made. But first, I have to have a conversation with my grandfather of blessed memory, Saba Yisroel Chmiel.

I wonder if he's still in the country.

1976: Tracking Down Saba

On a hunch, I journey to the big cities on the coastal plain. Perhaps Saba is visiting my cousins in Tel Aviv and trying to straighten *them* out for a while. I drop by Berl and Rachel's apartment in one of a forest of apartment buildings in North Tel Aviv. I could see the Mediterranean from here if there weren't a hundred or so similar apartment buildings blocking the view.

Rachel plants me in an armchair and quickly produces a plate of spice cake and a glass of tea. I tell them that I am leaving the country. For them, and maybe for me, leaving the country is a *yerida,* a descent, from the obligation to build a new State for the Jewish people. They are shocked, but polite. I find myself near speechless as I give them the news. This is going to be a hard thing to do and I'm not feeling very good anyway.

I've never told Berl and Rachel about my grandfather's ghost. Berl had known my grandparents back in Ostrolenka and, as a young boy, had helped them load their wagon with their meager possessions when the German army drove out the town's Jewish people. They also know that Saba and Grandmother and the rest of our Ostrolenka family were machine-gunned to death in the forest of Stolin in 1942. They knew that all of our relatives' bodies were buried in a pit with 10,000 other Jews. When I ask my cousins if they had seen Saba's ghost in Tel Aviv, they look at me as if I am hallucinating. They shake their heads and Rachel squeezes the handkerchief in her hands. Dead Jews rarely walk the streets of Tel Aviv.

I move on to Jerusalem.

Getting off the Egged bus at the main Jerusalem terminal, I begin my search for Saba in *Mea Shearim*, the ultra-religious quarter. Here, within the narrow streets frequented only by black coated orthodox men and shawled orthodox women, the life of the European ghetto remains alive amidst poverty and shabbiness. I go into one of the many little synagogues to search for my Saba among the old men standing in front of the ark of the Torah. They sway and chant their age-old prayers, each at their own rate of speed, covered with prayer shawls.

No one notices me, a secular madman walking among them, dressed like a heathen, peeking into their eyes, searching, searching. Saba, Saba, why have you abandoned me?

The synagogue has a faint odor of candles, rye bread, old men, and tobacco. Saba is not here.

Frustrated, I take myself through the gates of the old city, down David street with its Arab shops and covered markets, over to the Western Wall, and I poke a note into a crack between the dank Herodian stones asking God to please help me find my grandfather. The sun is setting and the color of old Herod's wall is changing to a shadowy iron oxide, just like ridges of the Golan.

"Oh my God (so to speak), I'm leaving Cfar Moshe, and my life is coming apart!" I say to the wall.

I find myself crying, then weeping, and then sobbing and I don't know why. This is strange behavior for an unbeliever like me. But these are strange times and I'm getting desperate. I need help.

I won't give up seeking Saba Yisroel. I know that I can trust him to be somewhere in this land, even though he is only a ghost.

My next stop is the dusty town of Beersheva, in the Negev desert. Perhaps Saba might be at the camel market hanging around with the Bedouins. There aren't many camels anymore. All the Bedouins have tractors and vans now. Instead of coming to Beersheva to draw water out the well, they come to fill up their gas tanks. I ask one of the Bedouins if he has seen an old man dressed in a Polish army uniform, or in a burial shroud. No luck. The Bedouin scratches his head and mumbles under his breath…perhaps a curse to ward off the devil. I speak to a group of young Bedouins, gathered in a circle, smoking hand rolled cigarettes and discussing the price of sheep and camels. They give me that same puzzled look.

I return to the North of the country, sleeping through the long drive on the back seat of the Egged bus—oblivious to the fellow passengers and the clucking chickens under their seats. I remember that Saba was interested in the Arab population of the Galilee. I get off the bus to Nazareth and ask my friend Ibrahim if he has seen the ghost of my grandfather, but Ibrahim doesn't believe in ghosts. He invites me to stay a while but I can't.

My friend Muhammad, who is now the Mukhtar (the village chief) of his Galilee town, has not seen any old Jewish spirits around either, although he has no doubt that such a thing could be possible. Sensing that I am in deep pain he offers to put me up for as long as I want.

"Let's sit on the balcony and have a bottle of *Arak Zachlawi* together," he proposes.

Even though *Zachlawi* is the best brand of *Arak* in the world and has to be laboriously smuggled in from Lebanon, and even though I love the minty flavor of this powerful spirit, I can't accept his offer. He can read the obsession in my eyes and so he isn't offended. He knows that I have to move on.

Next stop is Safed, where my two boys Hermon and Golan were born in the old Turkish hospital and where my broken leg was treated during the *Outhouse War*. No Saba there, either. I think about going over to the tomb of Rabbi Shimon Bar Yohai a few kilometers from Safed and asking for help. But I am too exhausted.

I take the bus back to my home valley (soon to be my ex-home valley), but instead of getting off at Papyrus Junction, I continue to the end of the line to the frontier town of Kiryat Shmonah. Arriving at the terminal, I spot my old friend and vineyard worker Saadia. As is his habit, he hangs around the bus station in the late afternoon, sitting with his buddies, watching people arriving from South of Rosh Pina. They comment on all the passengers, especially the women.

"*Ya*, Shimon," he calls, "come over here. Long time no see! I need to talk to you."

"*Ya*, Saadia," I answer and sit on the bench next to him and his fellow North Africans. We hold hands as part of our greeting.

"*Mah nishma?*" What's new? He asks.

"*B'Seder,*" (Everything's copasetic.)" I lie. Observing the ethnic commandment never to get directly to the point, I ask, "How's your family?"

"Thank God," he replies politely, still holding my hand, softly.

Now it's time to find out why he wants to talk to me.

"There's someone here that I want you to see."

"Who's that?"

"Your grandfather."

"You know where he is?"

"He's been here a long time. He prays in our synagogue. He's our only Ashkenazi (European) member."

"I've been looking all over the country for him."

Saadia and I walk over to the synagogue of the Jerban Jews on Jabotinsky Street in Kiryat Shmona and, sure enough, I find Saba Yisroel praying."

"What are you doing here, Saba?" I demand as I shake Saadia's hand.

Am I angry that I have found my grandfather only a few kilometers from my home—this home, this life that I'm about to give up?

Saba shrugs his shoulders and shows me the palms of his hands, as if he's been caught in the act.

"I wanted to keep my eye on you, but I didn't want to interfere in your life," says the old ghost. "These Jews from the Island of Jerba have welcomed me and, after all, they are the oldest clans in Israel that we have. They're the descendents of priests, you know, from the destruction of our first Temple, 2,500 years in exile, and now back in our Holy Land. I've learned a lot from them."

"But I've been looking all over for you."

"I know."

"Why didn't you tell me where you were?"

"I couldn't."

"Why not?"

Saba motions me to have a seat next to him in the back of the synagogue and Saadia begins praising God with his other worshipers—chanting the ancient prayers in their Tunisian-Hebrew accents.

"Because you're forty-years-old now, and you have to make up your own mind about things. I know that you're leaving the country. I know about the *tsuras*, the trouble you've had on your kibbutz. But I have my needs, too."

"Aren't you going back to America with me?" I hear a note of panic in my voice and so does Saba.

"No."

"Why not?"

"Look, I understand your problems, *boytchik*. But they're not my problems any more. You don't need my protection anymore. Go back to America and *Gei Gezunt*, best of luck. You're going to make your parents very happy. They'll be able to see more of their grandchildren. You'll be able to learn more about your profession. Your new woman will be happier over there, and the State of Israel will not collapse because you're not around. I'm staying here to see what will happen with this crazy Holy Land of ours. I've got a lot more time than you have to knock around. Go make a good life for yourself, and take care of my beautiful great-grandchildren."

Like at the Wall, tears cascade down my cheeks and I'm not sure why. I can't stop the flood. Saba takes his handkerchief out and dabs the side of my face.

"Don't take this all so hard," Saba counsels. "I understand you. You'll be back here before you know it."

1993: Slivovitz and Judaism

What am I doing back in Cfar Moshe after fifteen years of working in public health projects in the fleshpots of San Diego, California?

What else? A consultant.

My idea is to offer health education workshops to the good people of the upper Galilee, of course basing operations in Cfar Moshe. This way I get to do good things for the health of the local communities and, as a bonus, much time to schmooze around with my old friends.

One fine September day, I find myself sipping coffee in the apartment of Benesh, a bachelor who lives out in the kibbutz's periphery by the Jordan River.

"Crazy Americans," mutters Benesh as we watch the last few minutes of the Oprah Winfrey show late on Friday afternoon. "Why would someone want to stick a ring through his tongue? Who wants to see a thing like that anyway?"

"That's the price that you pay for having cable TV up here in the Galilee." I answer. "Pretty soon the kids here on the kibbutz will be piercing their lips, cheeks and other parts just like the American kids. The boys here are already wearing earrings and shaving their heads. I saw one skinhead going by on a tractor, on my way to your apartment."

"It's all part of the *matzav*—the situation—the whole country is headed down the drain." mourns Benesh.

He continues to mutter but doesn't click Oprah off. I know that part of his scowling mood has to do with the vote at the last general meeting of the kibbutz where the younger members had pulled off a major political triumph. From now on, managers of kibbutz industries will be paid more than the non-professionals. For Benesh and the other veteran members, it is the ultimate defeat of the communal ethic, sabotaged not by the rapacious capitalists in the city but by their own children now grown up and making their own decisions.

"What else?" I ask after a short pause.

"The religious maniacs."

"What about them, Benesh?"

"They're forcing us to kosherize our communal dining hall." He seethes out between his teeth.

"Screw them," I suggest.

"It's not that easy any more," he explains. "We've started a new business. We have all these tourist buses entering the kibbutz every day bringing shoppers to our shoe factory outlet mall. The mall is a good moneymaker and Eliezer and I suggested that we open up part of the dining hall as a restaurant, for the shoppers. The problem is that if we're going to serve the general public, all the food has to be kosher. That means that we have to hire a kosher inspector, probably some disgusting, primitive, religious fanatic with a white beard. Of course, all the food that we will serve in our dining hall will have to be kosher, too."

"Great God," I say, "I remember when I first became a member of the kibbutz- you people were serving pork chops on Yom Kippur. Now, you're going to have a kosher dining hall?"

"It looks like Socialism is dead," says Benesh with a grimace.

Poor Benesh, his ideology is crumbling. He's probably wondering why he left Argentina anyway or why he didn't settle in the city when he immigrated to Israel in 1952. Maybe he's kicking himself for not marrying and having kids. Maybe that's why he's a grumpy old bachelor. He might have even been thinking that unthinkable thought, why was he born a Jew?

I visit this sad character because no one else visits him. Most of the rest of the older members are busy with part-time work, grandchildren, puttering in their gardens, doing crafts or just hanging around the coffeehouse commenting on the news of the day. But Benesh has elected to shut himself up in his sad and tiny apartment on the Jordan River side of the kibbutz. He stares hypnotically into the TV set and mutters,

"*Shtuyot*," (Foolishness), he says.

After leaving Benesh's grim apartment, I need some positive inspiration. I walk across the kibbutz to drop in on Amnon. I knock on his door and hear a hubbub of voices inside. Olga, Amnon's spouse raises her voice to say "*yavo,*" (come in, whoever you are). Stepping over Lucky the dog (Dina's replacement). I find a gathering consisting of Avraham Cohen, Amnon, Olga and an unknown foreigner.

"It's Shimon—excuse me—Dr. Shimon Chamiel. Come in. Another crazy American." Amnon greets me. "Sit down and have a drink with us. We have one of your countrymen here."

I notice a serious bottle of Slivovitz on the table, some empty drinking glasses and trays of goodies including dates, apples and peanuts, spread out over the coffee table. My timing is perfect. All of those present have empty but wet shot glasses in front of them and grins on their faces. The foreigner is an American all right, a young looking fellow in expensive jeans and a tee shirt. I sense that this conversation will be the ideal antidote to the morbid conversation at Benesh's house.

"Shimon, we have here a rabbinical student, a Reform Jew from California," Amnon says gleefully as if he has caught an unusual butterfly specimen. "Jerry, meet Shimon, one of our own who has left us for the fleshpots of San Diego. Sit down, Shimon, have a drop of Slivovitz with us and join the fun."

"Slivovitz always brings fun in Amnon and Olga's house," I say. "Last time I was over, I almost broke my leg trying to get back down your stairs. But why not?"

Amnon pours some of the clear liquid out of its squat bottle and I take it down. It is a smooth variety of the poison. Only the best! I remember when, years ago, Amnon had brought an enormous stash of the stuff back with him from diplomatic duty in the Balkans.

"*L'chaim*," says everyone.

"*L'chaim*," I say back to them as Amnon mischievously pours another shot.

"It turns out that this is Jerry's first visit to a kibbutz and he has just asked me why we don't have a synagogue on our kibbutz," chuckles Amnon.

I realize that I have come just in time to join in a hot discussion. This one will be fueled by the basic inability of most American Jews to understand secular Israeli society, in general, and kibbutz society, in particular. Amnon and I have been over this ground many times before, but it will be fun watching the rabbinical student trying to grapple with our heretical ideas.

"There are several reasons why we do not have a synagogue on our kibbutz," begins Amnon, in a friendly if somewhat paternal tone of voice. "The main reason is that very few of our members are religious. If there would be public demand for a synagogue, a proposal could be brought up in our town meeting and a synagogue could be built. But no such proposal has ever been made."

Jerry thinks about Amnon's statement for a few seconds and then asks, "If there's no interest in having a synagogue here, does that mean that the members of the kibbutz don't believe in God?"

"I'm really not sure who believes what around here," continues Amnon. "The only requirements for someone to join the kibbutz are membership in the Israel Labor Federation, willingness to work according to the needs of the kibbutz, and a positive vote by the majority of members. The bargain is that we care for the member's needs for the rest of his life, given the resources we have and according to the democratic decision of the community. One member, one vote."

"I wish it was really as simple as that," interjects Olga, who enjoys playing the role of the Queen of Cynicism, "sometimes the biggest mouths decide who gets what."

"Back to God," insists the rabbinical student, "what percentage of the population of the kibbutz do you estimate believe in God?

I say, "My guess would be about two percent on any given day and most of them would be tourists buying shoes at the outlet shop. Let's be honest about it, Amnon, almost all of the members if you asked them, would say they were atheists."

"You're probably right about most of us being atheists," says Avraham Cohen, one of the few Polish members of the kibbutz who now has the big job of running our enormous fruit packinghouse. "But you'll find that we don't usually sit around discussing each other's religious beliefs. We're a practical bunch and our main interests are making a living and surviving our bad neighbors, the Syrians."

"What I don't understand," Jerry responds, "is how people can be part of Judaism and atheists at the same time?"

"How about some more Slivovitz?" suggests Amnon, picking up the bottle and waving it at the shot-glass. Knowing Amnon, this gesture means two things, one, he wants more Slivovitz and two, we have now reached the crucial point in the discussion where the American's knowledge of history is going to be painfully inadequate.

"You know, Jerry," begins Amnon, as he pours heavy doses of Yugoslav paint thinner into every available glass, "we came here in the late 1930s because we didn't have much of a choice. The soil of Europe was burning underneath us and there was no place that Jews could call their own on this earth. We were young people, young pioneers, wanting to take charge of our own fate, as Jews, instead of begging at everyone else's table. So we tried to reshape Jewish society in our own clumsy way. We believed that the only way to build a decent life for ourselves was do it ourselves. Just like your pioneers back in America. If God existed, He obviously wasn't being of much direct help during the 1930s and 40s. It was up to us to survive, to make the land fruitful, and to build and defend our own country. It was only after 1967 that some people in this country thought that God had personally arrived just in time for the Six Day War."

"But what about the idea of Jews as a people tied to God in a covenant? We are supposed to be a holy people on God's Holy Land. What other claims, besides that, do you have over this land that your kibbutz is sitting on?" protests the rabbinical student.

I know what's coming next and I hope that Jerry doesn't get his head too out of joint.

Amnon: "Actually, I don't think that we have any particular claim to this country. We came here because we had no other place to go where we could be in control of our own affairs. We like to think that we are peaceful people coming back to a historical homeland. But the truth is that we had to acquire it by force of arms. Something like your people taking half of Mexico and calling it Manifest Destiny."

Jerry: "What about Jerusalem? How can we claim that it is our holy city if there is no God?"

Amnon: "Some of us think that it isn't any holier than any other city. Not any more than San Diego." (Winks at me)

Jerry: "I just don't understand how you can have it both ways. Claim this country as our own and then say that we don't have a claim to it."

Amnon: "We have a claim to it. Just not a religious claim."

Jerry puts his hand to his brow in vast confusion.

At this point, Lucky decides that the discussion has exhausted itself and she abandons her perch by the door. She rests her head on Amnon's thigh and he gives her a little rub. Far over the Golan Heights we hear one of our jet fighters on its daily reconnaissance mission over Syria and South Lebanon. The argument has played out and neither Jerry nor the rest of us have found much of an answer. The heady effect of the plum brandy is beginning to wear off. We are all too used to debates that have no resolution and to opinions that cannot be changed. We all say that we hope for peace, but don't quite know how to achieve it. We all love this place, for various reasons, but we know that our enemies love it, too, for various reasons of their own. Perhaps the only thing that we can agree on is that it is a beautiful and peaceful afternoon. May we always have our friendship, and may we all be healthy and let us say Amen, whether or not God exists.

II

"OK, let's try it this way," I say to Jerry a few days later. He still has a confused look on his face even though he has already been busy flirting with the Danish girls over on Turkey Row. "Let's stand here on the sidewalk and when the members of the kibbutz come by on their way to eat lunch in the dining hall, let's see how they will answer your question about believing in God and being Jewish."

Our first victim is Dahlia, one of the nurses, pulling a cart behind her filled with trays of food for some of the homebound elders of the kibbutz.

"Dahlia," I say, half-blocking her way, "this young American friend of mine and I are doing a survey. Can I ask you two short questions?"

"Hurry up," she sighs, her good nature has led her into our trap. "I have to get this food to Grandma Schultz. She's a *yekke* (a German Jew) and wants her meals exactly on time."

"Are you Jewish?" I ask her.

She thinks about for a second and says, "No, I'm an Eskimo."

"Question number two, do you believe in God?"

"Not today," she retorts. "*Savta* (Grandma) Schultz is driving me crazy."

"Thank you," I say with a grin and Dahlia continues on her way shaking her head. The trays shake too as she pulls the cart along behind her.

Next is Bracha, who works in the laundry. As we see her coming, I tell Jerry that Bracha may have more time for us since the laundry house is closed today. She is a hefty woman, a mother of six kibbutz kids. She was born in Tunis but raised in Cfar Moshe.

"Bracha," I ask as she passes, "are you Jewish?"

"Are you crazy?" she looks at me as if I really *am* crazy. "Do I look like I'm a Danish volunteer?"

"Do you believe in God?"

"Sure," she says, anxious to get away from someone who is obviously drunk or hallucinating.

Clarita and Olga walk toward us with Lucky following them. They are busy discussing last night's film in our outdoor cinema.

"I hate Turkish films," I hear Olga saying. "Too long, too many characters and no plot."

Clarita pouts, "I fell asleep after the second murder, the mosquitoes ate me alive."

I suggest that Jerry try Clarita out on our survey question since she speaks good English. He accepts the challenge.

"Excuse me, *Geveret* (Ma'am) do you believe in God?" he asks as she slows down.

She gives him the same—what are you crazy?—look that Bracha gave me a few minutes before.

"No," she answers in her delightful Latin American English. "I'm an atheist."

"Are you Jewish?"

She stops, looks at Jerry and me once more and says, "No, I'm not. I just came out to live in this country because I like the weather. I also enjoyed losing my husband in the war not so many years ago. Don't ever ask me that question again."

The three of them walk on and I hear Clarita saying to Olga, "Are they on drugs?"

Jerry, in shock, says, "Jesus, what did I get into here."

I'm also embarrassed and make a promise to myself that I will beg Clarita's forgiveness. I explain to Jerry that this survey is costing me my reputation in the kibbutz. But I hope that now he gets the idea that out here, on the front line of Israel, one should be careful about deciding for others what it means to be Jewish.

1996: Close Call

Back in Promised Land again, I decide to stop by my cousin's house in Tel Aviv just before I take the Egged bus up to the Galilee.

You have to watch what you say around Israel these days. People are cranky about the *"Matzav,"* the "situation." One might have a hard time explaining just what the situation is but everyone knows that it's in the air and it's about to blow. The unmentionable words "Civil War" are mentioned although all sides say "God, forbid" when they hear it. I take a cab from North Tel Aviv to the Center of town and in the fifteen minutes we spend together the driver, who looks familiar, delivers a non-stop sermon on the situation:

"Corruption is everywhere. I'm a third generation Israeli, and I've seen it all. It's never been worse. Everyone is out for himself. When you walk on the sidewalk they push you into the street. When I'm driving down the street, the other drivers try to push me up onto to the sidewalk."

I cooperatively nod my head in order to keep him happy and he goes on.

"Now we're going to go to war to keep 400 orthodox fanatics living in the middle of Hebron. Now I have to pay a *shekel* every time I see a doctor or a nurse at the clinic when it used to be free. Now, everyone is moving out of Tel Aviv and moving into the suburbs. Now the trash workers are on strike and the whole city stinks of garbage. I'm fifty-five and all the other taxi drivers can't understand why I'm still working. No one wants to work anymore. I used to live in America and I should have stayed there."

Suddenly I realize where I have seen this taxi driver before.

"Mike! Don't you recognize me? I'm Shimon. We came over together on the *A.K. Galilee* back in 1959! What happened to the gas station that you inherited?"

"Don't ask," he replies. So I don't.

From all of this, I wonder where Mike is politically. From his attitude about Hebron, I place him to the left, but his attitude about the trash workers seems to swing him to the right. Anyway, before I have a chance to think much about it, we arrive at my destination. There is nowhere else to stop except the middle of the traffic flow so I pay my fare while a long line of cars honk their horns behind us. I get so nervous that I dash out of the taxi without counting my change. I also forget to tip Mike, but since I'm becoming part of the situation myself, I don't feel guilty about it. He turned out to be a big grouch anyway.

Later, I spend a few hours in front of the television set with Berl, my favorite Israeli cousin, at his apartment in the concrete forests along the Yarkon River. We have been getting on famously commenting on the dire news that flows endlessly out of the TV—floods in the south of the country, drunk teenagers jumping out of five story buildings, flying saucers observed over Nazareth and worse.

We both enjoy the story about the burial committee in the ultra-orthodox cemetery, walling off the fresh grave of a pious woman from the other orthodox cadavers around her. This took place after the religious authorities heard rumors that the woman had hidden a TV set in her room and indulged in the sin of peeking at the profane world through the boob tube. Never mind that the orthodox investigators had searched her apartment without finding the heretical TV set. Still, the head-high plywood dividers remain in place around the gravesite to preserve the maximum of modesty available for the religious dead.

Next item on our TV screen is another incident in Hebron where fanatical orthodox women are cursing the Israeli police for allowing Arabs to protest the occupation of their own city. For some reason—some say the recent elections—the deal made with the previous government has not been implemented and the Moslem Hebronites are much aggrieved. The Jewish protesters, mostly Americans, claim that not one inch of holy territory in Hebron can be given up. After all, our blessed patriarchs and matriarchs are stashed within shouting distance in the nearby mosque/synagogue. We're talking Abraham, Isaac, Sarah, Leah, etc.

"What do you think?" asks Berl, who is in his mid-seventies and has seen it all.

"I think that those women are out of their minds. I'm embarrassed that they are all Americans."

"If you give the Arabs one inch of Hebron, the next thing you know they'll be wanting Tel Aviv," he says. I can tell he is willingly or unwillingly shifting his blood supply from the rest of his body to his face.

"I thought that the Arabs were about 90% of the population in Hebron. Where would you like them to go?" I ask innocently, knowing what comes next.

"They can go to hell," he mutters, eyes fixated on the Israeli-made TV screen. He punches the volume up two more clicks as if he's firing a .50 caliber machine gun.

"I guess you're thinking of loading them on freight cars?"

I was immediately sorry that I said that; after all, we both have lost mutual relatives in the Holocaust and nothing good could come out of a remark like that.

He looks at me as if I am Cain and he is Abel.

However, the entrance of Rachel, my cousin's wife, with a tray full of cake and a bottle of orange pop saves the situation.

"You look like you're having a stroke," she says to her spouse. "Here, leave politics alone, and eat some cake."

She grabs the clicker out of his hand and Oprah Winfrey appears. If elections were held tomorrow, Rachel would be my candidate for Prime Minister with Oprah running a close second.

Whew.

1996: The Three Rebels

During this latest visit, I resolve to drop in at Kibbutz Yardena and renew my friendship with my old buddy Walter. I look him up in the kibbutz movement phone book and dial his number. An answering machine greets me indicating that high technology has entered his life. I leave a message that I will visit him the following Shabbat and that he had better be there or else.

If you follow the back road from Cfar Moshe south along the banks of the Jordan River, you will eventually end up at Kibbutz Yardena, a small settlement at the foot of the Golan Heights close to the Bailey bridge that spans the holy river. My friend Walter has lived here for the past 30 years. The two of us immigrated to Israel from Southern California around the same time in the mid 1950s.

When I was a permanent resident of the Upper Galilee, I saw Walter often; sometimes during my army service near his kibbutz and sometimes when I was showing tourists, relatives and friends the battlefield sites where I fought during those glorious old days. Those were the days when we were the good guys defending our territory and the Syrians were the bad guys trying to take it away.

On Shabbat, I head down the back road from Cfar Moshe in my rented car. In the old days, when the Syrian army was still on the Golan, this back road was taken only by the adventurous or the suicidal, but now it is just a neglected, rutted and narrow road along the banks of the Jordan.

I find Walter in the dining hall of his kibbutz. It is late in the morning and most of the members have finished breakfast and are hanging around the dining room smoking cigarettes and talking politics. Walter sits in his usual baggy blue shorts, sandals and an Upper Galilee tee shirt. Next to him sits a vaguely familiar man dressed in faded denims, an Israel Bank tee shirt, black socks and shoes. Obviously not a kibbutznik.

"Hey, Shimon," Walter yells halfway across the dining hall. "Look who I've got here for you." As I walk over to the table, I identify the guy in the black socks as Jacobs, another wild character who had emigrated from California about the same time as the two of us.

"Jacobs is a capitalist now," explains Walter, as he points to the Israel Bank tee shirt. I plop down and pour myself a cup of coffee out of a steaming tin pot. It is as if twenty years haven't passed since we have seen each other.

"We're all capitalists now," I say. "In our kibbutz people don't eat in the dining room anymore. They drive into town and shop at Greenberg's Super Market. Then they hole up in their rooms and eat their goodies with the shades pulled down so the neighbors won't want any."

"Not in this kibbutz," protests Walter. "We do it the old way here, dining hall, equal division of the wealth, children's houses, all the old stuff except communal sex, and bestiality." I laugh. The last time that communal sex and bestiality had taken place at this site was during the reign of the Canaanites.

"Worse than being a capitalist," interjects Jacobs, "I've become a government official. I use your tax money for trips to Europe now. I've come all the way up from Jerusalem to this wilderness for two reasons. One, to see you, Shimon, and two, to find out if Walter and his kibbutz are holding back on their taxes. I need another trip. This time to Sweden for some erotic experiences."

"Speaking of sex," I offer, "in our kibbutz they have abolished sex until our local bureaucrats finish their strategic plan—goals, objectives and evaluation strategies—for copulation. It probably won't get done this year because our kibbutz farm manager is finishing his MBA at Harvard Business School. He's majoring in jargon."

"I wish him luck," quips Jacobs. "And I hope that the bank doesn't take over your kibbutz before he comes back with his MBA."

"Who did you vote for in the election?" Walter asks Jacobs.

"Usually I vote for *Moledet* (a secular ultra-nationalist party), but I ended up voting for the Sephardic Torah Party, this time. I've decided to grow my beard back and I like their women better. Also the skullcap helps cover my bald spot."

"You're too white for the Sephardic Torah guys," I correct him. "Next time vote for the Georgian Immigrant Party list. The Mafia is much less corrupt than any of the other parties."

This is our old-time caustic banter mode left over from the wild times in Los Angeles when we were lampooning everything decent that was going on and getting ready to leave the USA forever. Forty years later, we still know how to slip into gear.

The dining hall cleanup squad is ready to mop up our table whether we remain seated or not, so we decide to take our political debate and tearful laughter to another venue and move under a tree in front of Walter's apartment.

You can guess what Walter's occupation is by the state of his garden. He has been in charge of the kibbutz's lush lawns and flowerbeds for the past 20 years and, of course, his own personal plot is a disaster. But there's plenty of shade from a row of poplar trees and on the neighbor's lawn the grass grows green as if it were imported from Ireland. After all, the irrigation system is Jordan River water guaranteed by *Elohim* to be especially wet and nurturing. Now that the three of us have kidded around for a while, I try to get the discussion into a more serious note and the topic I have in mind is as follows:

How was it that we three middle-class kids, two from Beverly Hills and one from San Diego, chose to give up on the idea of being lawyers, doctors or CPA's and uprooted themselves, to the dismay of their families, to settle in the wilds of Israel.?

Nowadays, American immigration to Israel is not such a rarity. There are all kinds of people doing it. There are the neo-orthodox, young Jewish people who, for spiritual reasons, settle in Jerusalem and in the West Bank and gum up the peace process between Jews and Arabs. There are old people who skip retirement in Fort Lauderdale and move to up-scale old age homes along the

Mediterranean coast. There are the fat cats: Americans and South Africans who buy up the million dollar apartments in the exclusive fortress of downtown Jerusalem (and live in them for three months out of the year). There are the sons and daughters of Israeli immigrants to the USA returning to do their military service and sometimes staying on. Then there is still an et cetera category of adventure hunters, socialist youth groupers, marriage partner searchers, dog owners, purse snatchers, archeologists, college professors, and even a few lunatics that still want to live on kibbutzim to show the world a new model of decent and ethical living.

One of the things that the three of us had in common back in Southern California was total disdain for the polite social norms of the day. I was a student at UCLA, living in a Jewish fraternity house and hating everything about it. I had joined because of the lack of student housing at what was then essentially a commuters' college. Somehow I made it through the humiliating process of hazing and harassment during my first semester.

Although I liked some of the members, I was appalled at the general atmosphere of social climbing and conformity. The overwhelming majority of the fraternity brothers were heading for careers in business, law, or medicine, motivated by how much money they intended to make rather than what good they might bring to the world. They seemed disinterested in the social issues of the day and even their love-lives seemed obsessively tuned toward dating girls from the right sororities and being seen at the right places. They were not untypical of the many other students on the campus who didn't care much about what was going on in the world around them and who were pursuing academic paths paved with conformity to bourgeois values.

To me, this was a world of boredom and irrelevancy. Worse was that it was exactly what my parents wanted me to be doing. They had long since abandoned the idea that I would be President of the United States. But a doctor, lawyer or CPA would be just fine. I didn't have the guts to totally discard the dead weight of what I perceived as a foolish life, so I tried to keep myself honest by adopting wild, rebellious, shocking and crude behaviors on one hand and a wretched academic record on the other.

One night, those many years ago, Walter and Jacobs dropped by the fraternity house and barged into my bedroom where I was studying for an exam—a somewhat rare behavior for me during my rebellious college days.

"Shimon," Walter said excitedly, "what do you think of Rosa Parks?"

"I haven't dated her lately. Why do you ask?" I answered as if he had been sitting in my room for hours rather than seconds.

"Are you for the liberation of Negroes or not?" he insisted.

"O.K., I am. So what?"

"How would you like to strike a blow for them right now?" Walter slammed his hand down on my table, dislocating my slide rule.

"I can't go to Alabama tonight," I protested, "got an exam tomorrow morning."

"Forget the exam and forget college, Shimon," said Jacobs. His eyes were full of mischief.

"We need to get into action. We're going to be kibbutzniks; anyway, not gray flannel suit guys like your fraternity brothers. C'mon!"

Jacobs grabbed me by my button-down collar and hauled me out into the streets of Westwood, around the corner where an old pickup truck was parked. He pushed me into the truck and off the three of us headed with Walter driving as if the revolution was about to take place on Wilshire Boulevard. As he hit the brakes at the first stop sign, I heard a heavy chain slide across the truck bed.

"Walter, what are you doing with this pickup truck and that chain back there?" I asked, knowing that he was capable of just about anything.

"Do you think that we ought to allow insulting images of Negroes to be set up in front of people's houses?" he said slowly while looking straight ahead as we gunned down Sunset Boulevard.

I sighed and leaned back to see what this madman and his accomplice were about to do. He turned the truck into an affluent Beverly Hills residential street, slowed down for a few blocks and then parked in front of a white-pillared mansion. At the entrance of the mansion's driveway, barely visible in the dark, I spotted an object and immediately understood what we were about to do. It was a little plaster statue of a colored man with a big watermelon grin on his face, bowing and extending his plaster hand to the carriages and Cadillacs that might visit this gracious mansion. The only thing missing on this degrading work of rich-racist-kitsch art was a sign saying "Yassuh." I flashed for a second on Rosa Parks defending her right to sit down on a Birmingham bus after a hard day's labor ironing good old boys' shirts. Then, I joined Walter and Jacobs in attaching the heavy chain to the statue's neck. We hooked the other end of the chain to the truck's bumper and the three of us popped back in the truck.

"Ready?" asked Jacobs, as if he was Robert Jordan in *For Whom the Bell Tolls*, about to blow the bridge.

"Let her rip," I nodded.

Walter revved up the motor and shifted into first. The plaster Uncle Tom cracked off his pillar and bounced on the Beverly Hills asphalt as we tore down the street.

"Down with racism. Rosa, this one's for you," said Walter."

Forty years later, stretched out on the cool green lawn of Kibbutz Yardena, after a morning and afternoon of laughter and talk, we settle into a moment of quiet, each of us thinking about where we had been and where we were going. Had there been a price to pay for leaving a life of security and comfort? Could our righteous battles have been fought on American soil taking Rosa Park's example? And where will this raw and unpredictable country take us next?

A warm afternoon breeze rolls down the Golan and ruffles the poplar trees.

1997: 50th Anniversary

I'm in a hurry to make it up to the Galilee just in time for the 50th anniversary of the founding of the kibbutz. To tell you the truth, I probably shouldn't be driving this day; I'm full of jet lag and by the time I get out of the snarl of Tel Aviv traffic and onto the coast highway, I'm ready to go to sleep again.

I pull into a roadside gas station restaurant and have a few cups of Turkish coffee while I read the morning newspaper. The headlines are all about the Syrian army's maneuvers up on their own end of the Golan Heights.

With the super dose of caffeine in my veins, I feel ready for the rest of the trip up to the Cfar Moshe. I zoom through the pass over the hills to the Yizrael Valley, and head into the rolling hills of the lower Galilee. Passing a rural McDonald's Golden Arches, I have the sudden urge for a kosher Big Mac, but conquer the urge by picking up a hitchhiking soldier, on his way to a tank base on the Golan. He doesn't have much to say and I detect that he wants to sleep, just like I did when I was a soldier hitch-hiking my way to the unpleasantness, lack of sleep and stress of military service.

Returning home, for me, begins with the view of the Hulah valley, Israel's northernmost frontier. Just as you pass Kibbutz Ayelet HaShachar, you stare into the face of Mt. Hermon, 30 miles north and ten thousand feet up—the Jordan River valley at its feet. I spot a little *yarmulke* of snow on its highest peak, winter is on its way and the entire summit of the mountain will soon be carpeted in white.

I pull over at the junction to the Golan Heights and wake the soldier up. He picks up his rifle and backpack, and mutters a sleepy thank you, "*toda raba.*" I say, "Thanks for protecting us." I watch him join the crowd of military boys and girls thumbing the last leg of their journey to the Syrian front.

I turn off the main highway onto the narrow, eucalyptus-lined side road crossing the valley west to east and leading to the kibbutz. The car and I pass the line of carp ponds on either side of the road that soon gives way to the stubbled fields of fluff in the aftermath of the recent cotton harvest. Two minutes later I turn into the kibbutz itself with its dusty carob trees standing guard on either side of the entrance road. Which kibbutz member will I see first as I roll into the scenes of my communal past? This time it is Mordecai Cohen, once the boss of the shoe factory. Semi-retired kibbutz-style, he chugs along on the Ferguson tractor #3, pulling a flat bed wagon stacked with boxes of fruit from the persimmon harvest. I wave as I drive past and he nods, but his expression seems to say, "who the hell is that?" Then his face comes to life with a sunshine smile under his idiot's cap. It's Shimon again.

I park the car in the little lot next to the cold storage building and watch a flight of pelicans coming down the valley in a precise V—yet another welcoming committee.

Alberto Cohen (no relationship to Mordecai), the head of the health committee, meets me at the kibbutz office, a one-story stucco building housing the telephone switchboard, the executive-secretary, the financial department, and a computer center (how times have changed). Alberto and I were never the best of friends when I was a member of the kibbutz. I suppose that he thought that I was "too American, not serious enough, lacking ideology, and mildly crazy"—the usual stereotype of Americans. But now he has to deal with me as a public health consultant.

"Blessed be your coming," says Alberto as we sit down on a bench in front of the office building.

"Blessed be those who are here," I answer, completing the formal greeting protocol—yet another welcome. Finished with the blessing thing, we get down to business.

"O.K., where do I sleep?" is my first question.

"Well that's a little complicated," says Alberto. "There's a little disagreement between the executive committee chairman and the health committee about your room. They want a place for the social worker, but I put my bid in for your housing first. For the present, you'll have the doctor's cottage since we don't have a doctor living here right now and I'll fight it out with the Housing Committee later." He looks a little embarrassed about this complication.

I see it as the usual lack of clarity between kibbutz committees—how quickly one gets drawn into their endless politics. But since I'm not a member any more I pull back from getting involved. An hour later I'm all set up and unpacked in the ex-doctor's house, clothes out of the suitcase, computer up on a table, and toothbrush in its bathroom holder. I flop onto the bed and drop off into a deep afternoon nap.

When I wake up, night has fallen and it's time to go to the party. I grab a quick bite from the plate of apples that Alberto has placed on the kitchen sink (another welcome), take a shower, put on a white shirt, khaki pants and sandals, and *chick-chak*, I'm on my way out to the 50th anniversary festivities.

The party is taking place in the "new" dining hall (now twenty years old), an eight- sided structure with a red tile roof built in the geographical center of the kibbutz and surrounded by lush lawns and children's playgrounds. During the day, there is a stunning view of Mt. Hermon, the Golan Heights and the ridge of Naftali visible from any of the tables in the dining area.

The old dining hall, built in the early 1950s, had been a crowded and noisy rectangular building, full of flies and inadequate for the population explosion of kibbutz families. Back then, in the 1960s, families with four or five children were common. It was as if the kibbutz members were furiously trying to replace the Jewish children lost in the holocaust. Or perhaps it was because of the Zionist dream of creating a new generation of strong, proud, agricultural, and socialist youth who would build the new State after 2000 years of exile.

Now, five decades after the beginning of the experiment, for this particular kibbutz, the dream is not as bright. Families are smaller. Many of the young people have grown up and left the kibbutz for the seraglios of consumerism in Tel Aviv or Los Angeles— the romance of agriculture has declined in its emotional appeal and has become just ordinary work that needs to be done in order to make a living.

Such disappointments notwithstanding, fifty years of kibbutz persistence under the Golan Heights deserves a big bash. Japanese lanterns line the sidewalks leading to the dining hall and by the time that I put in my appearance, it is filled to the brim with kibbutz members waiting for the show to begin. Kibbutz girls with festive flowers in their hair stand at the doors to the dining room pouring out cognac for each guest and member who enters.

"*L'chaim*," they say in unison as I bolt the stuff down and gasp.

Inside, the dining hall is heating up from the hundreds of warm bodies who have come to celebrate the event. The kibbutzniks are dressed in their holiday best. The older men wear their usual white shirts, dark blue pants, and sandals, but the women, younger members, and kids dress like Americans in their jeans and tee shirts. Searching for a place to sit down where I could see the stage, I see Marta and Aliza sitting on a bench. They wave to me and I squeeze in between them. The house lights dim and the entertainment begins.

The lights rise again and three old timers from neighboring Cfar Baruch appear on the stage in circa 1950 dress: cone shaped idiot hats, faded blue work shirts, mud stained work pants, airplane-gray work socks and exhausted work shoes. As the trialogue begins, thick, fake, Eastern European accents color their Hebrew.

"What's all the noise about?" asks One.

"The noise is about our neighbors in Cfar Moshe," answers Two, picking his teeth.

"The noise is about fifty years on the land," says Three.

"So what?" returns the first old farmer. "I remember when they were new in the valley."

"OK, Yankel, but fifty years is a good reason to celebrate," says Two.

"Why not?" says Three, "We would have done our celebration ten years ago if we hadn't run out of money because of the hail storm in the apple orchard..."

"Something about Cfar Moshe that I never understood," One interrupts. "Who are they named after? Was it Moshe Pipick, the first Jewish cowboy in the Galilee?"

The stage lights go out and a spotlight picks up Devorah Gurvitz, one of the founding members of the kibbutz, standing on a small podium within the audience.

Dvorah: "Cfar Moshe was named after Moshe Regensberg. Who was Moshe Regensberg? He was a rich man in Uruguay who gave the Jewish National Fund the money to redeem the land we live on from the Arab landowners. We were all in our teens and early twenties when we moved to this barren place by the Jordan River. It was 1947 and we were part of the movement to settle the Hulah valley. The British mandatory forces were supposed to stop any Jewish settlement in the area, but we managed to sneak onto our land like thieves in the night. The Arabs woke up in the morning to see the beginnings of a kibbutz sitting right next to them, and some of their hotheads opened fire on us. That's when we had our first casualties, two young boys from Tel Aviv both named David Cohen, who were part of the small military attachment assigned to us by the *Haganah* (Jewish Defense Force)."

Spotlight back to the three farmers on the stage: "Did you ever meet Moshe Regensberg, the man that your kibbutz was named after?" says One.

Spotlight to Eliezer the ex-pig farmer: "No, our benefactor died in Uruguay and never visited us. But the Jewish Agency sent a big photograph of him in a wooden frame. It used to hang in the old office shack. Once someone hung it in the toilet but it was rescued. I don't know where it is now. Maybe in the Archives."

Bracha, the boss of the kibbutz archives, stands up and declares. "No I don't have it. Maybe it's in someone's apartment."

"No, no, I saw it in the old dining hall," says Amnon.

"No, no, I saw it hanging in the laundry room," says another.

A spotlight shifts from one old timer to another.

"No, it's in the closet in the coffee house...."

The spotlight goes out and the stage lights return. The kibbutz choir comes up and sings the nostalgic songs of kibbutz life in the old days. There are love songs, work songs, but most of all songs about their new homeland—the mountains, the fields, the rivers, the lakes, the sky, the clouds, the sunsets. Now, for the first time they are able to breathe their own air and taste their own wine. They are to be a normal people on their own soil.

Then we watch a multimedia show, photos, films and videos of the kibbutz's history. Faces appear of young pioneers, now creaky old timers, of children who are now graying kibbutz farm managers, of youngsters who never came back from the wars (long silence) and of happy times and holidays. Old black and white films of Purim, the bacchanalian costume party; Pesach, with scythes flashing in the twilight, the symbolic cutting of the first wheat far out in the fields; Shevuot, the great harvest festival with a parade of the kibbutz's agricultural equipment and a proud display of the fruit of kibbutz labor. We see apples, grapes, pears, alfalfa, cotton, persimmons, bees and honey, potatoes, pigs, cider, shoes, plastic tarpaulins, turkeys, chickens, mushrooms and babies. The show ends with Chanukah, the winter festival of lights.

All the lights in the dining hall come back on, the chairs and benches are pushed to the periphery and the dancing begins— horas, jitterbugs, disco, macarenas, until the wee hours of the morning.

But, alas, I need to sleep. The jet lag has finished me off.

1998: Turtle Doves

I see Peter, the bird expert, picking up his mail in the kibbutz post office.

"Got a bird question for you," I say and continue, "what bird is it in the area that warbles something like 'for yooo tooo, for yooo tooo?'" Peter closes his post office box and strokes his long black beard.

"What time of the day did you hear it?" he inquires.

"I hear it every day in the morning when I walk around the security road and then yesterday I noticed it at Perkal's funeral in Cfar Baruch. I heard it in the middle of the day, so it wasn't an owl. But it made kind of a hoot."

"Sounds like a turtledove to me, Shimon; listen, is this it?" He warbles just like my mystery bird.

"Great, you solved my problem. It was so strange yesterday. As soon as they lowered Perkal into his grave, this whole group of turtledoves gave him a concert. It seemed to me that they were saying, 'for you, too,' they must have liked him a lot."

"Probably better than his students liked him," quips Peter, whose daughter hadn't liked the principal very much. "Consider what those birds were saying to us all," Peter points out. "Don't forget, it was a funeral. Gotta go back to the plastic factory," he says as we walk outside and climb onto our bicycles.

"Such a philosopher," I murmur to myself.

I ride my bike down the main road of the kibbutz and then cut through the persimmon orchard to the cemetery. I have decided to visit some graves and check out who died in the period since my last visit, a year ago. The founding group of the kibbutz had all been kids in their early 20's and now, 52 years later, the cemetery is becoming a frequent destination for the deceased and their mourners. One could easily lose track.

(A couple of years ago when I visited the kibbutz after a long absence, I looked around for my friend Yigal's apartment to sit down with him over a cup of coffee and review the demise of our Socialist ideology. I ran into Moshe from the plastic factory and asked him where Yigal is living now and without hesitation, with his exquisite sense of grim humor, Moshe said, "In the persimmon orchard." That's how I found out that my friend had died in the interim.)

There are about one-hundred-and-fifty headstones in the cemetery dating back to 1947 when the kibbutz members moved into this particular corner of the Jordan River valley. Many of the earlier headstones memorialize parents of members, the old *Sabas* and *Savtas* who had come to live on the kibbutz in their old age.

After wandering past the headstones of infants who died shortly after birth, the graves of older kibbutz members begin to appear, along with some war casualties and traffic accident victims. The later headstones marked the beginning of the gradual disappearance of the founding mothers and fathers of the kibbutz. May the remainder live to one hundred and twenty.

I am looking for Yigal's stone when I notice an older man standing next to a cypress tree (the dominant trees of the cemetery) looking intensely at the ground before him. It turns out to be Yigal himself, or rather his ghost, doing his usual thing, checking out the mouse holes in the soil. Among his other jobs—beekeeper, orchard worker, and tractor driver—he used to be in charge of rodent control in the apple orchards. His ghost is only looking at the mouse holes without exterminating the mice, probably because he lacks his most important tool, a long stick with a perforated cup wired onto the lower end of it. He would fill that cup full of poisoned, dark red grains and walk around the orchards shaking the stuff down into the mouse holes. He was very serious about this work and during the few times that I worked with him doing this incredible drudgery, he called me back innumerable times, to shake poison into holes that I had missed.

Yigal and I had a special relationship. We drew close to each other through our work in the orchard because we were the only members who had subscriptions to the same left wing daily newspaper, *Al HaMishmar*—On Guard. Little by little, as we got into our political discussions during our breaks at work, we began to hanker for more time together. My first wife and I lived in a tiny room across from the dining hall and I couldn't really invite Yigal and his extended family over for afternoon tea. But he was a *vatik* (old timer in the kibbutz) and had a lot more room in and around his house. We would go over to Yigal's house several times a week and sit around in the living room or on the grass outside to discuss the important things in life. Chava, Yigal's wife, knew how to bake good middle Europe cakes, especially apple strudel.

There were other family members involved in these soirees. There was an older man, Franta by name, a city person who had done much for the members of the kibbutz when they were struggling to make a living. For his help in difficult times, he had been invited to spend his old age on the kibbutz, and now he too resides in the persimmon orchard.

There was another kibbutz member, Peretz, a bachelor, a man who had been mentally damaged by the horrors of a concentration camp. He drank coffee with us and often walked aimlessly around the kibbutz most of the night, unable to sleep. We were all afraid that he might commit suicide on one of those long nights and so we took turns walking with him. From this man, who was an amateur astronomer, I learned the names of the stars and constellations and I learned how to follow the planets' paths in the clear sky of the Galilee.

Both of our families grew during this time. Yigal and his wife adopted more afternoon coffee drinkers, like stray cats, and my wife and I produced children. The scene out on the grass at four o'clock in the afternoon got to be a mass phenomenon. After coffee, politics, philosophy and lots of history, we would all go to the dining hall to eat dinner and talk some more.

Back in the persimmon orchard, I ask Yigal's ghost if he had spotted any mice.

"You know," he says, as if we had just seen each other yesterday morning at breakfast, "you have to keep at this work all the time to keep ahead of the mice. I don't want to complain, but the present gardening crew doesn't pay enough attention to this plot of land."

"There was an article in the paper yesterday about how all the money for housing and development in the country is going to build country club apartments for the affluent. The banks are getting rich and the kibbutzim are going broke. That's why the kibbutz can't even afford a gardener for your cemetery," I try to explain.

"I don't think so, Shimon," Yigal corrects, "You can't always blame it on the economy. The children of the kibbutz who are now running things don't have as much respect for the way the kibbutz looks any more. They're more interested in buying cars and fixing up their own houses. The other day, one of the mourners who walked though here on the way to Perkal's funeral in Cfar Baruch tossed a Coca-Cola bottle into the grass over here. It took two days until someone spotted it and cleaned it up. What a scandal for all of us out here! It's really a matter of education."

"No, Yigal, I don't agree, I think you're right about the second generation being obsessed with material things, but I don't think that you can educate them out of their capitalist thinking. They're exposed to a lot of western consumerism on the TV and many of them see the bottom line in life as personal profits so that they can buy more stuff. They have a whole other view of what this place should be in the future."

I was getting drawn into this ideological discussion out in the cemetery, so much so, that I couldn't find time to ask Yigal how he was feeling or what it was like to be a ghost. Just like old times.

"*Tachlis* (bottom line), Shimon," Yigal says, "if you want to have a commune, you can't let those members who don't want to live in communes, like some of the second generation here, dictate the future. Sooner or later you're going to have to ask them to leave if they don't like our equality. I know, they say that they love our community and the area and want to stay. So let them move to some other place in the valley or into town. Otherwise they are going to destroy our way of life—not that what we do out in this graveyard is much of a life," he quips.

"Glad you still have your sense of humor," I acknowledge his grim joke and continue to theorize.

"I guess we should have been more careful about who we send out from the kibbutz to learn to be managers," says my ghostly friend. "I'm not really sure what the solution is, if there is one at all. It's all very disappointing. Anyway, I better get on with my work here. Drop by again. When you do, could you bring me a copy of Friday's *Al HaMishmar*?"

"Sorry, my good friend," hating to give him the bad news, "the newspaper is dead, too. The last issue came out three years ago."

"What next?" said Yigal, staring down into the mouse hole.

On my way out of the cemetery, walking down the row of persimmon trees leading to the main road, I am feeling quite powerless to do anything about the imminent collapse of what, to me, once seemed an ideal way of life, the best example yet of a decent community based on cooperation rather than competition.

"Well perhaps," I say to myself, "if this kibbutz doesn't make it, some of the other kibbutzim may find the strength to revive themselves. Maybe new immigrants and the third generation will understand that quality of life built on a strong sense of community is the best way, rather than hoping that the free market, or the national lottery, or the information super highway, or the coming of the Messiah will fix this sad world."

Then, I think about my approaching sixty-third birthday. I play with the idea of becoming a ghost in the persimmon orchard someday in the not too distant future. I think about possible epitaphs (Ate Onions Like Apples), and about my death certificate (Cause of death: nodded off at age 95). But I find myself too immature or too frightened to seriously consider these realities. I suppose that I am not yet convinced that I will ever die. So what am I to do? I can't even bring myself to buy a burial plot. And would it be in San Diego or Cfar Moshe?

Just then the turtledoves up in the persimmon trees begin their song again:

'For you, too, for you, too.'

As I pass through the gate of the orchard, I notice a ladder propped up against one of the persimmon trees. An old man in kibbutz-issue clothes is standing on the top rung looking for persimmons left over from the late fall harvest. He turns and waves at me. It is my deceased grandfather Yisroel, now a ghost kibbutznik.

He calls out to me: "Come back to Israel soon, Shimon, there's still plenty of work to do."